P9-CQC-908

Evangelism

Made

Simple —

How To <u>DO</u> It!

Stephen W. Rogers

Manual

Printed in the United States Of America
© 1998

All rights reserved. No part of this book may be reproduced
without written permission from the author (except in the case
of brief quotations embodied in critical articles and reviews.

ISBN 0-9667521-0-4

Library of Congress 98-96675

A Product Of

Sain Publication
3120 Minor Hill Road
Mailing Address: P. O. Box 616 • Pulaski, TN 38478
931 ~ 363-6905

Appreciation

My heart is filled with gratitude for so many as I write this book. First, I am thankful for my parents, Jesse and Louise Rogers, who from my earliest days taught me the importance of the Lord, His Church, and evangelism. Secondly, my wife Vicky, has always been such a support in urging me to be evangelistic both in the States and overseas.

The elders at the Washington Avenue Church of Christ in Evansville have been tremendous in their support of me! For twelve and one-half years, I have been encouraged to be evangelistic, and have been given encouragement to teach evangelism classes, and to write this material.

The evangelistic growth of the members at Washington Avenue has been terrific. We have so many Christians who have applied themselves to learning God's Word and understanding how to teach it, and have become extremely adept in teaching His Word. More are eager to learn in the near future.

My gratitude is sincerely given to ten people who have read and re-read these documents for accuracy: Becky Barker, Alan Bush, Neil Kempf, Louise Rogers, Vicky Rogers, Jama Scherer, Hilary and Joni Schultheis, Margaret Shirel, Tony and Karen Tanner, Danny Weddle, and B.J. Woodring.

Also, I am so thankful for some of my dear brethren who are so busy and yet took time to read and evaluate this document for scriptural content. These respected brethren are Jerry Barber, Don

Brown, Earl Edwards, Garland Elkins, E. Claude Gardner, Tom Holland, James Meadows, Barton Rogers, Milton Sewell, Robert R. Taylor, Jr. and Clayton Winters.

Words cannot express my gratitude to some special brethren without whom this book could not have been published. These generous brethren, anxious for Christians to become more evangelistic, have financially made this publication possible. Thanks to Don Brown, Ray Wall, and Anna Whitmer.

Lastly, this document could not have been finished without the work of Margaret Shirel. She has been a patient and supportive secretary who has endured my determination to get this book published quickly and to have it done with excellence — as near perfection as we could get it.

Thanks to all of you; may our combined efforts bring glory to our God!

Table Of Contents

Foreword

The Gospel of Jesus is the most exciting, glorious message known to the world! Every Christian knows how precious his hope in Christ truly is. I rejoice that during my lifetime I have seen more and more brethren committed to understanding God's Word, to educating themselves in the most effective methods of evangelism, and to making amazing sacrifices to teach the Gospel throughout the world. This thrilling message of hope is one that every person in the world needs to hear!

Teaching the glorious Gospel involves assisting a student to know the facts about Deity before one can consider knowing Christ as his Savior. Too, teaching Christ involves emphasizing the commitment that true faith involves. This takes time and patience. If you are looking for a "quick fix," a "one shot approach," a fifteen minute method of teaching so you can quickly baptize the student, you will be terribly disappointed. I believe in cultivating true faith which results in commitment and determination that will cause one to obey Christ no matter what the consequences.

Through the years, I have observed many Christians who are eager to teach but who feel very inadequate. Two struggles seem to cause this feeling of incompetence. One of the struggles is trying to understand the religious confusions that pervade the world and how to assist those who have been entangled in those errors. Brethren long for a method to teach the Gospel in a way that will lovingly guide the student to look at the Truth while simultaneously comparing his false beliefs with that Truth. This book presents a method that will adequately address those problems.

The second struggle is even more basic. I could not enumerate the times I have heard brethren who want to be evangelistic complain, "I do not know where to start!" This book with its companion books, "Evangelism Made Simple — You <u>CAN</u> <u>DO</u> It!" and "The Gospel Made Simple — You <u>CAN</u> <u>KNOW</u> It!" are offered to assist you to be able to teach God's Word effectively.

This method is extremely effective in teaching the Gospel for people throughout the world. We have used it extensively in the States and in Belarus, a state of the former Soviet Union. To emphasize the effectiveness of this method, I have included statements from those who have taught the Gospel using it and testimonies of people who have been students and who have learned the Gospel and become Christians through this method. See Chapter 19.

My encouragement to you is, "YOU CAN DO IT!" I have seen Christians, who have never taught anyone and who were terrified, become excellent teachers of the Word. Commit yourself NOW to become a great teacher of the greatest message in the world. I have a motto that I use in every effort I attempt, "Excellence and Enthusiasm!" I urge you to adopt this motto as you study, learn, and practice to become a great teacher of God's precious Word!

Then go teach people God's Word! Many are

so intimidated; they believe the Bible is a terribly complicated, unapproachable, and impossible to understand book! My message to you: you are capable of assisting students to begin to realize that they CAN understand the Bible! The book containing the lessons for the students has blanks for them to fill in as they study. They can then take these lessons home to continue to review, study, and contemplate. My heart thrills as I see people learn that the Bible can be understood. Their hunger for God's Word escalates and their determination to obey it and to grow in faith multiplies!

Dear Christian brother or sister, let us be about God's business! Let us teach the Word, see its results in the hearts and lives of people, convince ourselves that the Word really is alive and powerful today, and delight as we can see people become convinced that they CAN KNOW God's Word!

Explanatory Notes

The following lists will explain the usage of abbreviations and capitalizations in this book, the accompanying student lessons entitled "The Gospel Made Simple — You <u>CAN</u> <u>KNOW</u> It!", and the teacher answer guides entitled "Evangelism Made Simple — You <u>CAN</u> <u>DO</u> It!"

If you are unfamiliar with abbreviations used to identify books of the Bible, the following list will assist you in finding the scriptural references used in these materials.

Old Testament

Genesis	Gen.	Proverbs	Pr.
Exodus	Ex.	Ecclesiastes	Ecc.
Leviticus	Lev.	Song of Solomon	So.
Numbers	Nu.	Isaiah	Is.
Deuteronomy	Deut.	Jeremiah	Jer.
Joshua	Josh.	Lamentations	Lam.
Judges	Ju.	Ezekiel	Eze.
Ruth	Ru.	Daniel	Dn.
I Samuel	I Sa.	Hosea	Ho.
II Samuel	II Sa.	Joel	Joe.
I Kings	I Ki.	Amos	Am.
II Kings	II Ki.	Obadiah	Ob.
I Chronicles	I Chr.	Jonah	Jon.
II Chronicles	II Chr.	Micah	Mi.
Ezra	Ez.	Nahum	Na.
Nehemiah	Ne.	Habakkuk	Hab.
Esther	Es.	Zephaniah	Zeph.
Job	Job	Haggai	Ha.
Psalms	Ps.	Zechariah	Zech.
		Malachi	Mal.

New Testament

Matthew	Mt.	II Thessalonians	II Thess.
Mark	Mk.	I Timothy	I Tim.
Luke	Lk.	II Timothy	II Tim.
John	Jn.	Titus	Tit.
Acts	Ac.	Philemon	Phile.
Romans	Rom.	Hebrews	He.
I Corinthians	I Cor.	James	Js.
II Corinthians	II Cor.	I Peter	I Pet.
Galatians	Gal.	II Peter	II Pet.
Ephesians	Eph.	I John	I Jn.
Philippians	Phil.	II John	II Jn.
Colossians	Col.	III John	III Jn.
I Thessalonians	I Thess.	Jude	Jude
		Revelation	Rev.

Abbreviations that have been used in reference to versions of the Bible are:

King James Version	KJV
New King James Version	NKJV
American Standard Version	ASV
New International Version	NIV

All quotations are from the King James Version unless otherwise denoted.

An explanation of usage of capitalization is also appropriate. Throughout this book, I have capitalized words to emphasize Deity and Their Names (God, Christ, Holy Spirit, Lord, Master, Lawgiver, Mediator, etc.), to show the significance of a certain event, place, or thing (the Flood, the Cross, Heaven, Hell, Blood, Law, etc.), to indicate God-ordained roles (Apostles, Elders, Deacons, Ministers, etc.) and to accentuate the uniqueness and exclusiveness of His Church (the Church, Church of Christ, etc.).

Some may consider the usage of the word "Church," especially when used in the phrase "Church of Christ" as a denominational usage. The word "Church" has been capitalized to show its Divine origin and its exclusiveness and uniqueness. When the word "Lord" refers to Christ, it refers to His being the One and Only Savior and Master in the life of a Christian. The word "Church" refers to the Divine Institution which He purchased with His Own Blood. It is the spiritual Body of Christ that is totally unique in the world. Men may have established religious bodies; Christ established HIS Church, the Church of Christ!

Blue highlighted words in this book coordinate with the answers in "Evangelism Made Simple — You <u>CAN</u> <u>DO</u> It!" These highlighted words will assist you to quickly find and restudy a particular passage or point in any lesson.

Marvelous Motivators!

"**M**otivation!" I love that word! Motivation is that drive that causes a person to be actively involved in a work. Motivation has two important components. It begins with one's mind being convinced about the value and significance of that effort. Secondly, it continues with a persuasion in a person's heart that he MUST be personally involved in that work!

True motivation is SO powerful! It will inspire one to action. It will cause one to be involved in an effort when others sit on the sidelines. It will force a person to keep going when others have stopped putting forth effort. It will stimulate one to sacrifice time that could be given to selfish concerns or interests. It will propel one to action when the message is not popular. It will provoke one to "stay the course" when persecuted and when it would seem much easier to just be silent.

Jeremiah, the prophet, was so tired of being ignored, despised, harassed, and persecuted that he decided he would no longer warn the people of Judah about the seriousness of their sins and impending judgment. "Then I said, I will not make mention of him, nor speak any more in his name. But his word was in mine heart as a burning fire shut up in my bones, and I was weary with forbearing, and I could not stay." Jer. 20:9. He had decided to stop urging repentance and offering God's mercy, but he could not keep his mouth quiet. He knew that his message was their ONLY hope! That was his motivation!

Christians today MUST find motivation that will force us to be actively involved in proclaiming the Gospel to people in our communities, our country, and the world! Many fine methods have been available for years. However, without true motivation, no method will be beneficial! What will convince you in mind and heart that you must find an effective method of teaching and will drive you to seek excellence in being able to teach the glorious message of the Gospel? Let me suggest several powerful motivators.

The Total Commitment of the Godhead to Man's Salvation! The tragedy of the sin of Adam and Eve in the Garden of Eden is immediately followed by the commitment of God to provide grace whereby man could be saved. Even in the midst of the curses in the Garden, God emphasized His grace that would furnish an antidote for man's sin. Gen. 3:15. Perhaps no verse in the Bible more beautifully portrays God's determination for man to be saved than John 3:16. "For God SO LOVED the world, that he gave his only begotten Son." He purposed to send the Son to this world to provide a means whereby His wrath could be appeased and sinful man could be justified. Imagine the heartache that the Father felt as the Son was in agony in the Garden and on the Cross. Yet, He HAD to allow Christ to die that we might have an atonement.

The total commitment of the Son is also heart-rending! He left the perfection and peace of Heaven to come here to die. As Deity, He knew what He faced. That knowledge caused His humanity to cry for release; yet, in that fear, He KNEW that He had to die in order for man to be saved! Although "He could have called ten thousand angels," He submitted to the Will of God, the Father because He understood that He, and He alone, could provide that saving sacrifice that man so desperately needed.

The total commitment of the Holy Spirit to reveal to all mankind the Gospel message and to validate it in order that it might be proven to be true is so amazing! He provided revelation and inspiration so that the pure Gospel would be presented. He provided the Apostles and first century Christians with the supernatural support whereby they could proclaim the Gospel to the whole world during their lifetime! Ac. 1:8; Col. 1:23. All of this was done because the Holy Spirit knew that sinners are eternally lost without the Gospel.

The Christian who is truly touched by the total commitment of the Godhead to man's salvation cannot help being motivated in mind and in heart to be personally involved in telling others of the Good News!

The Glory of the Gospel Message! The Gospel is the GREATEST message in the world! It is a message that every sinner so desperately needs to hear! "Gospel"— the GOOD NEWS! The angel emphasized its glory, "I bring you good tidings of great joy, which shall be to all people." Lk. 2:10. The Gospel is God's power to bring a sinful heart to salvation. Rom. 1:16. Christ, the virgin-born, crucified, buried and risen Savior is our hope, our justification, our salvation!

Every person in the world needs to hear about Him and how to receive salvation through His blood! I will never forget the reaction of an interpreter in Belarus named Tamara. Reared in a Communist family, she had never seen a Bible nor heard about Christ. After studying the Bible and seeing the love of Jesus for mankind and the hope He offers, I said to her, "Isn't this BEAUTIFUL?" I will NEVER forget her reaction that made me "sit up, take notice" and reflect upon my own appreciation of the Gospel. She said, "That word is not good enough." I was taken aback and was uncertain for a moment what she was really saying. Then she explained. "'Beautiful' does not do this message justice. Perhaps 'Marvelous' or an even greater synonym would be more appropriate." Tamara is right! And perhaps there is no word in man's vocabulary to describe the supreme sacrifice of Christ for mankind and the majesty of the message inherent in the Gospel!

Our Heart-felt Appreciation For Our Own Salvation! How long has it been since you paused and asked yourself, "Where would I be spiritually without Christ and His saving Blood?" The realization that we have been sinners against the Holy God of Heaven should rip our hearts apart! Remorse 'should always keep us humble and overwhelming gratitude for God's mercy and forgiveness should inspire us to holy living and to evangelistic zeal!

This heart-felt appreciation was the Apostle Paul's driving motivation! He never forgot his persecution of Christians and his attempt to destroy the Church of the Lord. Even as he faced death, he was still heart-sick that he had been "the chief of sinners." I Tim. 1:15. Yet, Paul had great confidence and hope in facing death and Christ at the Judgment. II Tim. 4:6-8. In II Corinthians 5:9-21 Paul gives the reasons for his motivation. He knew that EVERY MAN must face the judgment of Christ and answer for the actions done in the body while on earth. Verse 10. In the Judgment, a sinner will face the terror the Lord. Verse 11. The love of Christ is the ONLY HOPE for every sinner! Because Christ died for all, it means that every sinner is dead in his sins! Verses 14,15. Christ had provided justification for sinners that enabled them to be new creatures, reconciled to God, the Father. Verses 17-21.

My motto to describe my motivation is "For the love of Christ constraineth me!" His love is SO powerful; it propelled Paul like water gushing from a hydrant; it drove him as if he were a human cannonball shot from a cannon. Paul described this conviction, "for necessity is laid upon me; yea, woe is unto me, if I preach not the gospel." Oh, the powerful drive the love of Christ gives to an appreciative Christian!

The Messiah's Mandate to His People! Jesus gave a mandate to His Apostles and Christians of succeeding generations before salvation by His Blood was ever offered to mankind. He commanded that His Gospel be taught to every creature in the whole world for as long as the world stands! Mk. 16:15,16; Mt. 28:19,20. Every Christian is to "show forth the praises of him who hath called you out of darkness into his marvelous light." I Pet. 2:9.

This mandate is the duty of every Christian. Many Christians, because of the influence of today's culture, despise the concept of duty — performing actions in response to commands. However, before you criticize one responding to Christ's mandates out of duty, study the Greek Work "Ὀφείλω" and the numerous words by which it is translated. Christians are "behooved," "bound," they have "debt," they "must" submit to the Lord's teaching and commands. All these words suggest a sense of duty and obligation. Even if you are insecure about teaching, you can participate in spreading the Gospel by encouraging friends to seek the Truth and then have other Christians teach them. Even if you are uncomfortable teaching personally, you can financially support evangelism.

Determination to be an obedient child of God will give you great motivation to be evangelistic!

The Value of Each Soul! Realizing the eternal value of one soul will cause a Christian to place great value on teaching the Gospel. Jesus taught us that value, "For what is a man profited, if he shall gain the whole world, and lose his own soul? or what shall a man give in exchange for his soul?" Mt. 16:26. Mentally picture a scale with everything in the world on one side and a man's soul in the other side. The value and significance of the eternal spirit of a man immediately shows what is truly important! The things of the world are weighed in the balance and found miserably wanting!

The true value of one soul makes a staggering impact upon the motivation of a Christian. We realize that every time a sinner is converted, a God-created spirit is saved! Every time one chooses to leave sin, the Devil is thwarted in his attempt to eternally seize another soul in his destructive grip. This understanding compelled the Apostle Paul to long for the salvation of his own Jewish nation, Rom. 10:1, and to WISH that there was anything that he could do that might enable all Jews to see the Deity of Jesus and to turn to Him for salvation! Rom. 9:3.

How spine-chilling it is to think that by teaching the Gospel of Christ, you can make an impact on the eternal destiny of spirits. Imagine being in Heaven and having those you have taught trying to express to you their undying and eternal gratitude for your love, patience and sacrifice that they might know about the glorious Gospel and its unshackling freedom from the slavery of Satan and sin! What a thrill it is to be a part of such a wondrous and immortal mission!

The Swift Approach of Death, the Future Coming of Christ and the Judgment! One does not have to think for a moment to realize that we all are aging rapidly. That means death hurriedly approaches also. The Bible reminds us of some solemn realities, "And as it is appointed unto men once to die, but after this the judgment:" Heb. 9:27. God has warned all men of the impending judgment of Christ, "Because he hath appointed a day, in the which he will judge the world in righteousness by that man whom he hath ordained; whereof he hath given assurance unto all men, in that he hath raised him from the dead." Ac. 17:31.

That judgment is absolutely terrifying for the lost! II Cor. 5:11; II Thess. 1:7-9. However, for the righteous, it is a time of exciting anticipation! Faithful Christians should live "Looking for that blessed hope and the glorious appearing of the great God and our Savior Jesus Christ." Tit. 2:13. John reassured us of our confidence, "Herein is our love made perfect, that we may have boldness in the day of judgment." I Jn. 4:17. God's children are so excited and eager for that time when we will meet our Lord "face to face," and when we will meet our God and enter into the His abode!

Understanding the Glories of Heaven and the Horrors of Hell! God has given us glimpses into Heaven's glory that entice our hearts. Imagine being in the presence of Deity forever! Imagine being with all the redeemed of all the ages! Contemplate worshipping Deity with all of Heaven's hosts! And realize it is a home that cannot be lost once you are there. It is "an inheritance incorruptible, and undefiled, and that fadeth not away." I Pet. 1:4. And it can be the hope now for you and every person that you assist to come to faith in Christ and the realized reality after the judgment. How we should LONG for Heaven!

Conversely, how frightening are the glimpses God has given us of Hell. It is impossible to imagine a place where nothing associated with God exists. In this Divinely designed world, we see God's creative genius every day! Try to imagine "everlasting destruction from the presence of the Lord, and from the glory of his power." II Thess. 1:9. No beauty, no color, no rainbow, no joy! Rather, only everlasting torture, pain, and wailing, in the presence of the Devil, his angels and all unbelievers and wicked people from all the annuls of history. How can a Christian sit by unconcerned and untouched in his heart by the thoughts of people not being given the opportunity to choose Heaven instead of Hell?

Observe that I have suggested that we need to be touched in mind and in heart. Many Christians mentally acknowledge that God wants them to be evangelistic; yet, are not actively involved. Only when we are touched in the depths of our heart will we be driven to action. Hopefully, the motivating factors of this chapter and the methodology offered in this book will convince you in the depths of your heart that you can, yea you MUST, teach the Word!

I want to commend you for beginning on a journey with me in this book. Obviously you are interested in obeying God from your heart. You must be desirous of either learning how to teach others or to sharpen the skills you have already cultivated. If you are just beginning, I pray you will find zeal and conviction that motivates you for the rest of your life. If you have been involved but have been lethargic or lazy, my prayer is that this book will help to rekindle a fire in your bones that can never be extinguished!

Think about it — you can be a part of the GREATEST work in the world — assisting in the snatching of souls from Satan's grasp and the road to Hell, and showing them the Good News of God's eternal plan that offers them forgiveness, hope and the privilege to be in God's family and on the road to Heaven. Get fired up! Allow nothing to hinder you any longer. Determine that you will be God's instrument to guide souls to the salvation Christ offers and to the peace and security that can only be found in Him!

Take The Weight Off

Vicky and I went on a diet about fifteen months ago. We each lost about twenty-five pounds. It was amazing how much easier it was to mow the yard, hike, or just walk! It was SO freeing! We felt as if a load had been lifted from our lives!

Have you ever travelled on international flights? During the past three and one-half years, I have made ten trips to the country of Belarus. In fact, I began writing this chapter in Molodechno, Belarus. On the first trips, you overpack and stuff your carry-on just in case your luggage is lost and ends up in another country, on another continent, or even in a different hemisphere. That has actually happened to some of our team members in our overseas travels! On other trips, our carry-ons have been very heavy pieces of much-needed medical equipment to assist doctors and hospitals. We have literally run through airports with extremely cumbersome and weighty medical machines. Such burdens bring excruciating pain to tense shoulder muscles and aching cramps to arms and legs.

However, after running through airports to get through passport checks, customs checks and to make connecting flights, you learn to "Take the Weight Off!" The more I travel, the less weight I carry! Put the cumbersome load in the suitcase and travel in comfort!

With all the reasons to motivate Christians that we saw in the last chapter, why is it that so many Christians are so uninvolved and unmotivated evangelistically? I suggest it is because Christians need to "Take the Weight Off" too! God has encouraged Christians to lay aside every sin that would keep us from faithfulness. Heb. 12:1. Perhaps there is no area in which we need to work more diligently to take off cumbersome hindrances than in the area of evangelism!

Question: What has "Weighted YOU Down?" What hinders you in taking the glorious Gospel message to others?

Perhaps the greatest weight for most Christians is **FEAR**! Self-doubt has suffocated the motivation of so many. "Can I do it?" "I do not know enough." "Will I be mistreated?" "What if I am asked questions I cannot answer?" Fear has paralyzed more Christians in evangelism than anything else.

There could be no better time than now to lay your fears aside! Interestingly, we overcome our fears when we challenge them head-on! I have met some who had to challenge their fear of water in order to be baptized for salvation. They overcame that fear by being motivated to submit to Christ in order to be saved! I have faced such fears in bungy jumping. After talking my wife into going bungy jumping with me, she said, "YOU go first!" There is so much fear in jumping off a platform hanging by a big rubber band! You are taught all your life not to jump off high places. "What am I doing?" "Have I lost my mind?" It was terrifying to do it; however, when you lay aside the fear, it can be so exhilarating. I have now jumped five times and it has become less fearful!

However, a new type of jump, such a doing a backward flip, still demands laying aside my fear.

I challenge you to be like David! While his brothers were terrified of Goliath and fled, I Sa. 17:11,24, David was disgusted with such cowardice. He defended the Lord and His people, slew Goliath and delivered Israel from the Philistines! What helped him overcome his fear? HIS FAITH! Lay down YOUR FEAR; pick up FAITH and go do the Lord's work! The more you do it, the easier it will become!

Another terrible weight that destroys motivation for evangelism is any **EXCUSE** you may manufacture to soothe your conscience! A song, written about excuses people have for neglecting worship, might well be adapted to describe Christian's justifications for not being evangelistic, "Excuses, excuses, you'll hear them every day!" Ah, it is true — the Devil will supply them if you are trying to rationalize your lack of involvement in telling sinners about the Gospel!

Some of our excuses place the blame upon sinners. "People just do not care any more." "I just cannot find people who will study the Bible." "No one in this town is interested in the Gospel anymore."

Other excuses blame brethren. Some of these excuses may have some validity, but they still do not justify our inaction. "Others are not being evangelistic." "My brethren will not be enthusiastic in welcoming my guests to worship." "My brethren are not as loving as they should be."

Many of our excuses are about ourselves. "I don't know how." "I'm TOO YOUNG!" "...TOO OLD!"

"...TOO BUSY!" "I can't!" "I've had some bad experiences!"

Some even find excuses that blame the Gospel! "People in the first century obeyed the Gospel message the FIRST TIME they heard it!" "The Gospel just does not have the effect today that it had in the first century!"

STOP! Look at your excuses and realize how they have become a burden to your conscience and a millstone to your motivation to obey God! Sinners DO CARE; take your head out of the sand; look around; talk; see how people are interested in obeying the Lord. I have NEVER been in a community where there were no people interested in the Gospel message. I once preached in a community where the brethren lamented, "People are not interested in the Gospel in this town." Yet, that congregation doubled in attendance as people were converted to Christ.

Some brethren may be hindrances to evangelistic efforts; that does not give you any justification to be silent with the Gospel! The truth is, when a few brethren become evangelistic and start converting sinners, there can be a positive leavening effect on a whole congregation! Active, evangelistic brethren become more soul conscious, more loving, more committed, and more motivated.

We desperately need to lay aside our personal excuses and start living in faith. If you know enough to become a Christian, you know enough to begin to tell others about the Gospel. Some older Christians need to take lessons of zeal from some new Christians. A friend of mine told me about a nurse who was recently converted. She talks to every patient about the Gospel. Several in her family have become Christians since her conversion. Ludmilla, my daughter in the faith in Belarus, is on fire for the Lord. She has been a Christian for only six months, yet she is bringing many people to learn about the fantastic Gospel she has heard and obeyed. She wants everyone who will listen to learn of the love of Christ and of the glorious hope that can be theirs! She also has become determined to know these lessons so she can translate for me. And, she has committed herself to learn to teach others herself.

If every Christian uses the excuse "I can't because of my position in life," who will be the Lord's mouthpiece to tell sinners of the saving Gospel? The young are too young, the old are too old, and everyone else is too busy. Who is going to do the Lord's work? I challenge teens to learn NOW to teach the Gospel and do it the rest of your life! I urge older brethren to use your knowledge and wisdom to teach the Gospel and determine that you will do it as long as there is breath in your body! I encourage those of you who are spouses, parents, and employees to see opportunities that present themselves almost daily.

Those who say, "I can't," simply need to admit that I CAN be involved in evangelism. Many who say "I can't" are like Moses. When God called him to lead Israel, Moses had every excuse in the book. Read Exodus 3-4. His last excuse was, "I am not eloquent...I am slow of speech, and of a slow tongue." Ex. 4:10. Do you ever feel like Moses? He said in essence, "I get so nervous and I am not a person of words." Observe God's answer to Moses' excuse. Aaron "shall be thy spokesman." Ex. 4:16. If you feel you are not a person of words, then you be the interest piquer! Live a godly life that is blameless. Whet people's appetite for the Gospel through the use of tracts, correspondence courses, discussions and invitations to worship. Then let an "Aaron" be your spokesman to teach your friend the Gospel.

The excuse, "I have had bad experiences" simply will not hold water. Do you use that excuse about everything in life? Do you say, "I never drive a car because I had a wreck once." Or have you stopped using a computer because you lost some material? Have you lost material because you forgot to save it? Have you had a system crash and lost your work? I will never forget working on a sermon one day; I was on the last paragraph. Suddenly a power outage occurred and I lost the whole sermon. Trying to keep my cool, when the electricity was restored, I began retyping that whole lesson. After just a few sentences, the electricity went out again. I just got up; walked out of my office and went home so I would not get angry. Even with that bad experience, I still use the computer! In fact, these very words are being typed on a computer. We may have a FEW bad experiences in evangelism, but be certain you will have SO MANY wonderful experiences if you simply continue to tell sinners about Christ!

And how dare anyone blame the Gospel! It DOES have the same impact upon sinners today that it did in the first century! I see it constantly!

It is totally untrue that people obeyed the Gospel
the first time they heard it. Someone says, "But
what about the people on Pentecost? They obeyed
the Gospel after ONE SERMON!" That is SO untrue,
such a wrong assumption! Those Jews had heard
the Gospel of the Old Testament all their lives! They
knew a Messiah was coming; they were simply wrong
in ONE POINT! They thought Jesus was an
impostor, a FALSE Christ! When they understood
that He was the TRUE MESSIAH, they immediately
were ready to respond! Today, we need to educate
people about God, Christ, the Holy Spirit and the
Gospel before we can ever expect them to obey! So
many are so ignorant of Biblical Truths. We must
teach them so they can then make an informed and
intelligent choice by faith!

If excuses have been your burden, lay them
down, and you will be surprised how freeing it is
and how many opportunities you will find!

Another terrible weight that is destructive to
evangelistic motivation is the **ELEVATION OF
OTHER THINGS TO A MORE IMMEDIATE
AND MORE IMPORTANT PRIORITY**! Jobs,
hobbies, social activities, school events, sports,
recreation, reading, shopping — they may be
wholesome and good; however, we must not neglect
the souls of the lost! We MUST make evangelism a
priority in our lives! Would you be too busy to help
your neighbor if his house was on fire? Would you
be too busy to help him search for a lost child? Are
we too busy to care about his sinful soul that is on
the road to hell? When you allow true motivation to

cause you to become evangelistic, you will find the most rewarding work in the world!

Another great hindrance to evangelistic zeal in congregations is an **INTERNAL FOCUS UPON US**! Many congregations are so focused upon their OWN needs that they have forgotten their mission! Many Christians are satisfied in the Church as long as they attend one or two worship services a week, leave ON TIME, and have their OWN pew. Sadly, some brethren have decide that it is more blessed to care for themselves than to assist others! Such brethren need to lay aside selfish concerns and become interested in others! It is amazing how satisfying and truly inspiring it is.

Then there is the great hindrance of **CHURCH WORK**! Leaders of many congregations spend SO MUCH TIME in meetings, in concern for a particular program, in developing new programs to replace worn-out ones, and in busy work that they lose sight of their true purpose and focus. "Church work" is vital; however, it must never become a burden nor a hindrance to our focus upon the lives of people. When we stop being "people oriented," we lose our focus! We must never forget that we are about souls, salvation, and keeping the saved faithful! If you are a Church leader and "Church work" is interfering with your evangelistic zeal and opportunities to teach the Gospel, perhaps right now is the time to re-evaluate your efforts. Continue to be a leader; however, re-establish your priorities so you can truly be about the Lord's work!

Another awful burden is the present-day

attempt to **PAWN OFF DECEPTIVE DISGUISES AS TRUE EVANGELISM**! Some brethren are more interested in altering God-ordained worship, in practicing watered down fellowship, and in giving hope to those in error than they are in proclaiming the Gospel Truths! False doctrine will NEVER make one free! It will only enslave hearts in sin! Jesus reminds us that "the truth shall make you free." Jn. 8:32. Brethren need to STOP trying to find something new to teach; STOP trying to fellowship error, lay aside all man-made disguises; and just teach God's message! We have nothing else to preach; nothing else will provide escape from sin! We have no authority from God to offer another gospel! If we offer another gospel, it is a damnable perversion! Gal. 1:6-9. If you have been offering people hope from you own opinions and views and not hope based upon God's Truths, you may feel you are doing people a great favor. However, you are doing them and yourself great spiritual harm. Lay down error; pick up the Truth and be free at last!

Losing weight has made life less of a trudge and has increased my physical motivation. It took me several overseas trips before I finally learned to "Take the Weight Off" in travel. Since I have learned that, my trips are much more enjoyable and I am not nearly as tired. The same is true about those who are hindered in being evangelistic. What weight do you need to lay aside? If you will be courageous enough to "Take the Weight Off," your motivation will kick in, your zeal will blossom, your determination to teach the Gospel will multiply, and

God will give the increase! Once that happens and you see people converted to Christ through the Gospel, NOTHING will stop you from being involved in this great work for the rest of your life!

Will you do it? Lay your weight aside! Give yourself the freedom to teach the Gospel and see its power!

Understanding The World We Evangelize!

Before we begin to evangelize, we must have a strategy. Careful plans need to be made. However, before you make plans for your strategy, you MUST first understand the circumstances you are facing. I believe one of the great struggles of Christians today is the attempt to teach without understanding the circumstances that we are facing. Some zealous brethren are so frustrated because they are not having the results they did thirty or forty years ago. Years ago, many brethren were very successful beginning with a study of baptism because that was the biggest disagreement of the day. Years later, brethren began with the authority of scripture because many were questioning Biblical authority. However, things have changed drastically in the last twenty-five years. You must understand these changes before you try to teach the Gospel. Once you understand people's beliefs, then you can begin to lay a strategy to assist them. After studying this lesson, hopefully you will see the strategy in the lessons, "The Gospel Made Simple — You <u>CAN KNOW</u> It!"

Take a few moments mentally or with a piece of paper and identify traits of the world that you will attempt to evangelize. What are people's beliefs? ...Views? ...Philosophies? ... Lifestyles?

Let me suggest several traits that are

prevalent in our world:

The Godhead is SO Misunderstood!
Christians often ASSUME that almost everyone
believes in God. Most people will affirm that they
do believe in God. However, we must not assume
that they believe in the God of the Bible. In my
studies with people, I have become convinced that
if the Apostle Paul were here or in any other country
in the world today, he would proclaim that the God
of Heaven is an "Unknown God" to most of mankind
today.

The god of many is SELF! Man determines
that he has the right to do whatever he wants to do!
Choice has become god, just as was prevalent during
the days between the judges of Israel. "In those days
there was no king in Israel: but every man did that
which was right in his own eyes." Ju. 21:25. The
"Me Generation" has even driven those who claim
to follow God to decide they can make decisions
about how to be saved, how to worship God, what
a moral life is and how to live it, and how to define
sin. This is the driving philosophical premise of pro-
abortionists.

The gods of other's lives are materialism,
power, or pleasure. The driving force of that person's
life is whatever his focus and priority in life is. Then
he will put his all into gaining those material
possessions, that power, or having that narcissistic
pleasure at every moment.

Others who claim to believe in the true God
of Heaven have molded a God who pleases them.
They take one trait of God and elevate it as the

ONLY trait He possesses. When asking people, "Who is God?" the usual answer one receives is, 'God is love." There is NO denying that God is characterized by love. "God is love." I Jn. 4:8,16. He is the epitome and source of love. I Jn. 4:19. That love has been wonderfully exemplified in His sending Christ to die the atoning but horrible Death by Crucifixion. Jn. 3:16. But, why would one want to describe God by only one of His traits? Man wants a God who will look down on us with a smile, who will overlook our faults, and who is never going to be harsh. To describe God as only "Love" is like describing a man who is a husband, father, grandfather, mayor, hunter, wood-working enthusiast, and golfer merely by his hobby of being a "wood-worker." Some have so emphasized and exalted God's love that they have virtually espoused Universalism; others have denied the existence of Hell. God cannot be fairly described by ONE of His traits — He is the sum total of all His traits!

The god of others is the uncaring god of Deism. This theology believes in a god who had power comparable to the power of the God of the Bible. However, Deism's god supposedly created the world; then left the world and went to some far-off place, and presently has no care in the lives of individuals nor in the upholding of the universe. Deism's god has left man to fend for himself the best he can. Such an uncaring God is not even a scant image of the True God!

Others who speak often about God have such a false concept of the true God. The god of the

Mormons is a being living in a physical body;[1] the god of the United Pentecostals is Jesus who purportedly appears sometimes as a father and sometimes as a spirit, but who is always Jesus;[2] the god of the Jehovah's Witnesses is the only divine being[3] and Jesus is seen as "a created being"[4] while the Holy Spirit is defined as "God's impersonal spirit."[5] How wrong all of the ideas are!

Perhaps no present-day idea is more insidious, more dishonorable and disgusting than the "Jesus Seminar." This is a heretical lie by some "scholars" that claims that Jesus was a "Jewish Socrates" (just a philosopher), the "first Jewish social critic;" "the first stand-up comic;" or a "Jewish mystic."[6] They claim that only 20% of His sayings are authentic; even fewer of His deeds are authentic. They reject the Lord's Prayer, His sayings on the Cross, His claims of Divinity, His Virgin Birth, most of His miracles, and the bodily Resurrection![7] These men may claim to be Biblical scholars, but they are merely unbelievers who deny the very Son of Almighty God.

We must show people who God, Christ and the Holy Spirit truly are. We will accomplish this in Lesson 1, "Who is God?"; Lesson 2, "Who is Jesus Christ?"; and Lesson 3, "Who is the Holy Spirit?" When a student understands the Godhead, he will have an intense desire for God, just as David did. David expressed his desire for God, "As a hart panteth after the water brooks, so panteth my soul after thee, O God. My soul thirsteth for God, for the living God:..." Ps. 42:1,2. One who understands the Godhead will say with the songs, "Our God Is An

Awesome God," and "How Great Thou Art!" We must urge people to worship NO false gods, Ex. 20:3; but rather, to have intense desire for the True God who is deeply interested in the whole human race and in each one of us individually!

Calvinistic Theology and Its Influences! I know of no false theology that has had more insidious influence upon the thinking and religious views of men than this doctrine. Calvinism is based upon the premise that each person who is born is tainted with the guilt of the sin of Adam and Eve because of being in flesh. This doctrine is called "Total Hereditary Depravity." It is also known by the phrase, "Original sin." Here is a succinct statement of this tenet,

> Because of the fall, man is unable of himself to savingly believe the gospel. The sinner is dead, blind, and deaf to the things of God; his heart is deceitful and desperately corrupt. His will is not free, it is in bondage to his evil nature, therefore, he will not—indeed he cannot—choose good over evil in the spiritual realm. Consequently, it takes much more than the Spirit's assistance to bring a sinner to Christ—it takes regeneration by which the Spirit makes the sinner alive and gives him a new nature. Faith is not something man contributes to salvation but is itself a part of God's gift of salvation—it is God's gift to the sinner, not the sinner's gift to God.[8]

This depravity supposedly so contaminates the spirit of the child that it can never have any desire to approach or to turn to God. God's Word does NOT teach that babies are born in sin! Ezek. 18:4-20; Mt. 18:3-6.

Those influenced by this doctrine then immediately begin to seek ways to absolve the depraved child from its guilt. This is why religions practice "infant baptism." What is so extremely interesting to me it to see how many parents do not really believe this idea in the depths of their heart, especially after the birth of a new-born baby!

Once a theology begins with the premise that being in flesh taints a child's spirit, the next step is to devise a way to remove that depravity. Calvinism has devised work for each member of the Godhead that is totally unbiblical. God, the Father, supposedly predestined specific individuals to be saved without ANY RESPONSE upon their part. This tenet is known as "Unconditional Particular Election." Those who believe this view affirm,

> God's choice of certain individuals unto salvation before the foundation of the world rested solely in His sovereign will. His choice of particular sinners was not based on any foreseen response or obedience on their part, such as faith, repentance, etc. On the contrary, God gives faith and repentance to each individual whom He selected. These acts are the result, not the cause of God's choice. Election therefore was not determined by or conditioned upon any virtuous quality or act foreseen in man. Those whom God sovereignly elected He brings through the power of the Spirit to a willing acceptance of Christ. Thus God's choice of the sinner, not the sinner's choice of Christ, is the ultimate cause of salvation.[9]

The New Testament teaches predestination, but predestination of a group; those who, of their own personal choice, will turn to Christ in faith, submit to Him, and live holy and blameless lives! Eph. 1:4,5; Rom. 8:29,30.

God, the Son, supposedly died ONLY FOR THE ELECT! This doctrine is known by the phrase, "Limited Atonement." Read the words of those who aver this doctrine,

> Christ's redeeming work was intended to save the elect only and actually secured salvation for them. His death was a substitutionary endurance of the penalty of sin in the place of certain specified sinners. In addition to putting away the sins of His people, Christ's redemption secured everything necessary for their salvation, including faith which unites them to Him. The gift of faith is infallibly applied by the Spirit to all for whom Christ died, thereby guaranteeing their salvation.[10]

A cursory and unbiased reading of scripture will quickly affirm that Christ died in order to give all sinners, who choose, the privilege of being saved. Jn. 3:16; I Jn. 2:2; II Pet. 3:9; Heb. 2:9. I have found very few people who will affirm this premise.

God, the Holy Spirit, purportedly is sent, at the Father's chosen time, to instantaneously transform the depraved sinner's heart (called repentance), give him faith, and save him. This doctrine is described by the phrase, "Irresistible Grace." Proponents claim,

> In addition to the outward general call to salvation which is made to everyone who hears

the gospel, the Holy Spirit extends to the elect a special inward call that inevitably brings them to salvation. The external call (which is made to all without distinction) can be, and often is, rejected; whereas the internal call (which is made only to the elect) cannot be rejected; it always results in conversion. By means of this special call the Spirit irresistibly draws sinners to Christ. He is not limited in His work of applying salvation by man's will, nor is He dependent upon man's cooperation for success. The Spirit graciously causes the elect sinner to cooperate, to believe, to repent, to come freely and willingly to Christ. God's grace, therefore, is invincible; it never fails to result in the salvation of those to whom it is extended.[11]

This teaching denies Biblical Truths that declare that man has choice about salvation, that faith comes by hearing God's Word, and that sinners are saved by obedience to the Truth. Mt. 16:24,25; Josh. 24:15; Rom. 10:17; I Pet. 1:22; Js. 1:18,21.

The final and culminating tenet of Calvinistic theology is the claim of "Perseverance of the Saints." This proposition is typically described as "Once Saved, Always Saved." Proponents maintain,

All who are chosen by God, redeemed by Christ, and given faith by the Spirit are eternally saved. They are kept in faith by the power of Almighty God and thus persevere to the end.[12]

This dogma totally contradicts the New Testament's affirmation that man CAN fall from grace, Gal. 5:3,4; I Cor. 10:12; Heb. 2:1-4; 3:12,13; 4:1, and Christ's call for Christians to remain faithful. Rev. 2:10; 3:11; Js. 1:12; II Tim. 4:6-8.

Our obligation is to show sinners that they CAN come to faith and CAN choose to obey God. We must clearly assert that sin is a violation of God's Word, I Jn. 3:4; not an inborn trait. Sinners must realize that God's grace IS available and each person may choose to receive that grace through obedient faith. This will be addressed in Lesson 5. Then in Lessons 6 and 7, we will emphasize that the Bible is God's inspired Word, and the New Testament is the Law under which we now live. Therein, Deity has shown us of Divine grace and has urged us to choose to come to personal faith in the Gospel. In Lessons 9 and 10, the student will learn that he or she can choose to believe in Christ, repent of his or her own sins, confess faith in Christ, and be baptized to be saved by the Blood of Christ! The Truth can be SO freeing and exciting to those who have been taught the enslaving ideas of Calvinism.

As a teacher, you must realize that many religions will adhere to only certain points of the Calvinistic TULIP. However, holding to any one false premise of Calvinism will poison one's theology.

Immorality is SO Glorified! Sin was formerly viewed as "Sin." That is certainly not true today! Immoral practices are now justified and advocated. Homosexuality, fornication, living together, adultery, abortion, and euthanasia are totally accepted by a great part of our society. As we teach sinners, we must help them define sin, grasp sin's horribleness, and be convicted of their own sinfulness.

Why is sin so glorified today? People

throughout the world have lost their fear of Hell; many deny its existence; most have no fear of going to Hell personally. Secondly, sin has been redefined. It is no longer rejecting God's teaching and violating His Will; now, sin is breaking the Golden Rule,[13] oppression,[14] or violence.[15] Too, moral convictions are being abandoned. Examples of this moral bankruptcy and abandonment are noted: "29% of women who marry are virgins on their wedding night";[16] "62% believe there is nothing morally wrong with the affairs they are having";[17] "91% of Americans lie regularly";[18] and "for $10 million, one in four would abandon all their friends, or abandon their church, or turn to prostitution for a week."[19]

Those who have sold their soul to sin have tried to create a value-relative society where everything is seen as gray; nothing is seen as black and white. About the only absolute is that "There are NO absolutes!"[20] Too, the Bible as an objective standard of morality has been completely rejected.

In counteracting this, in Lesson 8, the student will realize that sin is a violation of God's Law in the New Testament. Also, we will emphasize that sin is an abomination in God's sight. Specific sins will be identified and the student will be called upon to comprehend the consequences of sin in his or her life. As teachers, we must stress that sin is STILL sin and call upon the sinner to repent.

The "Don't Judge" Phenomenon! This concept is based upon a misunderstanding of Matthew 7:1, "Judge not, that ye be not judged." This verse is falsely interpreted today to "stop the mouths" of anyone who might point out error in a person's life. It is advocated in the following affirmations, "You have NO RIGHT to tell me that ANYTHING I am doing is wrong!" "It's MY life; don't tell me it is wrong!" "You live your life; I'll live mine!" "One value system is JUST AS GOOD as another."

This is NOT a new phenomenon. When Lot chastised the homosexuals of Sodom, they cried, "You think you are our judge?" Gen. 19:9. This age-old phenomenon is rampant today. People attempt to condone and justify sin, false avenues of salvation, false religion, and false worship by crying, "Don't judge me."

Tragically, many Christians have become "closed-mouthed" and no longer attempt to evangelize sinners. However, we must stop being intimidated! It is NEVER wrong to call sin, sin; nor is it ever wrong to call a sinner, a sinner. If we love and care for people in sin, we will want them to realize that they are on the road to eternal punishment in Hell. Too, we will remind them that on the Day of Judgment, the standard of judgment will be the Word of Christ, not their own feelings! Jn. 8:24.

Changes in Religion! Change is the norm in most religions today! People of past generations would "roll over in their grave" if they saw the changes that have occurred. Many today are deeply confused and frustrated by changes occurring in their religions.

One specific example is the Roman Catholic Church. In recent year, the law requiring the eating of fish on Friday has been changed.[21] Some Catholic Churches in Evansville are now practicing immersion.[22] Perhaps the most amazing change now being advocated around the world is the attempt to make Mary the co-mediatrix and co-redemtrix with Christ.[23] Of course, such is impossible if we follow the Bible! I Tim. 2:5; I Pet. 1:18,19; Rom. 3:24.

The role of women in religions is rapidly changing. Women are leading in worship, becoming elders, deacons and preachers in many churches. There is even debate in the Catholic Church about the possibility of women being priests.[24] God in NO WAY demeans women. However, He has given specific roles to women. He ordained that men be the leaders in the Church. I Tim. 3:2,12.

Changes in worship are exploding. More and more instruments are being incorporated into worship services. When I was a boy, forty years ago, most churches that advocated the acceptance of instrumental music would only condone the use of a piano, possibly an organ at the most. Now, some churches have more equipment and instruments than huge rock bands.[25] Worship services are becoming more charismatic. There is more and more emphasis on emotion and less and less emphasis on proclamation of the Word of God.

Ecumenical fellowship is the chic cliché and belief being advocated today. Doctrinal differences are supposedly completely ignored, fellowship with all faiths is espoused, and people are encouraged to "agree to disagree." This is being seen in present-day programs like Promise Keepers. Differences in beliefs about standards of religious authority, in how to become a Christian, in doctrinal views about Deity, in methods of organization, and in views about morals are merely overlooked. In fact, some are now very near the belief of Universalism. Even the importance of belief in Jesus as the Divine Son of God is being seriously challenged.[26]

What is the driving force behind this ecumenical movement? The Word of God is not viewed as the FINAL standard and authority in matters of doctrine, practice, fellowship, and morals. Rather, society, culture, man's own emotions, and the desire to be liked and accepted by others are the real motivating factors. Truth is no longer seen as absolute; man's desires are most important.

However, to teach God's Truths to people, we must convince them of the UNCHANGING nature of New Testament Christianity. We must emphasize to students the unchanging and unending authority of Christ. Mt. 28:18. His Word is the unalterable Standard, the Truth! Jn. 12:48; 17:17. It will NEVER change its doctrine: neither about how to become a Christian, nor about the uniqueness of His Church, nor Its worship, nor Its organization. People must understand that leaving the teachings of Christ to follow the doctrines of men will make our religion vain, empty, worthless and unacceptable to God! Mt. 15:8,9. To change His religion is to bring His judgment upon ourselves. Rev. 22:18,19. We will emphasize the uniqueness of the Lord's Church in Lessons 11, 12, and 13.

Many Christians, eager to be evangelistic, have become disillusioned. Often, this discouragement occurs because we have begun our studies at the wrong place. We have not realized the impact of the thinking of culture upon the hearts and minds of the students. Once we understand the influence of the world upon men, we can begin to design a strategy to help them see the emptiness, shallowness, and worthlessness of what the world is offering them. Then we will be able to show them the Truths about God and His Will for our lives!

Our Attitude As We Evangelize!

Having the Truth is critical if we wish to guide one to the salvation Christ offers. Equally important is our attitude as we teach! Attitude is important BEFORE YOU GO, and AS YOU GO! Your attitude will either push you to be evangelistic or discourage you. Attitude will either cause people to respect you and listen to you or to resent you and to reject your message. Attitude will either cause you to grow or to be stifled and to quit. Remember, attitude determines altitude! Attitude determines effectiveness!

First, there are **Attitudes That We Must AVOID!** These are attitudes that can be SO DETRIMENTAL to evangelism. We must evaluate our hearts and make sure these are not a part of our lives.

We must never give an air of **"I know it all!"** Obviously, you have been blessed to know the Truth and to have become a Christian. Surely, as Christians, we continue to learn; we grow in our understanding of God's Word. Yet, we do not know it all! There will be questions that we are asked that we will never know how to answer. "What was the fruit Adam and Eve ate?" "When will the world end?" We do not have answers to these questions. God has not given us answers to some questions that people love to ask. No man will know those answers in this life!

We must never give the impression that **"I have all the answers!"** We surely will not have all the answers. Many things that we have studied, we may not understand. We will not remember every passage that we have studied. And we will not remember or may not know the context of some passages about which we are asked.

We must never put pressure upon ourselves by saying, **"I HAVE to have all the answers!"** This is inhuman pressure that you do not need to put upon yourself. NEVER be afraid to say, "I do not know; but I will find out." Students will respect you rather than disrespect you.

We must never enter a study with the attitude that **"I am going to prove you wrong!"** This makes it appear that you see a Bible study as an attempt to win an argument. That is NOT the purpose of evangelism. We are trying to lovingly guide a soul to Christ for salvation, not win a debate!

We must not be eager to tell one **"You are going to Hell!"** We do not have to condemn a sinner; he has already condemned himself by his sinfulness. Jn. 3:17. If we show the student his sins and the Truth, he will KNOW that he is lost. Obviously, if one is determined to reject the Truth, even though he understands it, he should be reminded of the consequences. There has been only one study in which the student and I had to discuss his absolute rejection of the Word and the eternal consequences.

We will be much more effective in evangelism when we avoid **fear and terror**. You very well may be nervous; that is human, understandable, and justifiable. Almost everyone I know is nervous when tackling a new project or job. However, fear and terror are a different matter. Be strong in your faith; trust the power of God's Word and do not feel that the success of the study depends upon you!

Also, avoid **putting pressure upon yourself**! Many teachers make themselves miserable as they prepare to teach God's Word. They see this as a task in which they must perform to perfection. Brethren ask themselves, "What if I fail?" This suggests that we are the most important factor in the spreading of the Gospel. I remind you, the power is in the Word, not in you! Many Christians put terrible pressure upon themselves before a study begins by asking, "What if they do not obey?" Remember that many did not obey the Lord Himself. Others will place undue burden and guilt upon themselves after a study is over if the student does not obey by asking, "What have I done wrong?" The answer likely is, "You did NOTHING wrong; what was the student's attitude toward God's Word?"

Secondly, there are **Attitudes That We MUST POSSESS!** These are absolutely critical if we want to be successful in teaching sinners the glorious Gospel of Jesus Christ!

We must realize that **there are prospects everywhere**! More Christians are so pessimistic, saying, "There are just no prospects or interested people anymore." We need to cultivate the optimistic attitude of the Christians in the first century who, when scattered by persecution, went everywhere teaching the Gospel. "Therefore they that were scattered abroad went every where preaching the word." Ac. 8:4. Paul was constantly looking for hearts that were tender and searching for the Lord. In Ephesus, he taught from "house to house." Ac. 20:20.

Many Christians are greatly intimidated by knocking on doors and trying to talk to people "cold turkey." However, every one of us has acquaintances who are excellent prospects. Friends, family, neighbors, co-workers, visitors at worship services, and people who are facing difficulty in life are potential students. Keep your eyes open; keep a continual list of people for whom you will pray, and who you will encourage to study. You will be amazed at the opportunities that are available!

As we teach the Word, we must teach in **love**! This demands a deep and abiding care for people who are lost! We want them to know the message of hope that will free them from guilt and put them on the road to Heaven. Loving sinners also demands that we care enough to point out error and sin. True love, "rejoiceth not in iniquity, but rejoiceth in the truth;" I Cor. 13:6. True love involves being a friend. "Faithful are the wounds of a friend." Pr. 27:6. A penitent sinner will be forever grateful that you cared enough to show him his need and the answer for his sin. "He that rebuketh a man afterwards shall find more favour than he that flattereth with the tongue." Pr. 28:23.

There are many Biblical examples of God's people having the courage to love those in sin. Paul reprimanded Peter for allowing prejudiced brethren to influence his heart and to cause him to withdraw from fellowshipping his Gentile brethren. Peter was more influenced to please his older brethren who had sinful hearts than to reach out and accept all who came to Christ. See Gal. 2:11-21. This love for sinners is also seen in Nathan's courage to tell David, "Thou art the man," II Sa. 12:7; and Philip's call for Simon, the sorcerer, to repent. Ac. 8:21,22.

Another vital attitude is **confidence** as we go and as we teach. As we look for students and as we go to teach, we must go with confidence in God's Word! It is the "power of God unto salvation," Rom. 1:16; and when it is taught, "God giveth the increase." I Cor. 3:7. It is the Gospel that converts sinful hearts! Realizing this truth will take so much pressure and stress away from you! Teachers realize the power is in God's Word, not in ourselves!

Because of false conclusions that have been taught for so many years by preachers and speakers in evangelism workshops, many brethren have concluded that something MUST BE WRONG with the Gospel today. We are constantly told that people in the first century obeyed the Gospel the FIRST TIME they heard it. You may have heard someone say, "The sinners on the Day of Pentecost obeyed the Gospel the first time they heard a sermon." That is such a false conclusion! The Jews at Pentecost had the Old Testament Scriptures which prophesied of the coming Messiah, His Kingdom, the salvation that He would provide, and the supernatural events that were occurring on that day. They had heard the Gospel in prophesy; they believed that a Messiah was coming; however, they had rejected and crucified Jesus, believing He was an impostor, not the promised Messiah. Peter's sermon corrected the one mistaken assumption of these Jews. As soon as they believed that Jesus was the Christ, they wanted to know how to be forgiven!

It is imperative that we slow down and ground people in the basics of God's Truths before we expect them to or encourage them to obey the Gospel. Realizing that the power is in the Word will take SO MUCH PRESSURE from you. You will then see yourself as a teacher, a presenter of a wonderful hope, not one who must FORCE people to obey. You will stop asking, "What did I do wrong" when one does not obey the Gospel. You will accept that your responsibility is to present the message, it is the responsibility of the student to be convinced in the intellect and in the heart of his own need.

Another important attitude is **enthusiasm!** We must be thrilled to know that there are people who really are interested in obeying the Lord. The Devil wants to persuade you to believe that NO ONE is interested any more. That is SO untrue. Many are interested!

We must also be enthusiastic about the glorious Gospel we teach. Realizing the precious gift of salvation that is ours, and the hope that is so powerful in our own lives, we should be so eager to tell sinners what we have found and encourage them to have the same redemption.

As we go to teach the Gospel, we must also go in **faith!** This demands that we believe the Truth ourselves before we try to teach it to others. It is imperative that you have a faith and confidence in which you trust the Truth implicitly. You must be convinced that it is the ONLY WAY by which sinners can be saved. Your heart must be filled with respect for God, His Word, and His promises. If you do not have certainty about the Truth, how can you ever influence others to obey it? People will "see right through" your doubt and uncertainty. If you do not believe that baptism must be for the purpose of seeking salvation or if you are not absolutely convinced that Christ authorizes singing as the only type of music in worship, stop now! Go back to the Word of God, study, be convinced, and THEN go teach the Word.

As you go in **faith**, NEVER apologize for the Truth. Our responsibility is to teach the Gospel. We must never compromise it, change it, nor be ashamed of it. Rather, love it, teach it, and trust it.

Perhaps the greatest blessing to our faith is to see the power of the Gospel in the hearts of sinners. Some of the greatest lessons in my life have occurred in Bible studies. There have been times when I had NO idea that one was so affected in the depths of his spirit by the message. There have been studies in which I have been shocked as people explained that they were ready to obey the Gospel. This proves that the power is not in ourselves, our ability to reason, nor our persuasion; the power is in the Word! NOTHING will strengthen your faith more than to see the Word in action! I hear many Christians complain, "I wish I could be stronger in my faith."

YOU CAN! James explains, "the trying of your faith worketh patience [steadfastness]." Js. 1:3. Put you faith to the test; see it work; see the Gospel convert hearts; then, watch your own faith and zeal increase, yea, even multiply!

Another important attitude is **humility**! There is no room nor reason for haughtiness as we teach the Word of God. Too, we should never act as if we think we are better than the student. Always strive to exhibit Christian graciousness that displays your gratitude to Christ for the privilege of being a child of God and for the opportunity to tell others of that saving message.

Too, try to approach every study with a desire to learn — **be teachable yourself**! One of the greatest blessings of evangelism is being challenged in your own knowledge and understanding of God's Word. Every time I conduct a study, students teach me by giving me more understanding about false religions and how to assist those caught up in such entanglements to see the light of Truth. Too, they challenge me to learn how to better explain God's awesome Truths in simple terms.

An extremely important trait in evangelism is **patience**! As teachers, we must be very patient and understanding with students. Never expect them to have to finish a lesson before you leave. Some studies may be very difficult for different students; allow them the opportunity to delve into, struggle with, and come to understand what they are reading.

Patience demands that we do not be alarmed nor dismayed if people do not grasp a Truth after the first cursory reading. This does not mean they are ignorant, nor feeble-minded. Remember, people learn at different rates, and that is okay. Think of the Lord's Apostles. They were with Him for three and one-half years. He told them over and over that He would suffer, be crucified, and rise; also, He continued to urge them to understand that His Kingdom was not an earthly kingdom. However, the concept of a Messiah establishing an earthly kingdom that would free them from Roman domination so permeated their minds that they never did "get it." Even after His Death and Resurrection and just before His Ascension back to the Father in Heaven, they were still asking, "Lord, wilt thou at this time restore again the kingdom to Israel?" Ac. 1:6. If it took them so long to "get it" with the Lord teaching them daily, are we being fair to a student to expect him to "get it" after one hearing?

Also, we must exhibit patience by never trying to FORCE a student to respond. Continually remind yourself that becoming a Christian is a decision of CHOICE, NOT OF COERCION!

Another important commitment is to determine to **make the message understandable**! Resolve that you will imitate the Lord and His teaching method. Jesus constantly used illustrations and parables to help students understand the vital Truths He brought to the world. You will notice in the following lessons many illustrations. Use those that you feel comfortable using; find others from your life that you can use to help the student grasp Christ's message. In every study, I try to think of illustrations with which the student may easily relate. This will make the message much more vivid to him.

Perhaps most of the attitudes that we should seek to cultivate could be summed up in this encouragement — in every study, **strive to practice the Golden Rule**. I know of nothing more vital to show how you are interested in the student. The Lord called upon us, "Therefore all things whatsoever ye would that men should do to you, do ye even so to them;" Mt. 7:12. Every time I sit in a Bible study, I ask myself, "How would I want to be treated if the roles were reversed?" This one trait will make such a difference in how you teach!

In conclusion, attitude is SO important in evangelism. It will either encourage you to be a teacher of the Word, or discourage you from doing so. If you are optimistic and soul conscious, you will be encouraged. If you believe people do not care, you will be pessimistic. A kind, considerate, caring attitude will motivate people to listen to your message; a harsh, inconsiderate, and hateful attitude will cause them to refuse to listen to your message and to reject anything you have to say.

Sincerely evaluate your attitude now before you go! How can you improve your attitude NOW so you can be more effective WHEN you go? Remember, attitude determines effectiveness.

Too, as we now turn to the studies, "Evangelism Made Simple — You CAN DO It!", what is your attitude? Are you eager to learn to be effective in teaching the Word? Are you determined that you will learn and will allow God to use you to bring sinners to Him? It will take time for you to absorb these lessons and to be well trained as a teacher. Are you willing to commit time, study and energy to being an outstanding teacher? YOU CAN DO IT! Come, let me guide you into an effective strategy for the GREATEST mission on Earth — teaching the Gospel and guiding sinners toward salvation and Heaven!

Do You Know God Exists?

Introduction to the Lesson:

A. Why study this topic?

    1. In conducting Bible Studies with people for years both in the U.S. and abroad, I have become convinced of the importance of this study. Without this lesson, people will never truly grasp the awesome significance God intended for man to gain about what we can know and what faith truly involves!

    2. Tragically, many see Christianity as a crutch for weak, dependent people, not as the anchor that it is for the human soul.

    3. I have studied with many religious people who see faith in God as good, just because of its impact upon the human existence. Some will advocate, "Even if there IS NO God, Christianity is still the best way of life."

       a. I DENY this affirmation!

       b. If there is NO God, we are, in Paul's words in reference to the Resurrection of Christ and our own resurrection, "of all men most miserable." I Cor. 15:19. Christians are to be pitied as deceived, gullible

> people who have NO certainty nor basis for our beliefs; we are simply people who believe fanciful theories that have no basis.

4. However, TRUE Christianity is built upon a SOLID ROCK based upon certainty that gives great comfort and strength to the heart of the believer!

5. This lesson's purpose is to assist people to understand Bible "Knowledge" and "Faith;" to see that Christianity stands upon a SOLID foundation, and to help us understand the premises of those who attack the validity of Christianity.

B. Do not omit this lesson with the assumption that the student will already understand these truths.

1. On numerous occasions, I have been flabbergasted to hear one who affirmed faith in God only to continue by saying, "No one can really know if God exists." My next question is, "Why be a believer then?"

2. Certainty about God's existence will produce great results later.

C. Purpose of the questions at the beginning of the lesson:

1. They are designed to get the student to begin to think.

2. Their responses give insight into their concepts of "Knowledge" and "Faith."

I. "Knowledge" As Used In the Bible!

Goals To Accomplish As You Teach This Topic:

- Show the difference between empirical knowledge and knowledge as used in the Bible.
- Emphasize that we can know facts and truths even though we have not seen them and even though we do not understand them.
- Identify empirical evidences that verify God's existence.
- Realize that we can have absolute certainty about spiritual truths once we understand knowledge as used by God.

Struggles That The Student Might Have With This Topic:

- Realizing that there are facts and truths he can know without having empirical knowledge.
- Getting beyond the realization that we can be easily deceived by people whether intentionally or unintentionally.
- Understanding that everything God tells us is true because of His nature.

Teaching Tools:

- True story about your family.
- Actual events from your past.
- Balancing illustrations like a "Jimmy Stick" or "Balancing Eagle."

A. We will begin by studying the WORLD'S definition of "Knowledge".

   1. It is knowledge based upon the experience of the five senses — called "Empirical Knowledge."

   2. Examples:

      a. People know that another human being, for example their neighbor, exists because they SEE him, TOUCH him and HEAR him.

      b. One may drive down the road, NEVER SEE a skunk and yet KNOW a skunk is near or has been run over by a car. How? "I SMELL it!" Even if he does not SEE the skunk, he KNOWS one is near. Why? THERE'S NOTHING IN THE WORLD THAT SMELLS LIKE THAT!

      c. You can KNOW a train is coming by HEARING the horn, FEELING the earth rumble, or by SEEING it.

      d. You can KNOW that a cook is baking lemon cake without tasting it. HOW? That lemon aroma will permeate a house. Obviously, you can know it later by TASTING the cake.

   3. Observations:

      a. With THIS definition of "Know," we are affirming that we can ONLY "Know" things that can be verified by the five senses.

b. Sadly, this is the approach many have to life: "If I cannot verify something by the five senses, it does not exist!"

c. Yet, I observe that NO ONE truly lives by that philosophy!

B. Bible "Knowledge."

1. GOD'S use of knowledge is knowing something based upon the **truthfulness** of the one relating the information:

a. WHETHER I CAN VERIFY IT OR NOT!

b. WHETHER I CAN UNDERSTAND IT OR NOT!

2. Illustrations — You can "know" something that you may not have verified.

a. ALWAYS begin these illustrations by asking "Do you believe that I am an honest person?"

b. Use illustrations from your own life. Here are two examples I use:

1. A red squirrel was eating bird seed from a bird feeder in my back yard. Trying to scare it out of my yard, I threw sticks at the squirrel where it had run to the top of the tree. The squirrel jumped out of the huge maple

tree right between my friend and me. It "belly-flopped" on the ground; I was certain it must be dead. About 10 seconds later, it got up and trotted out of my yard as though nothing had happened.

2. I tell about my two children and their mates.

c. The point of such illustrations: They can "Know" these things even if they cannot verify them by their five senses. How can they "Know" these facts? Because I am being truthful with them.

3. Illustrations where you can "Know" something you do not understand.

a. "Jimmy Stick"

1. This is a small piece of wood that looks like a "check mark."

2. I buy these at "Cracker Barrel" restaurants.

3. I ask the student if he has seen one; if not, I ask if he believes I am an honest person.

4. Then I proceed to tell him this "check mark" will stay on the end of my index finger without me holding it there with my left hand, thumb or other fingers on my right hand or with my teeth.

5. Even if he has never seen it

occur, he can "Know" it because I tell him in all truthfulness that it will occur.

6. I then ask him for a belt. If no one in the study has a stiff belt, I remove mine, "Hang" it on the "Jimmy Stick" and watch with excitement as the student's eyes widen with curiosity and his doubt grows almost simultaneously.

7. Once he sees it occur, I allow the student to hold the "Jimmy Stick" on his finger to see that there are NO tricks.

8. Now that he has "Empirical Knowledge," I ask him if he UNDERSTANDS what he has just verified.

9. Here is an example of him "Knowing" something he does not understand.

10. The explanation: This is a law of physics. The weight of the belt "Pulls" the "Jimmy Stick" right back up on my finger.

b. Balancing Eagle.

1. These can be purchased at "Cracker Barrel" restaurants or other novelty stores.

2. This eagle perches on a small stand on its beak.

3. Amazingly, you can tap the eagle's wings; it will twist and turn but will remain on its beak.

4. How does this happen? Almost all of the weight is in its nose.

5. For shock impact and a great laugh, you can even have someone to stand, hold their head back, and place the eagle on the person's nose. It will balance there perfectly.

c. Find other balance illustrations that you know.

4. Students quickly realize there ARE things they can KNOW whether they have seen them or not and whether they can understand them or not.

5. A quick realization that is usually made is that one who tells you information could be deceiving you whether intentionally or unintentionally! I give three examples:

a. A man who was told he had AIDS only to find out days later that the lab had given the same number to two different patients; HE DID NOT HAVE AIDS! It was an unintentional mistake.

b. A young nursing student was told she had an inoperable brain tumor. She got a second opinion from a leading medical center. It was an operable, non-malignant tumor; she is healthy and well after surgery. The doctor who gave her the first opinion was mistaken.

c. For 22 years, Jacob believed that his son Joseph had been killed by wild animals. All that time he had been alive in Egypt! Joseph's brothers intentionally deceived their dad. See Genesis 37 and 45.

6. God's nature is SO IMPORTANT in this discussion.

a. God is NOT ABLE to lie; He cannot lie! Tit. 1:2

b. It is impossible for God to lie; whatever HE tells me IS true! Heb. 6:18

7. In the creation, God has given empirical evidence by which we can KNOW that He exists!

a. The heavens with the sun, moon and stars declare to all men everywhere in the world the wisdom and orderly design of an all-wise Designer. Ps. 19:1-6

1. I ask students if they are like me — SO BUSY looking around and down that sometimes I do not stop to SEE God's wisdom and design all above me.

2. Did it JUST HAPPEN BY ACCIDENT or COINCIDENCE:

    a. That the sun is 93 million miles from the Earth? If closer, the Earth would burn; if farther away, it would be a ball of ice.

    b. That the moon is in the exact position to control the tides and keep them from inundating or flooding our earth?

    c. That the time of each day has such consistency? How is it that by that consistency man was able to design a watch dividing each day into 24 equal parts and most of us are so governed by a clock or watch? How often do you look at your arm each day? It is almost as if we are controlled by our watch.

3. Truly, the heavens are an empirical declaration of God's power, creative design and genius!

b. When the people of Lystra began to worship Paul and Barnabas after they had healed the crippled man, Paul and Barnabas quickly stopped that worship of themselves and directed the minds of the people to God who gave them miraculous powers. Ac. 14:17

1. The true God is a LIVING being.
2. He is the originator of our habitation — this planet.
3. He allowed the people of nations to make their own choices; however, He has always left empirical evidence of His existence for the people of all those nations.
4. That empirical evidence? He designed the world in such a way that man will have provisions for life.

   a. The Earth was made to be watered so man's very existence would continue — Water is for man's thirst; it also provides sustenance for the crops that provide man's food.

   b. The seasons were designed to provide for man. IMAGINE A WORLD IN WHICH THE SEASONS HAD NO ORDER! How could man survive?

c. God is enraged when man ignores the empirical evidences that He has placed all around us that so plainly declare His existence. Rom. 1:18-21

1. His existence, though invisible, is clearly known by observing the empirical evidence He has left throughout the created world.

2. The empirical data enables man to KNOW of God's AWESOME DIVINE POWER and DEITY!

3. Because of the magnitude of that empirical evidence, man is without excuse if he denies the existence of God.

4. How then could man deny God's existence? Man denies God's existence when he exalts himself and his own humanistic reasoning, decides that he himself is the all-wise one, and refuses to glorify God as he sees the empirical evidence RIGHT UNDER HIS OWN NOSE!

d. Yet, I wonder:

1. How much could I know about God if it were not for His divine revelation, the Bible?

2. One can see, in the reasoning of people who believe in a supreme being but who do not know the God of the Bible, the confusion that so quickly permeates man's thinking. People wrongly perceive storms, hurricanes,

volcanoes, and tornadoes as that supreme being's anger toward mankind.

3. How thankful man should be for the divinely inspired Bible that gives us SO MUCH MORE insight into and information about God than we could ever have with the empirical knowledge alone.

e. If we CAN know that God exists, WHY would one say, "I KNOW God does not exist?"

1. He is a logical positivist who declares that the ONLY KIND of knowledge is empirical knowledge.

2. Thus, because he does not SEE, he does not accept God, Heaven nor Hell as being REAL. To him, They simply DO NOT EXIST.

3. One wonders why he does not use the same logic about the existence of people in history such as George Washington, Abraham Lincoln, Winston Churchill, or Joseph Stalin.

    a. Did he SEE these men of history?

    b. Did he TOUCH them?

    c. Did he HEAR them talk?

    d. If not, did they exist?

4. Using his philosophy, why would he believe in anything or anyone whom he has not seen, past or present?

C. Once we understand Bible Knowledge, we realize that WE CAN KNOW:
1. The reality of **Heaven**, **Hell**, and the **Judgment**! Why? Because the God of Truth told us they exist and will occur.

2. That the world was **created**! Heb. 11:3
   a. God who designed the world and was there at its inception declares that the world was spoken into existence by the power of Deity and that the tangible, empirical evidences were instantaneously created; it did not come about through the restructuring or altering of matter that already existed (evolution).
   b. Thus, we can KNOW that the world was created; it did NOT come about by naturalistic evolution.
   c. God Himself reminds us that every house had to have a designer and **builder**. Heb. 3:4. This is also true with the design and order of the universe.
   d. Logical people would be insulted if someone tried to convince them that

a **watch** or **airplane** JUST HAPPENED — no designer, no builder; they just came about from a huge explosion in a junk yard or aluminum factory.

e. Why can man so quickly see the absurdity of such arguments and yet not see the absurdity of arguments that claim that the orderly designed universe, the order of our human bodies with all their systems working in harmony, and the phenomenal balance of the earth and atmosphere that provides a perfect habitation for mankind JUST HAPPENED?

3. That the **miracles** actually occurred!

a. The world-wide Flood, the Israelites crossing the RED Sea, Jonah being swallowed by a whale, Jesus healing the sick, raising the dead, and being raised from the dead Himself REALLY OCCURRED!

b. A skeptical human may deny these events — God, who cannot lie tells us they are true events.

c. Man may try to remove the supernatural but he only poses more problems for himself. For example, skeptics deny that the children of Israel left Egypt through the Red Sea; rather they claim the Israelites sloshed through about eight inches of water in the REED Sea. One question quickly arises: "How did the whole Egyptian army drown in the eight inches of water in the Reed Sea?"

4. That we have been **saved**!
   a. God tells us that we can KNOW that we have eternal life. I Jn. 5:13
   b. This is knowledge not based upon a bolt of lightning from heaven, nor from God speaking directly from heaven; rather, we know by the things He has revealed in His Word.
   c. When we have obeyed His Word, we can KNOW that we have eternal life.

5. What **sin** is!
   a. The world struggles today with the question, "What IS sin?"
   b. God has carefully identified sin in Scripture; we can KNOW if an action is sin or not.

6. That the world will NEVER AGAIN be **destroyed** by **water**!
   a. Genesis 6 tells of the universal Flood.
      1. It was God's punishment of a sinful world.
      2. Noah received God's grace and was spared from the Flood because of his godly heart.

3. Noah, his wife, his three sons and their wives were spared from the Flood — they spared the whole human family from extinction.

b. When the flood waters abated, God made a promise to Noah and all generations of mankind in the future: He would never again destroy the whole earth by water.

c. Then God gave empirical evidence as proof of His promise: He placed the rainbow in the heavens as a sign of His promise.

d. Sadly, mankind often sees a rainbow and thinks of the "Old Wives' Tale" that if you can get to the end of the rainbow you will find a pot of gold.

e. What a pitiful deception!

f. Rather, every time man sees the rainbow, he KNOWS that God has left empirical evidence that His Word is ABSOLUTELY true.

g. If He is true in the things we can verify, and if He cannot lie, we can be CERTAIN that the things we cannot see or the events that He has promised, but that have not yet occurred, are JUST AS CERTAIN and JUST AS SURE TO OCCUR!

II. What is Bible Faith?

Goals To Accomplish As You Teach This Topic:
- Contrast the solid nature of Biblical faith with the hopelessly inept and shallow concepts that are prevalent about faith.
- Accentuate the confidence and trust of true faith.
- Stress that true faith is based upon the very nature of God Himself.

Struggles That The Student Might Have With This Topic:
- Overcoming presuppositions and previous definitions about faith that he brings to this study. That may hinder him seeing the glory of true faith!
- Accepting the commitment of true faith.
- Struggling with his inability to have empirical evidence of Jesus. This may cause him to struggle with faith in Jesus.

A. Ideas People Have About Faith.
1. The concepts that most have about faith are hopelessly inadequate and inept.

2. Most see faith as one of the following ideas:
   a. **A crutch on which weak mankind leans.**
   b. **Belief in something that is not real but that man wants SO DESPERATELY to see as real — Tooth Fairy, Santa Claus, or God.**
   c. **A blind "leap in the dark."** This

is the view of the existentialist who sees faith as man making unwarranted conclusions from a few evidences that will not really support those conclusions.

d. Probability. This person tries to figure if it is more probable mathematically that God exists or does not exist; if he concludes there is more probability, then he believes.

B. What BIBLE FAITH REALLY IS!
1. Hebrews 11:1 gives great insight into the nature of TRUE faith.
   a. "Assurance"
      1. This word in the original Greek meant "guarantee," "reality."
         a. How can "faith" be a "guarantee" or "reality?"
         b. Because when God, who cannot lie, tells us something, we KNOW it is true.
      2. Faith is the reality "of things HOPED for."
         a. Here is another term that is SO misunderstood.
         b. How do we typically define "hope" today?
            1. What I WISH would occur, but would never really expect.
            2. I usually use the

illustration of receiving the Publisher's Clearing House Sweepstakes in the mail.

a. I always fill it out and enter the sweepstakes.

b. I ask the student if he has received the forms and did he fill them out and mail them?

c. I am excited when he did not fill his out; it gives me a better chance of winning.

d. Then I ask "Do you think I am at home on Super Bowl Sunday waiting anxiously and wringing my hands saying, 'I sure HOPE I am going to win that $10 million today?'"

e. What do I mean by "hope" in that context? "I WISH; IT SURE WOULD BE NICE!"

f. Do you think I

EXPECT to win? Will I be heartbroken if I do not win that money? Certainly not!

3. Bible hope is "expectation." I **expect** God's promise to happen because HE PROMISED AND HE CANNOT LIE; therefore, I KNOW it will happen!

b. "Conviction."
   1. The Greek word here means "**proof**"
   2. Bible faith is the proof even of the **unseen**.
   3. How can I have the proof of the unseen? How can I KNOW the unseen really exists? Because God, who cannot lie, has told me it is true and real.

2. II Timothy 1:12 is a MARVELOUS explanation of the nature and depth of true faith.
   a. Paul is in prison as he, by inspiration, pens these words.
   b. The death decree has already been given; he knows he will die, but the specific day is still uncertain.
   c. Observe the CERTAINTY of Paul's faith.

1. It begins with KNOWLEDGE —
   He KNOWS the promises of God
   concerning a coming Messiah.

2. Added to that knowledge is
   PERSUASION — Paul's heart is
   absolutely convinced that Jesus
   is that promised Messiah, the
   Son of God.

3. He is so convinced that he is
   willing to COMMIT his very
   soul's salvation and his
   justification before God in the
   hands of Jesus.

d. His conviction is so strong that he
   will stand firmly upon the truths of
   Christianity and is WILLING TO
   SUFFER persecution, rejection,
   imprisonment and even death for his
   conviction.

e. Paul is so certain that Christ is the
   true Messiah that he has NO
   SHAME for what he believes — NO
   MATTER WHAT PEOPLE THINK!

f. THAT IS BIBLE FAITH — Not some
   superficial wish, doubt or
   uncertainty.

3. The trust of genuine faith.
   a. Noah prepared an **ark**. Heb. 11:7
      1. Imagine what his neighbors
         thought when Noah began to
         build that huge boat — "Crazy
         Old Man!"

    2.   However, God told Noah that it was going to rain and there would be a universal flood. Even though he had never seen such a flood, Noah KNEW it would occur!

    3.   Based upon that knowledge, he built the ark and his life was spared.

b. Abraham left his **homeland**. Heb. 11:8-10

    1.   God called him in Ur of the Chaldees to leave his homeland and go to a land in which he would be a pilgrim, but which would be given to his descendants. Gen. 12:1-3

    2.   Abraham obeyed, not even knowing to what land he would travel.

    3.   However, he KNEW that God would keep his word!

c. Abraham **offered** Isaac. Heb. 11:17; Gen. 22:1-18

    1.   In this story, God was testing the depth of Abraham's faith.

    2.   Obviously, God would never have allowed Abraham to slay Isaac — He HATED child sacrifice.

    3.   When God told Abraham to go offer Isaac, he went.

4. He was so faithful that he built the altar, laid Isaac on the altar and drew his knife to slay him.

5. How could Abraham do that? He KNEW that Isaac was the son of promise.

   a. Earlier he had tried to "help God" by conceiving Ishmael.

   b. Immediately he was told, "This is NOT the son of promise."

   c. By supernatural blessing, Abraham and Sarah bore Isaac when they were 100 and 90 years old respectively.

   d. God declared that Isaac was the son of promise.

   e. Thus, Abraham KNEW that Isaac was going to bear children and through them a great nation was going to arise.

   f. He KNEW that if God allowed him to slay Isaac that God would also raise him from the dead because this WAS the son of promise!

d. Joseph made mention about his **bones**. Heb. 11:22

   1. He KNEW God's promises to Abraham, Isaac and Jacob about the land of Canaan. Gen.

50:24,25

2. He KNEW that God keeps His promises.

3. Therefore, Joseph commanded that his bones be returned to Canaan and buried when Israel returned.

4. It occurred.

    a. Moses took Joseph's bones with him when Israel left Egypt. Ex. 13:19

    b. Joshua buried them in Canaan. Josh. 24:32

e. Moses and Israel left Egypt and walked through the **Red Sea** on dry ground. Heb. 11:29; Ex. 14:21-31

1. In the ten plagues, God showed His mighty power to the Israelites.

2. He promised to deliver them from Egypt.

3. Yet, imagine their fear as the Israelites approached the Red Sea, with the wilderness on both sides and the enraged Egyptians pursuing them and determined to destroy them.

4. Moses encouraged them not to fear because they could KNOW they would be delivered — God had promised!

    f. Israel walked around Jericho for seven days. Heb. 11:30; Josh. 6:12-20

        1. What would you do if I told you to walk around a stadium in your town once a day for six days, seven times on the seventh day, blow trumpets and shout and the walls of that stadium will fall? Would you do it? Obviously not!

        2. Yet, when God told Israel to walk around Jericho, they KNEW He would give them the city and He did!

4. Does faith involve empirical knowledge?

    a. Sometimes it does; sometimes it does not.

    b. Illustrations:

        1. The woman of Samaria and the people she told. Jn. 4:7-42

            a. As the woman talked with Jesus and He told her about her past life, she believed. Verses 7-26

            b. Her faith was based upon empirical knowledge — She SAW Him, TALKED with him.

            c. Later, she returned to the city and told the people about Jesus who "told me all things that ever I did." Verse 29

    d. Many of the Samaritans believed because of her testimony, verse 39; others went to hear Him for themselves and believed after hearing Him. Verse 41

       1. Those who knew the woman and believed her testimony KNEW because of her truthfulness.

       2. Those who went to hear Jesus themselves KNEW by empirical evidence.

2. **Thomas** and Us. Jn. 20:19-29

    a. The evening of the Resurrection Day, Jesus appeared to the Apostles but Thomas was not present. Verses 19-25

    b. When they told Thomas that the Lord had risen, Thomas refused to believe.

    c. He stated that he would only believe if he could put his finger in the prints of the nails in Jesus' hands and stick his hand in the sword-pierced side. Verse 25

    d. The following Sunday, Jesus appeared to the Apostles and this time Thomas was present. Verse 26

    e. When Jesus spoke to him and offered to let him feel His wounds, Thomas breathlessly cried, "My Lord and my God!" Verse 28

    f. There is NO SUGGESTION that Thomas actually touched Jesus.

    g. Jesus then commended Thomas for his faith — even though it was based upon empirical knowledge. Verse 29

    h. He gave a greater commendation to those who will have faith without the privilege of empirical knowledge — That's all those after Jesus' Ascension to Heaven. That's YOU and ME!

  c. We today can **know** just as surely as the Samaritan woman and Thomas knew that Jesus IS the Christ and the resurrected Son of God even though we cannot see Him!

Conclusion!

  A. HOW IMPORTANT IT IS TO TRULY UNDERSTAND BIBLE KNOWLEDGE AND FAITH!

B. Sadly, the concept that many have of faith is so shallow that doubt is constant.

C. True Bible faith gives us GREAT CONFIDENCE!

D We can confidently, yet without arrogance say, "I KNOW God exists!"

E. Assignment for the next lesson: "Who is God?"

Who Is God?

Introduction to the Lesson:

    A. Why study this topic?

        1. One of the greatest mistakes we often make in teaching the Bible is to assume that the student already understands spiritual truths that we regard to be SO basic and elementary.

        2. NEVER assume that the student already knows the God of the Bible; you may be astounded when he tells you later what he truly thinks.

        3. If he has an incorrect view of God, he may later suggest, "I do not believe in God like that!", or he may reject plain Bible teaching by stating, "The God I believe in would never ask man to do that or expect man to understand it that way!"

        4. Most teachers will never have a student answer the question, "Who is God?" as a physician answered me in Belarus. She declared, "God is just an idea passed down from parent to child. God is merely a figment of man's imagination." Now imagine a teacher continuing by saying, "GOD tells you to do this." If God is only

a fictitious character, the student will NEVER give any serious consideration to your teaching!

5. Another reason to study this topic is that many students will identify God with only one of His traits; usually they will mention "Love!"

B. Our goal as a teacher is to assist the student to "**know**" God!
   1. There are two types of knowledge mentioned in the original Greek text!
      a. One type of knowledge is "knowing the **facts**."
         1. This is the Greek word " γινώσκω" (ginosko).
         2. This type of knowledge is the acquainting of our minds with the facts about a person, place or thing.
            a. "I know Michael Jordan." He is a basketball player for the Chicago Bulls; he attempted to become a baseball player; his father was murdered.
            b. "I know about my computer."
      b. The second type of knowledge is "knowing by **personal experience**."
         1. This is the idea of the Greek word " οἶδα" (oida).
         2. It involves taking the facts we

know and USING them.

3. Examples of this type of knowledge:

   a. One may know the facts about the operation of a machine such as a computer from having read the manual, but he has absolutely NO practical, first-hand knowledge of how it truly operates. If a problem arises, he may be clueless as to what the problem is. Then he has to call for help from one who truly "knows" the computer.

   b. One who truly "knows" computers is amazing to watch. He has no fear of computers, can immediately tell you what is wrong with a program, can "set up" or "clean up" a computer so it will operate much more efficiently, and can easily repair or "up-grade" your machine.

2. Paul's message at Athens vividly shows the importance of people knowing the facts about God before they can believe in and worship Him properly and

acceptably. Ac. 17:22-31

a. Paul was impressed with the extremely religious nature of the people of Athens.

b. At the same time, he was deeply distressed by the idolatry that was prevalent there.

c. Upon observing an altar dedicated "To The **Unknown** God," Paul saw his opportunity to teach the Athenians about the true God of Heaven.

d. Paul's sermon at Mars' hill presented the facts to these idolaters about the true God and contrasted His nature with theirs.

e. The idols were inanimate; the true God is a **living** God!

f. For one to worship God without knowing the facts about who He truly is, makes one guilty of "ignorant worship."

C. Our goal as teachers: we want to help the students **know** the **facts** about God and then apply these facts to their lives so they can **know** Him **personally** or make Him the God of their lives.

I. Coming to Know the Facts About God!

Goals To Accomplish As You Teach This Topic:

- Assist the student to know the facts revealed in Scripture about God.
- Portray God as a living being.
- Help the student to see the correlation between Deity and man. Man is the only part of creation made in the image of God. As such, man is much more like God than many have ever considered. Understanding ourselves helps us understand God.
- Encourage the student to begin to grasp the concept of God being eternal as he realizes he will never cease to exist.
- Glorify God for His Divine Nature that is so much greater than man! His being all-sovereign, and all-knowing about everything everywhere quickly shows us the glory of His Deity and our own finiteness.
- Magnify both the love and justice of God's nature.

Struggles That The Student Might Have With This Topic:

- Seeing God as a living being or person.
- Comprehending "spirit."
- Wondering "why" if God is all-sovereign He allows bad things to happen in our lives.
- Overcoming previous teaching about God being everywhere instead of His being in Heaven but knowing everything that happens everywhere.
- Accepting the fact that God is a being of justice who always has and always will punish sin. This is so difficult because of the present-day belief that God loves man SO MUCH that He could not possibly bring judgment upon anyone.

Teaching Tools:

- Chart #1
- Chart #2

A. God is a **living spirit**.
    1. He is **alive!**
        a. This is Paul's declaration in Acts
            17:28,29.
        b. Paul's reasoning is SO interesting
            — he affirms that we can understand
            the nature of God by looking at our
            own nature.
            1. He quotes one of the Athenian
                poets who affirmed, "We are also
                his offspring."
            2. Then Paul reasons like this: if
                we are the offspring of God, and
                if we are living, our God must
                also be alive.
            3. I have never studied with a
                student who would trust me for
                a minute if I told him that a baby
                came from a rock or from a totem
                pole. We all realize that a living
                baby comes from a living mother.
        c. Paul also affirms:
            1. That the true God had the
                wisdom to design the whole
                universe.
            2. That the true God does not
                depend upon man to serve Him
                and care for Him! An idol needed
                someone even to wipe the dust
                off its nose, but the true God can
                care for Himself.

2. He is a **spirit**!
   a. This is clearly stated in John 4:24, "God is a spirit."
   b. But, what does "spirit" mean?
      1. This word elicits all kinds of definitions and thoughts in a student's mind.
      2. Some think of God as gas, air, or Casper the ghost — something ethereal, mysterious, mystical, unfathomable and imperceptible.
      3. God has provided help for us to understand "spirit."
         a. "For as the body without the spirit is dead," **Js. 2:26**
         b. James explains that faith separated from works is not a living faith, just as a human body separated from the spirit is dead.
         c. Man is SO MUCH MORE than just a human body.
            1. "Body" refers to our human tabernacle.
            2. "Spirit" refers to the part of man made in the image of God.
            3. "Soul," although sometimes used in reference to our nature made in God's image, may refer to the fact that we are

alive or have life. See Genesis 2:7 where man became a living "soul" or "creature." This refers to his "being alive."

d. Consider the difference between one who was alive earlier this week, died, and today you visit his family at the funeral home.

1. How often have you heard someone say as they walk up to a casket, "He just looks like he is lying there asleep."

2. Yet, there are some drastic differences.

3. What traits did he have when he was alive that are missing now that he has died?

a. Intelligence.

b. Emotions.

c. Ability to communicate.

d. Conscience.

e. Ability to choose between right and wrong.

4. These traits describe the inherent nature of a spirit.

e. Chart #1.
1. This chart has been prepared to explain to the student that man is a spirit and not a mere human body.
   a. It explains what happens to the spirit and body after death.
   b. I realize it is a BUSY chart; however, it describes many events!
   c. BE SURE TO BEGIN THE EXPLANATION OF CHART #1 BY STARTING IN THE BOTTOM LEFT HAND CORNER.
2. Here we have a man alive; he dies; what happens at death?
3. The body is placed in the grave and left there.
4. The spirit leaves the body and goes to the realm of departed spirits, Hades, prepared by God Himself.
5. Hades is vividly described in Luke 16:19-31.

a. The spirits of the righteous go to Paradise at death. This is where Jesus' spirit went at His Death. Lk. 23:43

b. The spirits of the wicked go to Torment at death.

c. A great gulf separates these two realms; there is no changing of destiny after death.

d. These spirits have consciousness; they have awareness and memory.

e. All who die will go to Hades until Christ's second coming.

f. At that time, He will destroy Hades. Rev. 1:18

6. Christ will return on the LAST DAY.

a. Jn. 6:39,40,44,54

b. I Thess. 4:13-18

c. When He returns, He will bring ALL the spirits from Hades with Him — both righteous and wicked.

 d. Some wrongly have concluded that there will be two separate returns because I Thessalonians discusses the resurrection of the righteous.

 e. However, Paul is addressing the concern of the Thessalonian Christians who thought their deceased brethren would miss Christ's second coming.

 f. Paul reminds them that the living and the dead will all witness that glorious event together.

7. The spirits that Christ brings with Him will be re-united with the bodies that have been changed into incorruptible bodies.

 a. I Cor. 15:12-24; 50-54

 b. Those who are alive

will have their bodies instantly transformed into eternal resurrection bodies.

8. Then simultaneously, the whole human race will be caught up to meet the Lord in the air. I Thess. 4:17

9. Then the Judgment will occur.

   a. All those who have been in Hades already know their eternal destiny. Those in Torment will be sent to the tortures of Hell; those in Paradise will be invited into the glories of Heaven.

   b. It is at this time that those who are living on Earth at the Lord's Second Coming will learn of their eternal destiny.

f. As a spirit, He cannot be confined to any **building**. Ac. 17:24

4. Remember Paul's argument in Acts 17 — we can understand

much about God by understanding ourselves. I am a spirit made in the image of God who also is a spirit.

3. How glorious — God is a LIVING SPIRIT!

B. God is an **eternal** Spirit!
    1. In Romans 1:20 the Bible affirms His "eternal power and Godhead [divinity — ASV]."

    2. What does "Eternal" mean?
        a. This seems to be SUCH a difficult concept for mankind to grasp.
        b. I remember when I was young that this seemed SO difficult.
        c. Everything we know has a beginning and an end.
        d. Yet, "Eternal" means "FOREVER."

    3. God is a Being who is NOT **governed** by time.
        a. To Him, a day is no different than a thousand years; a thousand years is no different than a day. II Pet. 3:8
        b. How can that be? He is not governed by a watch or clock as we are.
        c. One caution: be careful that the student does not conclude that time references in the Bible cannot be understood by man. Some conclude

that because a day is as a thousand years in God's sight that we can never understand time references in the Bible. However, God has spoken in words and concepts that man can understand.

4. Chart #2.
    a. Remember Paul's argument in Acts 17 once again — we may be able to understand more than we think about God when we truly understand ourselves.
    b. The eternal nature of God may seem SO unfathomable to us.
        1. He ALWAYS WAS in the past.
        2. He ALWAYS WILL BE in the future.
    c. But what about man?
        1. Obviously, you have not always existed in the past.
        2. But what about your future?
            a. You were conceived when perhaps no one but God Himself knew you and that you existed.
            b. Some nine months later, you were born.
            c. Today you are alive.
            d. At some point in the future you will die. But is that the end of you?

      1. Obviously not.
      2. Remember Chart #1.
      3. At death, you will go to Hades.
      4. At the Lord's second coming, you will be judged and will then enter Heaven or Hell.
      5. How long will you be there? FOREVER!
   3. Suddenly, "eternal" begins to take on a personal concept!
   4. The eternal God, who designed mankind and provided the means whereby your parents could conceive you, knew that from the point of your conception you would NEVER end.

C. God is an **all-sovereign** Spirit!
  1. Ac. 17:25,26
    a. The Creation was all determined by His Sovereign Will.
    b. He made the choice to give man life and all the blessings of life.
    c. He also sets limits on the boundaries of a nation's growth and aggression against other nations and the times when nations will rise or fall.

  2. This attribute of God is often described by the word "omnipotent."

    a. I am uncomfortable with this word because of the connotations that many students attach to it.

    b. The word "omnipotent" simply means "all powerful."

    c. Many who have heard this word and define it as "all powerful" have become extremely bitter toward Him, turned against Him, or have even rejected Him and denied His existence.

        1. This is especially true of those who have had calamity in life.

        2. Parents whose baby has died may be heard to say, "If God is omnipotent, why did He not save my baby's life?"

        3. One with a terminal illness may be heard to say, "I have prayed and prayed to God. If He is omnipotent, why is He letting me die?"

    d. The false conclusion that is often drawn is that if God has the power, then He MUST use it or He is an unloving or even non-existent being.

3. The original Greek word would better be translated "**All Sovereign**."

    a. That means, "He can do whatever **HE CHOOSES** to do" within the confines of His Will.

b. Does God have the power to stop death? ABSOLUTELY!

   1. However, He has not chosen to do that.

   2. Rather, He chose to send His Son to come to this earth to die to secure a means of salvation for man and to be resurrected to assure us of our own resurrection.

c. Does God have the power to destroy the world today? ABSOLUTELY!

   1. Sometimes as we see wickedness in the world, we may wonder why He tolerates the world continuing to exist.

   2. However, He allows the world to stand because He wants to provide an opportunity for more people to become Christians. II Pet. 3:9

d. There are some things that God cannot do.

   1. He cannot overlook sin!

   2. He cannot become Satan!

e. As we studied earlier, we may learn much about the nature of God by learning about ourselves; however, when we come to this trait and the next two, we quickly realize the supernatural nature of Deity. We realize that God is SO MUCH

GREATER THAN MANKIND!

1. We cannot possibly do anything we choose to do.

2. We cannot say, "I want to fly by using my arms as wings; therefore, I will jump from the Empire State Building or Mt. Everest." We realize we would kill ourselves.

D. God is an **Omniscient** Spirit!

    1. "Omniscient" means "**all knowing**."

    2. Perhaps the greatest chapter in the Bible to explain the vastness of His knowledge is Psalm 139.

       a. Read Psalm 139:1-6; 13-16.

       b. God knows everything we do: when we stand, when we sit, what we think or say. Verses 1-6

       c. He knew us from the point of conception, before any human had an idea that we were conceived and growing toward birth, childhood and adulthood. Verses 13-16

    3. He knows:

       a. All our **goings**. Pr. 5:21

       b. All our **thoughts**. I Cor. 3:20

       c. The number of **hairs on our head**. Mt. 10:30

          1. Imagine the magnitude of such knowledge.

    2. He knows how many hairs are on my head in the morning when I rise; how many are there after I shower, towel dry and blow dry my hair.

    3. Such knowledge is humanly unfathomable when we realize how many hairs we lose every day.

    4. Obviously, some of us have so few hairs it might not be such a huge job to count the number of hairs on our head — especially if one is nearly bald.

  d. The number of **stars** in the universe. Ps. 147:4

4. Hebrews 4:13 describes the magnitude of His knowledge.

  a. God knows EVERYTHING about us.

  b. We cannot cover up nor hide anything from Him.

  c. We can hide NO SIN from Him — He knows all our actions, all our thoughts.

5. Once again we marvel at God's greatness and glory and realize that He is SO MUCH GREATER than mankind.

  a. We realize how little we really do know.

  b. What parent has not wished for just a little more knowledge of what small children were doing in another room or outside in the yard, or what teens were doing when on a date or when out of our sight?

6. This word "omniscient" is another word that is often misunderstood and causes great confusion in the minds of men.
   a. People often wrongly conclude that if He knows everything, then He must be responsible for everything and He causes everything.
   b. These are false assumptions.
   c. Although He knows everything (past, present, and future), this in no way suggests that He predetermines everything we do.
   d. God has given man free will and choice.
   e. This ties back to His being "All sovereign."
      1. Could He predetermine everything we do? Yes.
      2. But He has not chosen to do that.
      3. He never intended for man to be a robot nor a puppet on His string.
      4. He wants man to make the choice to love Him, honor Him and obey Him.

E. God knows everything that happens **everywhere**!

1. This idea is often expressed by the word "**omnipresent**."

   a. Here is another definition that causes EXTREME confusion in the minds of men.

   b. The word "omnipresent" means "all-present" or "everywhere."

   c. I have been amazed at students who immediately conclude from the word "omnipresent" that God is not a literal spirit or being.

      1. They conclude that God is like air, gas or that He is a force.

      2. They believe that God is in every mind, in every room and in every car in the world.

      3. This is an attempt to make God like man because we realize that we cannot know what is happening in another place unless we are there.

      4. Thus, the assumption is made that unless God is everywhere, He could not possibly know what is happening in every place.

   d. However, these are false assumptions.

2. This trait simply affirms that we can NEVER escape God's **knowledge**.

   a. Ps. 139:7-12

   b. This text is often lifted out of context to affirm that God is everywhere.

      c.   However, remember the theme of Psalm 139 — the KNOWLEDGE of God.

      d.   This text is simply stating that one cannot escape His knowledge in this life nor in Hades.

      e.   Ask the following people if you can ever hide anything from God:
1.   Jonah.
2.   Ananias and Sapphira. Ac. 5:1-11

3.   In reality, most people know where God is; but, may have forgotten.

      a.   As Jesus taught His disciples how to pray, He began, "Our Father which art in heaven." Mt. 6:9

      b.   In Acts 7, Stephen saw and declared that God was on His throne in Heaven. Ac. 7:56

4.   Once again, we marvel at God's supernatural nature and our own finiteness. It is incomprehensible to us to know EVERYTHING THAT HAPPENS EVERYWHERE!!

F.   God is love!

1.   This is perhaps the best-known trait of God.

      a.   However, it is also GREATLY misunderstood.

      b.   Many believe this is the ONLY trait of God!

1. That is comparable to saying a man is a policeman. That may be his occupation; however, there is much more about him. To fully understand or know him, you would also need to know that he is a husband, father, Christian, golfer, etc.

2. To mention only one trait does not mean that you know the person.

3. To mention only one trait of God does not mean that you know Him.

c. Others believe that His love means that He simply ignores man's sin. Those who hold this view will nearly espouse the concept of universalism — He will save everyone. Nothing could be further from the truth.

2. God first **loved us** when we were sinners; He showed us what true love encompasses when He cared about man being in sin and provided a way of redemption. I Jn. 4:19

3. Examples of His Divine love.
   a. God SO loved the world that He gave His Son to die for us. Jn. 3:16
   b. Instead of hating sinful man, God extended His love by providing His

Son to die that forgiveness might be made available. Rom. 5:8

4. He still loves mankind even though we often wonder, "Why?" "How long will He allow the world to stand?"
    a. Because He was longsuffering, He allowed the world to exist for 120 years while Noah built an ark whereby he and his family might be saved from the flood.
    b. He is a God of truth; He keeps His word; the world WILL BE destroyed in the future. The reason the world still exists is because He is "**longsuffering** to us-ward, not willing that any should perish, but that all should come to repentance." II Pet. 3:9
    c. He wants every person today to have the opportunity to turn from sin and to be saved.

5. His love exists today — He truly **cares** for all men.
    a. "For he maketh his sun to rise on the evil and on the good, and sendeth rain on the just and on the unjust." Mt. 5:45
    b. The sun and rain are examples of His daily care in providing for the very existence and continuance of the human race.

    c. "Casting all your care upon him: for he careth for you." I Pet. 5:7

      1. He knows every person.

      2. He is interested in every person.

      3. He wants you to be His child and to eagerly come to Him with all of your concerns and cares.

6. Truly, "GOD IS LOVE!"

G. God is **justice**!

  1. Here is the almost completely overlooked trait of God today.

  2. People want Him to be a God of love so desperately that they totally ignore His justice.

    a. What is "justice?"

      1. He is fair in His judgments.

      2. In judgment, man receives what he deserves based upon his obedience or disobedience to God's will.

      3. He keeps His word.

        a. He will extend His grace to those who obey His commands.

        b. He will punish those who do not obey His words.

    b. Ac. 17:30,31

      1. He commands sinful man to repent of his sins.

      2. He has appointed a day when

the world will be judged by His Son, Jesus Christ.

3. "Behold therefore the goodness and severity of God: on them which fell, severity; but toward thee, goodness, if thou continue in his goodness: otherwise thou also shalt be cut off." Rom. 11:22

   a. God's nature is inherently both **goodness** and **severity**.

      1. "Goodness" — grace and love.

      2. "Severity" — sternness, harshness.

   b. He extends severity to those who become unbelievers.

      1. This is what happened to the Jews in this context.

      2. God, in His grace, gave the Jews the privilege of His special promises and of bringing the Messiah into the world through their nation.

      3. However, they rejected Jesus; therefore, God's severity was brought upon them.

   c. He extends goodness to faithful believers.

      1. God has shown His grace and kindness to the Gentiles by sending Peter and Paul to preach to them the Gospel.

      2. Because of their faithful, loving

response, God had extended His saving grace to them.

3. However, if the Gentiles became unbelievers, God would then punish them in His severity just as surely as He had the Jews earlier.

4. Think of Biblical examples of God's severity.
   a. **Cain**. Gen. 4:1-16; Jude 11
   b. **The wicked in the Flood**. Gen. 6:1-7
   c. **Sodom and Gomorrah**. Gen. 19:24,25
   d. **Nadab and Abihu**, sons of Aaron. Lev. 10:1,2
   e. **King Saul's** rejection as King of Israel.
      1. After he unlawfully offered the sacrifice. I Sa. 13:14
      2. After he rebelled against God's command to utterly destroy the Amalekites. I Sa. 15:28
   f. **Those who continue to live in the works of the flesh**. Gal. 5:21
   g. Christ will come in severity upon **unbelievers at His second coming**. II Thess. 1:7-9

II. We Need to Know These **Facts** About God!
A. They declare who He **is**.

B. Only by knowing these facts can we then make the choice to make Him our **God**.

C. However, one may know the facts about God, yet refuse to faithfully react to those facts so that he can **know** Him as his God. Rom. 1:21

III. For One to Truly Know God, He Must Not Only Know the Facts, but He Must Also Proceed to Make God HIS God!

Goals To Accomplish As You Teach This Topic:

- Encourage the student to strive for understanding of the facts about God.
- Urge him to understand the emptiness of facts without acting upon them.
- Challenge the student to have an awe for God that inspires him to want to obey Him.

Struggles That The Student Might Have With This Topic:

- Absorbing these facts. Many of these facts may be very new for him; allow him time to go home and absorb these truths.
- Contemplating God's justice. God's justice may be difficult for the student to accept because of the constant emphasis he has heard during his life that a loving God would punish no one.
- Beginning to see his need for God. By the end of this lesson, the student may already begin to struggle with commitment, realizing the consequences of not knowing God as his own God.

A. Heb. 8:11
1. Under the Law of Moses, Jewish children were automatically under the Law of Moses. After birth the child had to be taught the facts about the God who was His God.

2. Under the New Covenant of Christ, one has to be taught the facts about God, then he must proceed to make God his own God. No Christian has to be taught to know the facts about who God is. He not only had to know the facts but he also had to make the choice to submit to God; God is now HIS God. This is true of **all** Christians under the New Testament of Christ.

B. We truly KNOW God when we are willing to become His **children**.
1. This occurs when we become true believers in His Son Jesus. Gal. 3:26,27

2. Because of our response to the amazing love of God, we are privileged to become His children. Those who do not know the facts about God will not understand us either. I Jn. 3:1

C. When we truly KNOW God, we will determine to give to Him our praise, respect and awe.
1. Who is like Him?

2. We can only reverentially and humbly assert, "HOW GREAT THOU ART!"

D. For one not to know the facts about God or to know the facts and refuse to know Him as his own God is to bring the severity of Christ's vengeance and **everlasting destruction** or separation from God upon himself! II Thess. 1:7-9

Conclusion:

A. Determine to know who God is as He has revealed Himself to us in Scripture.

B. Also, determine to know Him as your God by believing in Him, loving Him, trusting Him and obeying Him.

C. Assignment for the next lesson: "Who is Jesus Christ?"

Who Is Jesus Christ?

Introduction to the Lesson:

  A. Why study this topic?

      1. As I mentioned in the last lesson, it is a critical mistake to assume that the student surely believes in God or must certainly know who He is.

      2. Another great mistake we make in teaching the Bible is to assume that the student understands who Jesus Christ is.

      3. The first two facts about Jesus are not known by a great percentage of the students.

  B. Begin by asking the student, "How would you answer the question, 'Who is Jesus Christ?'"

      1. Allow the student to give answers without making comments.

      2. The purpose is to get his mind focused on what his understanding is about Christ; later he will compare his ideas with what is revealed in Scripture.

      3. At this point, some may see Him as a prophet, just a man, or think that He came into being as a baby. Do not be critical here; rather, proceed to teach the

student who Jesus Christ truly is.

C. It is as important to **know** Jesus Christ as it is to know God!

   1. It is imperative to begin by knowing the facts about Christ; these facts are what we will study in this lesson.

   2. We must know the **facts** before we can know Christ **personally** as our Lord and Savior.

I. Knowing the Facts About Jesus — Who IS Jesus Christ?

Goals To Accomplish As You Teach This Topic:

- Convince the student of the Deity of Jesus Christ. The student needs to see that a Divine Being came to Earth because it was the only way for us to have salvation.
- Persuade the student that Jesus was the Creator.
- Emphasize that Jesus is the Virgin-born Savior who died on the Cross, was raised and ascended back to Heaven. There He now reigns as the Lord and will come back on the last day for the resurrection and judgment.
- Accentuate His being the Word, a Lawgiver, an Intercessor who pleads to the Father for His people, and man's only Mediator.

Struggles That The Student Might Have With This Topic:

- Grasping the Deity of Christ. This truth is not understood by a great percentage of students. Rather,

they see Him as beginning as a baby.
- Accepting the fact that Jesus created the universe!
- Realizing the difference between an "Intercessor" and a "Mediator."

Teaching Tools:

- Chart #3
- Chart #4

A. Jesus is **Deity**.
1. He is one member of the **Godhead**.
2. In Genesis 1:1 the word "God" is a **plural** noun.
   a. It is vital to understand this point!
   b. One may quickly complain, "But I do not know a word of Hebrew."
   c. That is not necessary at all.
   d. Read Genesis 1:26,27.
      1. "And God said, Let US make man in OUR image, after OUR likeness."
      2. What kind of pronouns are "Us" and "Our"? PLURAL.
      3. What do plural pronouns imply? More than one person.
      4. These verses are explaining that there is more than one Being who is Divine.
3. Jesus is **God (Deity)**.
   a. "In the beginning was the Word, and the Word was with God, and the Word was God." Jn. 1:1

1. This passage is extremely confusing for many students.
2. Take plenty of time to assist the student to comprehend the truths in the text.
3. Who is "the Word" in this text?
   a. Students may make many different guesses.
   b. Read verse 14: "And the Word was made flesh, and dwelt among us, (and we beheld his glory, the glory as of the only begotten of the Father,) full of grace and truth."
   c. Could this refer to the Father? NO! Why? He never dwelt in flesh.
   d. Could this refer to the Spirit? NO! Why? He never dwelt in flesh.

b. Truths from this text.
   1. Jesus existed before the world began.
   2. He was co-existent with the Father.
      a. He was WITH the Father.
      b. Consider the implication of "WITH."
         1. Would you say, "I sit here WITH myself?" Obviously not.

2. To be "WITH" someone suggests that there are two or more persons together.

c. Jesus was WITH the Father before the world was brought into being.

3. Jesus is also "God."

a. This phrase seems to be the most confusing in the text.

b. Students typically struggle with this, "Is that saying that Jesus IS the Father?"

c. "God" is being used in two different senses in this passage.

1. The phrase "and the Word was WITH God" affirms that Jesus was with the Father in eternity.

2. The phrase "and the Word was God" is affirming that Jesus is a Divine Being just as the Father is Divine.

4. His name "**Immanuel**" means "GOD with us."

a. "Behold, a virgin shall be with child, and shall bring forth a son, and they shall call his name Immanuel, which

being interpreted is, God with us."
Mt. 1:23

b. This is a quote of Isaiah's prophecy 600 years before Jesus came to the world. Is. 7:14. Often I will read the Isaiah passage while the student reads the fulfillment in Matthew 1:23.

c. His name, "Immanuel," speaks of His nature — Deity.

5. Jesus affirms His Deity in another way to Philip in John 14:9.

a. Philip asked Jesus to show him the Father.

b. Jesus replied, "he that hath seen me hath seen the Father; and how sayest thou then, show us the Father?"

c. Jesus is NOT stating that He IS the Father; He IS affirming that He is Divine; one who sees Him can understand **the Father**.

1. Imagine being on a spaceship to Mars and upon landing, there really were Martians.

a. When you step off the spaceship, you are immediately approached by the Martians.

b. They are amused about you as a human being.

c. Then they ask, "Tell us about

your leader."

    d. You might reply, "If you have seen me, you have seen my leader."

    e. You certainly are not suggesting that you and the President are the same person.

    f. Rather, you are explaining that the President is a human just as you are a human.

  2. The thoughts, teachings, and actions of Jesus will be consistent with the Father's thoughts, teachings, and actions because both are Divine.

6. Chart #3.

  a. Begin by explaining the right side of the chart.

    1. All the beings identified in this circle are human.

    2. In explaining this circle you might say:

      a. You (the student) — The Human.

      b. Me (the teacher) — The Human.

      c. The President — The Human.

    3. The point of this illustration: All

in this circle have the same nature — they are humanity or human beings.

b. Next, turn to the left side of the chart.

1. All of the Beings in this circle are Deity or Divine Beings.

2. By way of explanation:

a   God, the Father.

b. God, the Son.

c. God, the Holy Spirit.

3. All three of these Beings possess every inherent trait of Deity — each one is a Divine Being.

c. The point: Jesus is JUST AS DIVINE as the Father!

1. He possesses every trait of Deity.

2. This suggests that Jesus is a living spirit; He is eternal; He has the power to do whatever He chooses to do; He knows everything that happens everywhere; He is love and justice.

3. Therefore, He is SO MUCH MORE than mere mortal man — He is a member of the Godhead.

4. HOW we should RESPECT, HONOR, and LISTEN to Him!

B. Jesus is the **Creator**.

    1. As soon as you make this affirmation, be ready for reactions of disbelief.

        a. Some will look at you with disbelief; some will glare at you with cocked head and squinted eyes.

        b. This is an almost universally unknown trait of Jesus Christ.

        c. "BUT," argues the student, "GOD DID IT!" Then very kindly turn his mind to what he learned earlier in this lesson, "Remember, the word "God" in Genesis 1:1 is **plural**.

    2. Passages that declare Christ's work in the creation.

        a. "God, who at sundry times and in divers manners spake in time past unto the fathers by the prophets, Hath in these last days spoken unto us by his Son, whom he hath appointed heir of all things, by whom also he made the worlds." Heb. 1:1,2

            1. God, the Father, at many times during the Old Testament days, spoke to the fathers in many different ways; however, today He speaks through His Son.

                a. He spoke during the days of Adam, Noah, Abraham, Isaac, Jacob, Moses and throughout the existence of the Nation of Israel.

      b. He spoke directly to some, through angels, through a flaming bush that did not burn, and even through a donkey.

      c. Today, His messenger to the world is His Son, Jesus.

2. God's Son, Jesus, is the One "by whom also he made the worlds."

      a. Jesus is the agent God used to create the world.

      b. Illustrations:

            1. Imagine you are buying a house; today is the time for closing the deal, and you cannot attend.

                  a. What do you do? You hire an attorney or representative to act as your agent.

                  b. Who buys the house? YOU do! How? Through your representative.

            2. Imagine that you have a law suit against you, but you have to be out of the country.

                  a. What do you do? You hire an attorney to represent you in the litigation.

      b. You defend yourself through an agent — your attorney.

    c. The truth here: God, the Father, designed the creation of the world; Jesus Christ did the creating.

      1. In Genesis 1:3, when it is stated, "And GOD said, Let there be light:" to whom does it refer?

         a. Obviously God, the Father planned for light to exist.

         b. JESUS is the member of the Godhead who spoke that light into existence.

      2. How AMAZING this is!

      3. The student at this point may be uncertain and want more evidence. That is a legitimate desire and God has given us more evidence.

b. Jn. 1:1-3

    1. We read verse 1 earlier; now, we will read further and learn more about Christ, the Word.

    2. "In the beginning was the Word, and the Word was with God, and

the Word was God. The same was in the beginning with God. All things were made by him; and without him was not anything made that was made."

3. Truths from this text:

   a. Jesus existed before the world began.

   b. He existed with the Father in eternity.

   c. Jesus is a Divine Being, just as the Father is Divine.

   d. The Word, Jesus, created everything.

c. Col. 1:12-19

1. This is perhaps the clearest passage to explain Jesus' work in Creation.

2. Truths from this text:

   a. Christians should give thanks to the Father because He has given us the privilege to be partakers of His inheritance and has delivered us from the power of sin and has placed us in the Kingdom of His Son. Verses 12,13

   b. Who is His Son?

      1. He is the One in whom we have redemption through His Blood. Verse 14

2. He is the exact image (has all the inherent traits) of the invisible Father. Verse 15

3. He is greater than everything that has been created. Verse 15

4. Why is He greater than all that was created? Because HE IS THE CREATOR OF EVERY-THING. Verse 16

5. As Creator and Sustainer, His authority presently upholds the world's continued existence. Verse 17; II Pet. 3:7

6. He is the head of the Church. Verse 18.

7. Through His Blood shed in His Death on the Cross, He made reconciliation available. Verses 20,21

3. What do these facts about Jesus mean to us?

a. I will never forget the statement of one young adult man when he learned these truths: "I always thought Jesus came into being as a baby. If Jesus is Divine and the Creator, this changes my whole perspective about Him. I must get serious about Him and what He teaches!"

b. This means that the Divine Creator came to this Earth to die for me! AMAZING!

C. Jesus is the **Virgin-Born** Messiah and **Savior.**

1. He is the virgin-born Messiah.

a. The Old Testament prophesied His virgin birth in **Isaiah 7:14**

1. "Therefore the Lord himself shall give you a sign; Behold, a virgin shall conceive, and bear a son, and shall call his name Immanuel."

2. He would be born to a virgin — a supernatural event.

3. He would be called Immanuel or "God with us."

b. His virgin birth occurred. Mt. 1:18,22,23

1. Mary was a chaste virgin.

2. Her conception was a supernatural event.

3. The angel told Joseph that Mary was not a sinner; her conception was brought about by God.

4. Joseph was reminded that this

was a fulfillment of the Messianic prophecy of Isaiah 7:14.

2. He is our Savior.
    a. Man NEEDS a Savior.
        1. Sin **separates** us from God. Is. 59:1,2
        2. **All** have sinned. Rom. 3:23
    b. Jesus is Our Savior.
        1. He was named Jesus, which meant "Savior." Mt. 1:21
        2. John the baptizer professed that Jesus was "the Lamb of God, which taketh away the sin of the world." Jn. 1:29
        3. God SO loved the world that He gave Jesus to die that those who believe in Him might be saved. Sinful man has already condemned himself by his own sin; Jesus is our only hope for a Savior. Jn. 3:16,17
        4. Jesus explained His mission, "For the Son of man is come to seek and to save that which was lost." Lk. 19:10
        5. Paul knew that Christ Jesus came into the world for the purpose of saving sinners. Paul was convinced that he was the WORST sinner of all time. I Tim. 1:15

       a. If God would save the WORST sinner, surely He will save us!

       b. If God would save those who killed His Son, surely He will save us!

    c. Titles that describe this saving work.

       1. **Mediator**. I Tim. 2:5. His work was to restore sinful man back to Holy God.

       2. **High Priest**. Heb. 3:1. He offered His Blood to the Father for our sins.

       3. **Redeemer**. Heb. 9:12; I Pet. 1:18,19; Eph. 1:7. By His Blood, He purchased us from our sinful condition.

    d. WHAT A SAVIOR!

D. Jesus is the **crucified** Son of God!

   1. **Isaiah 53:4-6** is the Messianic prophecy that foretold His Crucifixion for us.

      a. He died because of OUR sins.

      b. The Father "laid on him [bombarded Him with] the iniquity of us all."

   2. His Death by crucifixion on the Cross was **prophesied** hundreds of years before crucifixion was practiced in the world. Ps. 22:16

   3. Jesus' Crucifixion indicated the enormity of His **love** for us. Jn. 15:13

    a. The greatest love a man can have for his friends is to die for them.

    b. Jesus died for US when we were in sin and did not deserve such love at all.

E. Jesus is the **resurrected** Lord.

  1. Jesus **promised** that He would be raised. Jn. 2:19-21

    a. Early in Jesus' ministry, He cleansed the temple of the money changers.

    b. The Jews wanted a sign to give proof that He had a right to perform such an action.

    c. Jesus responded by promising, "Destroy this temple, and in three days I will raise it up."

    d. Standing in Jerusalem, the Jews immediately thought He was referring to the Jewish temple.

    e. However, He was referring to His Body, His Death and His Resurrection.

  2. He arose! The **angel** declared it HAD happened. Mt. 28:6

    a. This is one of my favorite passages in the Bible.

    b. The women who lovingly came to the tomb on that Sunday morning were given an astounding message of hope: "He is not here: for he is risen, as he said, Come, see the place where the Lord lay."

       c. It has happened exactly as He said it would occur; HE IS RISEN!

3. He was seen for **40** days after His Resurrection.
   a. He was seen by so many that the fact of His Resurrection was infallibly proven. Ac. 1:3
   b. Some twenty years later, Paul affirmed that over 513 witnesses had seen the resurrected Lord and most of them were still alive. I Cor. 15:5-8

4. HALLELUJAH, HE AROSE!

5. His Death on the Cross was absolutely critical; however, without His Resurrection, He would have been no different that any other man who shed his blood in his death! His being the Messiah, the Son of God was confirmed by His Resurrection.

F. Jesus is the **reigning** Lord.
   1. He DID **ascend**.
      a. Ac. 1:9-11
      b. He was with His Apostles, informing them to go into Jerusalem to receive the baptism of the Holy Spirit and then take the Gospel to the whole world.

   2. He is in Heaven **now**.
      a. As Stephen was stoned and about to

die, God enabled him to see Christ standing at the right hand of God, the Father in Heaven. This was about A.D. 36, three years after His Ascension. Ac. 7:56

b. Before His Death and Ascension, Jesus was trying to prepare the Apostles for the horrible events they would witness and for His departure to Heaven. He informed them of His work in Heaven, preparing a home for the faithful, and He promised them He would return and take them to Heaven to be with Him. Jn. 14:1-3

3. He reigns now in Heaven as "the only Potentate, the King of kings and Lord of lords." I Tim. 6:15

G. Jesus is the returning **resurrector**.
   1. He will return as He **ascended**. Ac. 1:11
      a. He went up in the clouds.
      b. He will return in the same way.

   2. When will He return? On the **last day**.
      a. Jn. 6:29,40,44,54
      b. What will happen on the day of His return? The world will be destroyed by fire. II Pet. 3:10-12
      c. There is NO TIME for people to live on the Earth after His return; neither is there any time for Him to have a

premillenial reign of one thousand years on earth.

3. Who will be resurrected on that day? **ALL**!
   a. All the dead, righteous and wicked, will be brought from Hades and raised in the same hour. Jn. 5:28,29
   b. The righteous will be raised to eternal life in Heaven; the wicked will be raised to eternal damnation or punishment in Hell.

4. All will meet Him in the **air**. I Thess. 4:13-18
   a. The Thessalonians were distressed, thinking that their deceased loved ones would miss the Lord's second coming. Paul reassured them that there is no need to worry.
   b. In the same hour that the dead are raised, the living will be changed. I Cor. 15:50-52
   c. The resurrected ones and those who are alive at His coming will all be taken up together from the earth to meet Christ in the air. I Thess. 4:13-18
   d. Christ will never set foot on earth again; He will return to take the whole human race to the Judgment; then each will be sent to his eternal home — Heaven or Hell.

H. Jesus is the **Word**.
1. "In the beginning was the WORD." Jn. 1:1

2. Why is He called the "Word?" Jesus is the **declaration** of the will of the Father.

I. Jesus is a **Lawgiver**
1. He has **all authority**. Mt. 28:18
   a. He was given that authority by the Father Himself.
   b. He has that authority in Heaven and on Earth.

2. He has given the world His **Law**.
   a. It is important that we help the student to understand that Christ has a Law today.
      1. Tragically, we are living at a time when people perceive Christ as only grace but not a lawgiver.
         a. Verses like John 1:17 are distorted to suggest that the Old Testament was all law and the New Testament is all grace.
         b. Such assumptions are gross misunderstandings!
            1. Grace existed under the Patriarchal age. Gen. 6:8
            2. Grace also existed under the Law of Moses. Ps.

103:8

3. Certainly grace exists under the New Covenant. Eph. 2:8

2. However, Christ also has laws (rules, precepts, statutes, ordinances) for man to obey today.

　　a. Paul commands Christians to bear each other's burdens — this is the Law of Christ. Gal. 6:2

　　b. In I Corinthians 9:21, Paul explains his work among the Gentiles (those without law). They may have been raised apart from the Law of Moses; however, they ARE UNDER LAW TO CHRIST.

b. Those who deny that Christ has law or statutes for man to follow today have placed themselves in the position of affirming Universalism.

　　1. How could I make this statement?

　　2. "For where no law is, there is no transgression." Rom. 4:15

　　3. If there is NO law, no one can sin — thus, all are righteous.

J. Jesus is an **Intercessor**.

　　1. What does the word "intercessor" mean?

One who pleads the cause of another.

2. Here I emphasize the word "AN."
    a. This suggests there is another intercessor beside Jesus.
    b. We will study about that intercessor in the next lesson.

3. He makes intercession to God, the Father at the throne in Heaven. Rom. 8:34

4. He is our **Advocate**. I Jn. 2:1
    a. He is the "Lawyer" who pleads to the Father for Christians when they sin, repent, confess that sin and plead for God's forgiveness.
    b. He is a "righteous" Advocate — He is fair and just.

K. Jesus is man's ONLY **Mediator**.
    1. Here contrast Christ being the "ONLY" Mediator with His being "AN" Intercessor.

    2. What does the word "mediator" mean? He is a "**go between**" who attempts to restore harmony between those who have been separated.

    3. "For there is one God, and one mediator between God and men, the man Christ Jesus;" I Tim. 2:5

    4. Chart #4.
        a. The usual usage of the word

"mediator" is seen in disputes between management and unions in contract negotiations or disputes.

1. When management and the union are at odds, a mediator is selected to negotiate a settlement.
2. Questions:
    a. Is he a member of management? NO! The union would NEVER agree to that!
    b. Is he a member of the union? NO! The company would NEVER agree to that!
    c. Is he an impartial person equally connected to both parties? ABSOLUTELY!
b. The Biblical usage of "Mediator" describes the work of Christ seeking to restore sinful man to holy God.
    1. By our sins, we separate ourselves from God.
    2. Christ came to reconcile us to the Father.
    3. Questions:
        a. Could the Holy Spirit be our mediator? NO! He is not equally connected to both parties. He is Divine, but not human.
        b. Could any man be our mediator? NO! He is not

equally connected to both parties. He is only human.

    c. Christ is the ONLY ONE who is equally connected to both sides (God and mankind)! He is Deity and humanity. He understands both sides.

  c. Often people explain Jesus' Incarnation as simply an opportunity for Him to experience temptation and struggle and to understand our lives.

    1. However, He is Divine; He knows everything.

    2. His Incarnation was for the purposes of living a perfect, sinless life so He could offer His Blood for our sins and being our ONLY Mediator.

II. Our Goal — Know Christ Personally.

A. It is possible to know the FACTS about Christ but NOT to **KNOW** Him as our Savior.

  1. People in the first century knew facts about Jesus, but they did not know Him as their Savior. Jn. 1:26

  2. Under Christianity, people not only know the facts about Christ but they know Him as their Savior; they have submitted to Him for their salvation. Heb. 8:11

B. Knowing Christ involves:
1. Knowing His **Will** or teachings and **obeying** them.

2. Knowing His **promises** and having hope in them.

C. Assigment for the next lesson: "Who is the Holy Spirit?"

Who Is The Holy Spirit?

Introduction to the Lesson:

A. Why study this topic?

    1. In the last two lessons we have observed the lack of knowledge students have about God and Christ. However, the misunderstanding of the first two members of the Godhead pales in comparison to the confusion concerning the Holy Spirit!

    2. Most students are anxious to talk about indwelling of the Spirit (literal or figurative), supernatural gifts such as speaking in tongues, and the baptism of the Spirit.

        a. However, these are studies that need to come much later.

        b. First, students need to know who the Holy Spirit is and what His works have been and are.

B. Our goal is to assist the student to KNOW the facts about the Holy Spirit, and to KNOW Him personally as the Divine Spirit whom we respect, adore and follow.

I. Knowing the Facts About the Holy Spirit — Who IS the Holy Spirit?

Goals To Accomplish As You Teach This Topic:

- Help the student to realize that the Holy Spirit is a Divine Being just like God, the Father and God, the Son.
- Emphasize His traits of personality that clearly affirm that He is alive.
- Remove from the student's mind the concept that the Holy Spirit is an "IT!"

Struggles That The Student Might Have With This Topic:

- Understanding that the Holy Spirit is a living Being.
- Getting out of their mind the "IT" concept.
  Wanting to get to topics such as "indwelling," "supernatural gifts," and "Holy Spirit baptism" before he even knows who He is.

Teaching Tools:

- Chart #3

A. Concepts many have about the Holy Spirit.

1. I begin this lesson by asking the student, "How would YOU answer the question: 'Who is the Holy Spirit?' How would your friends answer?"

2. Here is a sample of answers I have received in answer to that question (only six blanks are left in the student lesson):
   a. **"I have NO idea."**
   b. **"I cannot understand."**

  c. **"There is no such being."**

  d. **"A mysterious force."**

  e. **"God, the Father, Himself."**

  f. **"An angel."**

  g. **"A Ghost."** (This view may come from the usage in some translations of "Holy GHOST." The word "ghost" is from the Anglo-Saxon word "gast" meaning "spirit.")

  h **"An impersonal force."**

  i **"Man's own spirit."**

  j. **"Man's conscience."**

  k. **"The written Word itself."**

  l. **"A glorified 'IT.'"**

B. HE IS NOT AN "IT!"

 1. The Holy Spirit is a Person.

 2. He is a **living** Being.

 3. He has **will** or can make choices. I Cor. 12:11

  a. This passage is in the context of I Corinthians 12-14 that discusses supernatural gifts and their proper use.

  b. After naming the nine supernatural gifts, Paul affirms that the Holy Spirit was the giver of these gifts and that He chose which gift or gifts each Christian received through the means of the laying on of the Apostles' hands. Ac. 8:18

4. He accepts **responsibility**.

    a. Jesus reminded the Apostles that the Father would send the Holy Spirit to be a Comforter after Christ ascended to Heaven. Jn. 14:26

    b. The Father would send the Holy Spirit at the request of the Son. Jn. 15:26

    c. The Holy Spirit would accept that responsibility and fulfill the will of the Father and of the Son.

    d. He would teach the Apostles "all things" that the Father gave Him to teach them.

5. He **hears**.

    a. The message that the Holy Spirit would bring to the Apostles would be the message He heard from the Father. Jn. 16:13

    b. An inanimate "it" does not have that capability.

6. He **speaks**.

    a. The Holy Spirit would "testify" or "bear witness" of Christ. Jn. 15:26

    b. He would speak the message He heard. Jn. 16:13

    c. As Jesus sent out the twelve Apostles on the "Limited Commission" to the lost sheep of the house of Israel, He promised them that the Spirit would give them the message they should speak. Mt. 10:20

d. The Holy Spirit, speaking in words, emphatically promised through Paul's inspired writing that an apostasy from the Truth would occur. I Tim. 4:1

7. He **teaches**.

a. The Holy Spirit would teach the Apostles all things that the Father would give Him to relate to them. Jn. 14:26

b. He would guide or instruct the Apostles into all Truth and He would show them events that would occur in the future. Jn. 16:13

8. He **glorifies** Christ.

a. The Holy Spirit would give glory to Christ when He brought the Heaven-sent message to the world. Jn. 16:14

b. He would direct all mankind to understand that Jesus is the Christ, the Son of God, the promised Messiah, man's ONLY hope.

9. He can be **grieved**.

a. Paul cautions the Ephesians against grieving the Holy Spirit by whom they had been sealed. Eph. 4:30

b. What does "grieved" mean? To grieve means "to cause pain to," "to offend," "to hurt one's feelings."

        c.   Can you "hurt the feelings" of a chair, table, floor, or a tree?

           1.   ABSOLUTELY NOT!

           2.   Why not? Because these are inanimate things — "ITS!"

        d.   Can a person be grieved? Have we not all been hurt, pained, or offended?

        e.   The Holy Spirit as a Divine Being certainly can be grieved.

   10. He can be **lied to**.

        a.   Acts 5:3,4 relates the story of Ananias lying about the amount of money he and his wife had received for a piece of land they had sold.

        b.   Peter accuses Ananias of lying to the Holy Spirit.

        c.   Can you lie to a chair, car, or a flower?

           1.   ABSOLUTELY NOT!

           2.   Why not? Because these are inanimate things — "ITS!"

        d.   Can you lie to a person? ABSOLUTELY!

C. He is **Deity**.

   1. Acts 5:3,4 gives clear understanding about the nature of the Holy Spirit.

        a.   Because of a famine in Judea, Christians were struggling to survive.

b. Many wealthy Christians, of their own volition, determined to sell some of their possessions in order that they might financially assist their struggling brethren.

c. Ananias and Sapphira, a husband and wife, sold a piece of land.

d. They connived a scheme to make themselves seem to be SO generous.

e. We might illustrate it like this: They sold the land for $20,000. They decided to contribute $15,000 to help their brethren and keep $5,000 for themselves. However, publicly, they claimed that they had sold the land for $15,000 and they were donating all of it to assist the brethren. This was a deceitful attempt to make themselves seem to be much more caring than they truly were.

f. Ananias came to Peter, telling this lie.

g. Peter indicted Ananias of lying to the **Holy Ghost**. Verse 3

h. In verse 4, Peter accuses Ananias of lying to **God**.

i. The great truth affirmed here: when one lies to the HOLY SPIRIT, he is lying to GOD! How can this be? It is true because the Holy Spirit is a member of the Godhead. (See Chart #3 again).

2. Other passages clearly affirm that the Holy Spirit is Deity, just as the Father and the Son are Divine.

   a. Just before His Ascension back to the Father in Heaven, Jesus commissioned His Apostles to teach the Gospel to all nations and to baptize believers into the name of (into a relationship with) the Father, and the Son and the Holy Ghost. Mt. 28:19

   b. I John 5:7, although questioned by some as to its textual authenticity in the book of I John, states a truth that cannot be denied Biblically. There are three bearing witness in Heaven — the Father, the Son and the Holy Spirit.

   c. **Paul** believed with certainty that there were three Divine Beings.

      1. In the benediction of II Corinthians, he prays that the triune Godhead will bless his beloved Corinthian brethren. II Cor. 13:14

      2. He calls upon the grace of the LORD JESUS CHRIST, the love of GOD, and the communion (or fellowship) of the HOLY GHOST to be with these brethren.

3. The conclusion from these texts is

UNDENIABLE — the Holy Spirit has every trait of **DEITY**!

a. Take the student's thoughts back to the lesson entitled, "Who is God?"

b. The Holy Spirit has every trait of Deity: He is a living Spirit; He is an eternal Spirit; He is an all-sovereign Spirit; He is an omniscient Spirit; He knows everything that happens every-where; He is love; and He is justice.

c. He is in Heaven with the Father and the Son. I Jn. 5:7

II. The Work of the Holy Spirit!

Goals To Accomplish As You Teach This Topic:

- Identify His work in the past and in the present.
- Magnify His role in bringing the Word of God, the Father to the world in perfection through revelation, inspiration and confirmation.
- Explain how that Word works in the hearts of sinners in conviction, conversion and sanctification.
- Emphasize His role now in interceding to the Father for Christians.

Struggles That The Student Might Have With This Topic:

- Coming to understand that the way the Holy Spirit operates upon the hearts of mankind is through the revealed Word.
- Overcoming the desire to have something more than and more mystical than the Word He revealed.

A. He was present at the **Creation**.
   1. Genesis 1:2 says, "And the Spirit of God moved upon the face of the waters."

   2. If this phrase is referring to the Holy Spirit, all we can know for certain is that He was present at the Creation.

   3. Some, in attempting to explain this, have suggested a cooperation of Deity in the Creation.
      a. The proposed cooperation of Deity seems to accurately portray Their roles in the plan to provide salvation to the world. In making salvation available:
         1. God, the Father designed the plan.
         2. God, the Son created it by His Death on the Cross.
         3. God, the Holy Spirit was the Organizer who revealed the message so that all mankind might know about the Gospel and be convinced of its validity.
      b. From the above model, many have worked backwards to the Creation and suggested the following roles in the creation:
         1. God, the Father — Designer.
         2. God, the Son — Creator.
         3. God, the Holy Spirit — Organizer; assisted in providing order.

154

4. The first two seem extremely accurate and plausible; the third suggestion about the work of the Holy Spirit seems difficult to solidly affirm.

B. **Revelation**.
1. The Holy Spirit revealed God, the Father's Will to mankind.
   a. The Father gave Him that responsibility after the Ascension of Christ.
   b. Passages that explain His work of revelation:
      1. II Pet. 1:21
         a. The Apostle Peter explains the authenticity of his message and of Biblical prophecy.
         b. Scripture did not just "happen," nor did the writers of Scripture invent their messages by their own volition.
         c. These men spoke when the Holy Spirit revealed to them God, the Father's message that He wanted conveyed to the world.
      2. I Cor. 2:7-16
         a. This is one of the most misapplied Scriptures in the

Bible.

b. Commentators often suggest that this passage is talking about a sinful, depraved, unregenerate man who cannot approach God unless there is an operation of the Holy Spirit upon his heart.

c. This interpretation is totally inaccurate and not contextual in the immediate passage nor in the whole Biblical context!

d. Observe the context and message of the text:

1. Paul is discussing HIS PREACHING of the Gospel message.

2. His work as an Apostle was to preach the Gospel. I Cor. 1:17

3. Paul did not try to bring glory to himself by eloquent oratory; he wanted in no way to detract from the Cross and by so doing to bring glory to himself. I Cor. 1:17

4. The preaching of the Cross, of a suffering, crucified, and resur-

rected Divine Being, seemed absolute nonsense to the mind of man; however, Christians KNOW that Christ's sacrifice provides God's saving power. I Cor. 1:18

5. God chose the preaching of the Gospel to tell man about the salvation that was available and to bring him to that salvation. I Cor. 1:19-21

6. Jews sought a miracle to persuade them to believe; Gentiles wanted a message that "made sense" to them before they would believe. However, God chose preaching the Gospel about Christ to call men to salvation. I Cor. 1:22-24

7. God, in His wisdom, chose the preaching of the Gospel message to convict sinners' hearts so that man would only glory in the Lord!

8. Paul emphasized that he did not use eloquency of

speech to influence the Corinthians, he only proclaimed the message about the crucified Jesus. I Cor. 2:1-2.

9. Paul faced the weakness of human emotions; however, his message was validated by supernatural manifestations to convince his listeners that the message was absolutely true.

10. Now notice the theme of I Corinthians 2:7-16:

   a. Paul was speaking the wisdom of God. Verse 7

   b. His message is one TOO MAGNIFICENT for man to originate! Verses 8-10

   c. The Holy Spirit revealed the very mind of God, the Father to teach man His Truths. Verses 11-13

   d. Man, without revelation from Deity,

could not know God's mind and Will. Verse 14

    e. Paul absolutely affirms that the Holy Spirit has revealed to him the mind of Christ. Verse 16

e. This is a lengthy explanation of I Corinthians 1,2; as a teacher you may choose not to point out all of these passages. However, it is critical that the student understand that this passage refers to the revelation of God's Truths.

2. Two words describe revelation.
    a. **"Prophecy"**
        1. The typical definition given to "prophecy" is "foretelling of the future."
        2. However, the word properly suggests the revelation of all of God's Will to mankind. Only a very small part of this revelation involves the foretelling of the future.
        3. The Holy Spirit directed the Apostles and others with the gift of prophecy to speak the message

of God to the world in the first century when no Bible existed.

4. Because of that prophecy, now mankind has access to that Word.

b. "**Mystery**"

1. This word suggests a message previously "hidden" or not made known.

2. That message was kept secret until God, the Father, chose to reveal it to the world through the third member of the Godhead, the Holy Spirit.

3. Without revelation, SINFUL MAN WOULD GROPE ABOUT with NO WAY to know how to find salvation!

C. **Inspiration**.

1. Bible "inspiration" is much different than the concept of a creative person's being "inspired" to write poetry, music, or drama.

a. The creative person must "get in the mood" to write.

1. Sometimes that is extremely difficult.

2. His emotions and external circumstances can have great positive or negative impact upon his "being inspired."

b. Bible "inspiration" is a work of the Holy Spirit, where He not only revealed the message, but also directed the preaching of the speakers and the writing of the sacred authors so that mankind has the exact message of the Father.

2. Scriptures that teach "inspiration."
   a. ALL SCRIPTURE is "inspired of God." II Tim. 3:16,17
      1. The phrase "is given by inspiration of God" comes from one compound Greek word "θεόπνευστος" (theopneustos).
      2. The word means "God-breathed."
      3. The message is EXACTLY what God, the Father wants man to know!
   b. Here Jesus promised THE APOSTLES inspiration of the messages they would preach after His Ascension. Jn. 14:26
      1. The Holy Spirit would teach them all of the Will of the Father.
      2. He would remind them of everything Jesus taught them while He was with them on the Earth.

3. Return to II Timothy 3:16,17 to learn more about Biblical inspiration.
   a. It is "plenary" inspiration.

    1.   That means **"complete," "in totality."**

    2.   "ALL scripture is inspired of God," not parts, not most of it; ALL OF IT is **"God-breathed."**

  b. It is "verbal" inspiration.

    1.   Bible inspiration is NOT "thought inspiration."

       a. "Thought inspiration" involves the Holy Spirit giving the ideas to the inspired writers; then they wrote down their understanding of those thoughts.

       b. This is SUCH A DANGEROUS teaching!

       c. Give the example of sitting in a room of friends and playing the game "telephone." The first person makes up a message and whispers it in the ear of the person sitting beside him. This continues as each person passes on that message by whispering it to his neighbor.

          1.   What happens in this game?

          2.   I have never seen the message received by the last person to be

identical to the message that was first passed.

3. Why does this happen?

    a. You always have some "jokester" who enjoys passing on a message that is totally different than what he received.

    b. Some are hard of hearing and misunderstand what has been whispered to them.

    c. Others do not communicate clearly what they have heard.

    d. If Bible inspiration is "thought inspiration," why should we trust its message? Do we really believe they never inserted their own ideas into the message as they tried to remember what they had been told?

2. The **Words** were inspired by the Holy Spirit!

    a. Paul's message was not with enticing WORDS; it was delivered with WORDS chosen by the Holy Spirit and validated by supernatural powers. I Cor. 2:4

b. Paul affirms that the WORDS of his message were carefully selected by the Holy Spirit to explain spiritual Truths clearly and precisely. I Cor. 2:13

c. This means that EVERY WORD of the Bible is vitally important and should be carefully considered by mankind!

4. Some struggle with the topic of Biblical inspiration because different inspired authors use different words and have different styles of writing

a. Therefore, many quickly conclude that Bible inspiration MUST BE "thought inspiration."

b. However, the Holy Spirit revealed the **thoughts** to the inspired men and selected the words from that author's **vocabulary**.

c. Thus, the very WORDS were chosen by the Holy Spirit.

d. This provides us SUCH SECURITY; we know that the very message of God has been given to the world!

5. Many will immediately mention another concern about God's revelation: "How do

we know God's message has been preserved purely and that it will continue to be preserved throughout future ages?"

   a. The amazing number of documents in the original languages STRONGLY SUPPORTS the validity of the text today.

   b. The GREATEST comfort to me has always been the promise of Jesus Christ Himself in Mt. 24:35: "Heaven and earth shall pass away, but my words shall not pass away." The inspired Word will be **perpetuated**!

   c. Jesus promised that the inspired revelation will be perpetuated. Although Jesus does not explain HOW that would occur, we know He cannot lie; it IS the truth. Whether that Word was perpetuated by the Holy Spirit, the Father, the Son or God's angels, it has been done and will continue to be preserved as long as the world stands!

  6. The GLORIOUS message of Bible inspiration — I CAN COMPLETELY TRUST the inspired Word of God!

D. **Confirmation** (Validation) of the Word.

  1. This was the purpose of the miracles that the Holy Spirit provided to

Christians in the first century. Mk. 16:20

a. The "signs" were for the purpose of confirming the Word preached by the Apostles.

b. Imagine someone knocking on your door tonight and saying, "I am from the police department, and I am here to search your house."

    1. Would you immediately open the door and allow him into your house? I hope not.

    2. If you are thinking carefully, you will ask for validation. "Give me proof that you are a policeman. Show me a search warrant."

2. The purpose of the supernatural spiritual gifts in the first century was to confirm that the Gospel message was truly from Heaven and that is was man's answer for his sins. Mk. 16:17-20

a. Jesus had just given the "Great Commission" to His Apostles.

b. He then promised miraculous powers to those who heard the Apostles' message and obeyed it. Mk. 16:17,18; I Cor 12:8-10

    1. These powers were NOT JUST FOR THE APOSTLES.

    2. They were for those who became Christians in the first century.

    3. Other passages like Acts 8:18

explain that these new Christians received these gifts when the Apostles laid their hands on them.

c. The Holy Spirit, through these gifts, has proven to all men of all ages the veracity of the Gospel and the certainty of the availability of salvation through the crucified Son of God.

3. Once the Word was written and confirmed, these supernatural gifts ceased! Eph. 4:11-14; I Cor. 13:8-12

E. **Conviction**.
1. The Holy Spirit convicts the **hearts** of men of their need for God.

2. The question is NOT "Does the Holy Spirit convict the hearts of men?" Rather, the question is "**HOW** does the Holy Spirit convict our hearts?"

3. The Holy Spirit has revealed that it is through the **Word** that He penetrates our hearts to draw us to God.
a. In the discussion of the Christian armor provided to assist the child of God to ward off the dangerous attacks of the Devil, the Holy Spirit reveals how He convicts men's hearts. Eph. 6:17

1. "And the sword of the Spirit, which is the word of God;"
2. The sword He uses to work on the heart of man is His revealed Word.
3. I give an illustration of two people fighting. If I took a sword and stuck it into your body and cut out your heart, WHO killed you? I did! HOW were you murdered? By means of the sword.
4. Man's heart is convicted by means of the Spirit's sword — the revealed Word.

b. "For the word of God is quick, and powerful, and sharper than any two-edged sword, piercing even to the dividing asunder of soul and spirit, and of the joints and marrow, and is a discerner of the thoughts and intents of the heart." Heb. 4:12

1. His Word is alive, and SO powerful!
2. The Word of God, inspired by the Holy Spirit, penetrates so much more deeply than any physical sword could possibly reach! A literal sword can pierce flesh and bone; the inspired Word can penetrate to the very depths of a person's being. It can prick our

heart, cause us to change the direction of our lives, and motivate us to turn to Christ for salvation.

    a. This convicting power is vividly seen on the Day of Pentecost in the hearts of Jesus' crucifiers. Ac. 2:37,41

    b. Weeks earlier, these Jews had shouted, "Crucify Him; crucify Him!"

    c. When Peter, by inspiration of the Holy Spirit, preached the Gospel message and convinced them that Jesus WAS the Messiah, they were cut to the heart.

    d. How did the Holy Spirit convict their hearts to bring them to change? It was by hearing the message Peter preached. Verse 37

F. **Conversion** and **Sanctification**.

    1. Once a heart is convicted of sin and of its need for a Savior, the Holy Spirit, through the inspired Word, has revealed God, the Father's message to show man how to be **converted** to Christ.

    2. That revealed, inspired Word, is Deity's **power** to salvation.

    a. "For I am not ashamed of the gospel of Christ: for it is the power of God unto salvation to every one that believeth; to the Jew first, and also to the Greek." Rom. 1:16

        1. The Gospel is God's power to bring all mankind unto the salvation planned and brought into being by Deity!

        2. That Word will not only convict, but will also convert us to Christ!

    b. "Seeing ye have purified your souls in obeying the truth through the Spirit unto unfeigned love of the brethren, see that ye love one another with a pure heart fervently: Being born again, not of corruptible seed, but of incorruptible, by the word of God, which liveth and abideth forever." I Pet. 1:22,23

        1. Sinners' souls are purified by obeying the Truth that was brought into the world by the Holy Spirit.

        2. That conversion, called a new birth, is not a physical birth. It is a spiritual birth brought about by the Word convicting that sinner's heart.

  3. The Word also produces sanctification — directing man's life to be "set apart"

for the service of God.

    a. "Sanctification" is from " ἅγιος " (hagios), the same Greek word that is translated "holy," "sanctify," and "saint."

    b. These words do not mean "moral purity" nor "perfection."

    c. Our lives are sanctified at conversion ("set apart" to serve God), and this "setting apart" **continues** as we apply His revealed**Word** to our lives.

    d. Sanctification is NOT an instant operation performed by the Holy Spirit after conversion that makes man sinlessly perfect! It is the impact of the Word that brings man to conversion and then challenges him to seek to be more and more like Christ as long as he lives in this life.

4. Again, we see the awesome importance of the inspired Word of the Holy Spirit for our lives.

G. **Intercession** .

1. "Likewise the Spirit also helpeth our infirmities: for we know not what we should pray for as we ought: but the Spirit itself maketh intercession for us with groanings which cannot be uttered. And he that searcheth the hearts knoweth what is the mind of the Spirit,

because he maketh intercession for the saints according to the will of God." Rom. 8:26,27

    a. Paul is discussing the struggles man faces as he lives in a world where pain, illness, and death are constantly attacking our body of corruption in which we are now enslaved. Verses 18-22

    b. Struggling man, including God's own people, LONGS for deliverance from these burdens. Verses 23-25

    c. The Holy Spirit intercedes (pleads) for us to the Father.

2. "Intercession" is NOT something He does **TO** us; rather, it is something He does **FOR** us! Where does He do this? IN HEAVEN, TO THE FATHER, AT THE THRONE OF GOD.

Conclusion:

A. It is SO VITAL for us to understand WHO the Holy Spirit truly is.

1. He is Deity, a member of the Godhead; He is as surely Divine as the Father and the Son!

2. May we NEVER see Him as "AN IT" again!

B. It is also vitally important that we understand the means through which He affects men's lives and hearts today — it is through His precious Word.

C. We need to see His work today in caring for us and in wanting us to obey His revealed message. We also need to appreciate that He is pleading to the Father for us because He wants us to be successful and to see the end of our hope — the salvation of our souls in Heaven! That is in reality the purpose of everything the Godhead has done for us.

D. In the next lesson, we will study the relationship between Deity and mankind in salvation.

E. The next lesson will be more difficult that the previous lessons. I tell you now, so you will not be discouraged as we study Lesson #5. Too, the subsequent lessons will be easier.

The Relationship Between God And Man In Salvation!

Introduction to the Lesson:

A. This lesson may seem extremely complex and quite unnecessary to many teachers.

    1. However, consider how many times you may have tried to talk to someone about his responsibility only to have him act as if there is nothing he can do in obedience to God.

    2. Also, consider how many times a student may have asserted that salvation is God's work and God will "gift him faith" at God's own choosing and time.

    3. Can you remember someone suggesting that repentance must occur before faith? Were you confused and unsure of what the student was saying?

    4. You MUST realize that perhaps 95% of religions in America have been influenced by Calvinistic theology.

        a. Most religions will only hold to portions of the total Calvinistic package.

        b. However, a person who holds any

one of these points will be greatly influenced by this false theology. He will also likely struggle as he tries to correspond his theology with verses that suggest that man has responsibility in salvation.

5. This is the only time in this series of lessons that we will place such focus on FALSE teaching.

6. However, I have found that this lesson is critical to helping the student have a proper understanding of his own role in salvation.

7. Once the student grasps the truths of this lesson, it is amazing how quickly he will understand and readily accept God's Truths!

8. I urge you to understand this lesson and do not omit it.

B. The purpose of this lesson:
   1. To help the student see the correlation between Deity and mankind in relationship to salvation.
      a. Is salvation made available by the Godhead and do the Divine Beings determine which specific people will be saved and when they will be saved?
      b. Or has Deity made salvation

available and then given each person the choice to either accept or reject that offered redemption?

2. To see that man can and must personally respond to God's directions in order to receive His grace.

C. Question for the student: "Do you believe God has given man requirements to obey in order to attain salvation and to remain faithful?"

1. What are YOUR thoughts about that question?

2. What have you heard in the past?

3. What do you believe?

D. Our goal: to compare what is taught by most religions with what GOD teaches.

I. The Five Points of Calvinism — T U L I P! [27]

Goals To Accomplish As You Teach This Topic:

- Identify the points of Calvinism.
- Explain the five points of Calvinism clearly.
- Help the student understand the doctrine of "original sin" and its consequences.
- Define the roles of Father, Son and Holy Spirit in salvation as purported by the doctrine of Calvinism.
- Assist the student to grasp Calvinismic "predestination."

- Show the supposed work of the Holy Spirit in the doctrine of irresistible grace – an instantaneous religious experience.
- Emphasize the results of this doctrine – "Once Saved, Always Saved."
- Explain the struggles people have with this doctrine – most do not want to hold to all five points of the theology.

Struggles That The Student Might Have With This Topic:

- Accepting the idea that HIS OWN babies were born in sin.
- Seeing the consequences of these doctrines very quickly.

Teaching Tools:

- "The Five Points of Calvinism: Defined, Defended, Documented" by David N. Steele and Curtis C. Thomas.[28]

A. **T**otal hereditary depravity!
   1. Total — **Complete**.

   2. Hereditary — **Inherited**.

   3. Depravity — **Inability** to approach God.

   4. Summation of the doctrine:
      a. "Babies are born in sin; they can do nothing to approach God."
      b. This is commonly known as the doctrine of "original sin."
      c. Supposedly Adam and Eve's sin is transferred upon every child at birth. Original sin is the child's

condemnation because it was born in flesh. That child is supposedly totally incapable of desiring or being able to respond to God's offer of salvation.

B. **Unconditional particular election!**
  1. Unconditional — **No** conditions expected.
  2. Particular — **Specific** individuals.
  3. Election — **Predestined** or chosen by God before the world began.
  4. Summation of the doctrine:
     a. This is supposedly the work of God, the Father.
     b. Presumably, God made selection of SPECIFIC PEOPLE to be saved.
     c. The suggestion is that He made these selections before the world was ever created.
     d. The word "predestination" is used by the advocates of Calvinism to describe this purported choice of the Father before the world began.

C. **Limited atonement!**
  1. Limited — not for **everyone**; for specific individuals.
  2. Atonement — expiation of sin; making amends for man's sin and **restoring** him to a proper relationship with the Father.

3. Summation of the doctrine:
    a. This is supposedly the work of God, the Son.
    b. The claim is that He died on the Cross only for the elect.

D. Irresistible grace!
    1. Irresistible.
        a. It cannot be rejected. You do not desire it; you cannot stop it!
        b. Often I tease people with the illustration of a couple dating. They find each other absolutely irresistible! They are so magnetized to each other that they are irresistible; they cannot stop the attraction.

    2. Grace — God's bestowal of salvation.

    3. This doctrine is often referred to by the phrase "religious experience."

    4. Summation of the doctrine:
        a. This is purportedly the work of God, the Holy Spirit.
        b. At the time the Father has chosen, the Holy Spirit supposedly instantaneously transforms the depraved sinner's heart, gives him faith and saves him.

E. **P**erseverance of the saints!
  1. Perseverance — **steadfastness**, continuance.

  2. Saints — Those specifically chosen by the Father, purchased by Christ as He died for them, and instantaneously saved by the Holy Spirit.

  3. Summation of the doctrine:
      a. Once the Holy Spirit has changed the sinner's nature and saved him, he CANNOT lose his salvation!
      b. This doctrine is often known by the phrase "Once saved, **ALWAYS** saved."

II. Passages Used to Espouse This Concept, Their Context, and Proper Interpretation!

Goals To Accomplish As You Teach This Topic:

- Show the error of each point of Calvinism.
- Properly interpret passages that are mis-interpreted by Calvinists to teach the Calvinistic theology.
- Magnify the nature of man – made in the image of God, not born in "original sin."
- Give the student great hope, enthusiasm, and confidence as he realizes that God has given him the privilege to choose his eternal destiny.
- Explain the work of the Holy Spirit in salvation through His sword – the inspired Word!
- Show the consequences of Calvinistic theology – man supposedly is unable to fall away from God.
- Explain the danger of accepting any one of the five points of this doctrine.

Struggles That The Student Might Have With This Topic:

- Being intimidated by the seeming technicality of this study.
- Understanding the proper interpretation of the Biblical passages.
- Grasping the significance of Calvinism's doctrine; on the contrary, being convinced that each person really does have choice.
- Seeing the far-reaching implication of this doctrine even beyond the study of salvation, as man may believe that every event in life and every decision is supposedly already pre-determined by and is directed by God.
- Comprehending the greatness of the Bible and its power and importance for man's life.

Teaching Tools:
- Chart #5.

A. Total hereditary depravity!
   1. One of the favorite passages used to promote total depravity is Romans 5:12.
      a. The passage reads: "Wherefore, as by one man sin entered into the world, and death by sin; and so death passed upon all men, for that all have sinned."
      b. At first reading, what does this passage seem to be saying? It certainly may sound as if it is stating that Adam sinned and thus, all of us have become sinners.
      c. The context of this passage is critical

to understanding it.
1. Chapters 1-3 affirm that Gentiles and Jews are guilty of sin.
2. Chapters 4,5 explain that justification (being considered as just in God's sight) is only available through faith in Jesus Christ.
3. The immediate context in Chapter 5 explains that sin and spiritual death existed before the Law of Moses ever came into being! Spiritual death has existed since Adam disobeyed God. As head of the human race, Adam led humanity into disobedience.
4. Christ as another head of the human race leads man into justification.
d. The critical word in understanding Romans 5:12 is the little word **"SO!"**
1. See Chart #5.
2. Adam lived in the Garden of Eden. Satan tempted him to disobey God by eating of the forbidden fruit of the tree of the knowledge of good and evil. Adam acted upon that temptation by eating.
3. Adam plus the temptation plus

the action of eating equaled SIN or disobedience to God's command. That sin brought spiritual death or separation from God.

4. The word "SO" is critical to understanding this verse!
   a. It does not mean "therefore."
   b. It is an adverb that means "in the SAME WAY."

5. Man today is tempted by Satan to sin. We, too, can act upon our temptations just as Adam did!

6. Man today plus the temptation plus the acting upon that temptation (lying, stealing, fornicating) equals SIN or disobedience to God's command. That sin brings spiritual death or separation from God in our lives.

7. Paul's point is that we become sinners in EXACTLY THE SAME WAY Adam became a sinner!

8. This passage gives ABSO-LUTELY NO SUPPORT WHAT-EVER to the false doctrine of "Original Sin!"

2. A second favorite passage of Calvinists is Psalms 51:5.

a. David said, "Behold, I was shapen in iniquity; and in sin did my mother conceive me."

b. As with Romans 5:12, at first reading this passage seems to clearly advocate original sin.

c. However, as we will see later, this doctrine is completely contradicted by other Scriptures.

d. What COULD this verse mean?

1. Some suggest that David is stating that his mother committed sin at his conception, that his parents were committing fornication (that they were not married), and that he was a product of that sinful action.

   a. However, I know NO suggestion in I Samuel 16, in I Chronicles 10,11 or in Psalms that even hints of such a sinful tryst.

   b. This seems to me to be such an ugly, unnecessary, unwarranted conclusion!

   c. In fact, was not David the YOUNGEST of Jesse's eight sons? I Sa. 16:10,11. This does not prove that Jesse did not commit fornication but it seems unbelievable that God would not have noted such a sinful act.

2. Others suggest that David is stating that he was born into a world that is SO SINFUL.

    a. Psalm 51 is David's heart-broken cry to God for forgiveness after having committed adultery with Bathsheba and in trying to cover up that sin, having her husband Uriah murdered in war. II Sa. 11:2-17. Subsequently, Nathan the prophet came and convicted David of his sin. II Sa. 12:1-14

    b. If this proposition is true, David is bemoaning the fact that all men are born into a world that is so wicked and sinful and is acknowledging that he, himself, has been overcome by temptation and sin.

3. Another plausible postulation is that David is using **hyperbole** (literary exaggeration) to express the horrible sense of shame and guilt that he feels.

    a. Personally, I believe this explanation is the best

interpretation of this passage.

1. The idea of original sin is wrong because it is completely decimated in Scripture! See point 3 below: "The Bible DOES NOT TEACH total depravity."

2. The suggestion that David's parents sinned has no scriptural support.

3. The idea that he is simply affirming that he was born into a world of sin does not seem to fit the immediate context in which David confesses HIS OWN SINS.

b. Most of us use hyperbole every day.

1. Sometimes we use it to emphasize a point.

2. At other times we use it to show the depth of emotion that we feel.

3. Examples:

a. In Psalm 22:6, David declared, "I am a worm, and no man." Is this verse to be taken literally? Was David saying he was a "woolly worm," "silk worm," or a "fishing worm?" Obviously not!

b. David was using hyperbole to describe his feelings brought about because of the shame and reproach his enemies were heaping upon him.

c. When feeling great, have you ever said, "I am HIGHER THAN A KITE!"

d. When discouraged, have you sadly bemoaned, "I feel LOWER THAN A SNAKE'S BELLY!"

e. If you have done that, you are using hyperbole.

b. David, in Psalm 51:5, is overwhelmed with personal grief and shame.

1. He KNEW that adultery and murder were sinful.

2. He is flabbergasted and disgusted with himself

that he would commit such atrocious sins!

3. He is feeling SO ASHAMED that he is saying, "I just feel like one BIG OLD SINNER!" Or to say it differently, "ALL I EVER DO IS SIN!"

4. I suspect most Christians have had the same feelings at times when personal shame overwhelmed us.

3. The Bible DOES NOT TEACH total depravity!

   a. Likely the plainest passages to refute "total hereditary depravity" are **Ezekiel 18:4,20**!

      1. "Behold, all souls are mine; as the soul of the father, so also the soul of the son is mine: the soul that sinneth, it shall die." Verse 4

      2. "The soul that sinneth, it shall die. The son shall not bear the iniquity of the father, neither shall the father bear the iniquity of the son: the righteousness of the righteous shall be upon him, and the wickedness of the wicked shall be upon him." Verse 20

3. Verses 5-19 are SO clear and insightful.
   a. I use the illustration of a man, his son, and his grandson.
   b. If the man is a righteous, obedient child of God, he shall live. Verses 5-9
   c. If that godly man has a son who is a wicked sinner, that son will be held guilty for his own sins. Verses 10-13
   d. If this wicked man has a son who despises his father's sin and is a righteous, God-fearing person, he will live. Verses 14-17
4. The message of these texts describes any situation that could occur spiritually in a family.
   a. The righteousness of a godly man will NOT transfer down to bless his son.
   b. The sinfulness of a son will not revert backward to condemn his father.
   c. The sinfulness of a father will not be passed down to nor inherited by his son! The son does not inherit his father's guilt.

   d. The righteousness of a son will not revert backward to improve the condition of his sinful father.

   e. The message: each person has to answer to God for his OWN sins!

 b. It is also critically important to see HOW a person becomes a sinner.

   1. I John 3:4 explains how we become sinners.

   2. Sin is "transgression"(KJV) of God's law. That means stepping across the line, disobeying God. Thus, each person becomes a **sinner** when he, himself, violates God's law.

   3. Other translations use the word "lawlessness." That is a refusal to obey God's law.

   4. Sin is NOT an inherited quality; it is our personal disobedience.

 c. God declares that man is made in a holy, pure state at birth!

   1. Man has been created just a little **lower** than the angels (KJV); other translations have "God." Ps. 8:5

   2. Man was given dominion over all the rest of the creation! Ps. 8:6; Gen. 1:28

        3. Man is the only created being made in the image of God! Gen. 1:26,27; Ecc. 12:7; Zech. 12:1

    d. Jesus called upon sinful adults to become like little children before they will be allowed to enter into the kingdom of Heaven. Mt. 18:3

        1. If babies ARE born with original sin, consider what Jesus is saying!

        2. He would be telling men that they must become like depraved, sinful little children before they can enter heaven. ABSURD!

    e. THANK GOD that we only have to be responsible for our OWN sins! That burden is so heavy and so damning without adding Adam's sin to our lives!

B. Unconditional Particular Election!

    1. Ephesians 1:4,5 is used to advocate this position.

        a. "According as he hath chosen us in him before the foundation of the world, that we should be holy and without blame before him in love: Having predestinated us unto the adoption of children by Jesus Christ to himself, according to the good pleasure of his will,"

    b. Calvinists interpret these verses as proclaiming that God predestined specific individuals to be saved before the foundation of the world.

    c. These verses DO teach predestination, but NOT Calvinistic predestination!

        1. God placed the privilege of all spiritual blessings IN CHRIST. Verse 3

        2. God's predestination is the plan that sinners would only be saved by submitting to His Son, Jesus Christ.

        3. This is NOT individual election, choosing specific people to receive that salvation; rather, it is election of a GROUP — any who will submit to and obey Christ.

        4. It is a predestination of a people of holy character, those who determine to reject sin and to live lives of purity.

    d. The whole message of the book of Ephesians affirms that salvation is "in Christ," that is, in His eternally planned Church.

2. Passages that refer to specific people being chosen to a specific work for God are also misunderstood as referring to specific individuals being chosen for salvation.

a. One example is John 15:16.
   1. "You have not chosen me, but I have chosen you."
   2. There is no discussion of salvation in this text; Jesus is discussing His choosing the twelve to be His **Apostles.**
b. Romans 9:11-13 in another example.
   1. Paul here discusses the selection of Jacob instead of Esau as the son of Isaac through whom the Abrahamic covenant would continue.
   2. The decision that "the elder shall serve the younger" was made before the sons were born to Isaac and Rebekah.
   3. Again, **salvation** is not being discussed in this text.

3. The Bible DOES NOT TEACH "unconditional particular election!"
   a. There is **NO QUESTION** that the Bible teaches predestination.
      1. Sadly, some have denied that the Bible teaches the doctrine of predestination as they try to disprove the doctrine of Calvinistic predestination.
      2. We must NEVER deny Bible truth in trying to disprove error.
   b. The important question is, "Does the

Bible teach **particular** or **group** election?"

c. God elected a group — **"those in Christ."**

4. The doctrine of "unconditional particular election" has some DANGEROUS consequences!

   a. It makes **God** responsible for our being saved or lost!

      1. If I am saved, it was by HIS choice, not my response to His grace nor my love for Him.

      2. If I am lost, it was because HE did not choose me; I could do nothing to change my destiny.

      3. Such a doctrine seems very comfortable to sinful men who are always trying to blame someone else for their own sins. Adam and Eve did this in the garden. Gen. 3:12,13

      4. However, if I am lost, what benefit is there in blaming God; I am still lost.

   b. It makes God a **respector** of persons in salvation! He is giving some the privilege while withholding the privilege from others.

5. THANK GOD that Bible predestination is for all those who choose to be "in Christ!" That means I have the privilege

of being saved by His grace if **I** choose to obey Jesus Christ.

C. Limited atonement!
1. Many passages show the relationship of Christ to His disciples.

2. Examples:
   a. His name suggested that He would die for His people. Mt. 1:21
   b. He prophesied that He would die for His sheep. Jn. 10:11,14,15
   c. He asserted that He died for His friends. Jn. 15:13

3. Calvinistic theology affirms that Christ died ONLY FOR THE ELECT. These verses do emphasize that He died for **His disciples** Many other verses explain that these are not the only ones for whom He died. Sacred Scripture emphatically affirms that He wants **all** to become His **disciples**

4. The Bible DOES NOT TEACH Limited Atonement!
   a. So many familiar Bible passages are "death nails" to this teaching.
   b. Examples:
      1. "For God so loved THE WORLD, that he gave his only begotten Son, that WHOSOEVER BELIEVETH IN HIM should not

perish, but have everlasting life."
Jn. 3:16

2. "And he is the propitiation for
our sins: and not for ours only,
but also for the sins of THE
WHOLE WORLD." I Jn. 2:2

3. "The Lord is not slack concerning
his promise, as some men count
slackness; but is long-suffering
to us-ward, NOT WILLING
THAT ANY SHOULD PERISH,
BUT THAT ALL SHOULD
COME TO REPENTANCE." II
Pet. 3:9

4. "But we see Jesus, who was made
a little lower than the angels for
the suffering of death, crowned
with glory and honor; that he by
the grace of God should TASTE
DEATH FOR EVERY MAN."
Heb. 2:9

c. For whom did Jesus die?
EVERYONE, not just the elect.

D. Irresistible grace!
1. Calvinists seek verses to affirm that man
is instantly called by an operation of the
Holy Spirit and that man cannot turn to
God without this instantaneous
experience.

2. Passages that supposedly teach these ideas:

    a. Rom. 8:30. This passage affirms that those predestined are called in order that they might be justified.

        1. Remember that predestination is election of a GROUP — those who will submit to Christ.

        2. They ARE called! But the question to ask is, "**HOW** are they called?"

        3. Calvinism declares that this is done by an operation of the Holy Spirit upon the sinner's heart. But what does the BIBLE say?

    b. I Corinthians 2:9-16 is a favorite passage of Calvinists!

        1. They claim that the "natural man" of I Corinthians 2:14 is a man depraved by original sin.

        2. That is an impossible conclusion since original sin does not exist!

        3. The context of I Corinthians 1,2 is a discussion of **Paul's** inspired PREACHING and of his message being inspired by the Holy Spirit.

        4. The "natural man" is an uninspired man; one not inspired by the Holy Spirit to preach.

    c. Romans 8:14 says that the sons of God are led by the Spirit of God.

The question is not ARE we led, but HOW are we led?

3. The Bible DOES NOT TEACH "irresistible grace!"
   a. The Bible definitely affirms God's grace to be essential to man's salvation.
      1. "By grace are ye saved." Eph. 2:5
      2. "For by grace are ye saved through faith...." Eph. 2:8-10
         a. Grace — Deity's provisions that salvation might be made available.
         b. Faith — Man's response to that grace.
      3. "Being justified freely by his grace through the redemption that is in Christ Jesus." Rom. 3:24
      4. The Gospel is to be preached to every person. Each person has the choice to believe or not to believe! Mk. 16:15,16
   b. Faith is NOT God's gift to man. It is man's response to God's Word.
      1. Calvinist's often use the phrase, "God GIFTS YOU faith!"
      2. However, Romans 10:17 clearly explains the responsibility of faith!

      a.   "So then faith cometh by hearing, and **hearing** by the word of God."

      b.   Faith is MAN'S response to the inspired Word of God as his heart is convinced and convicted of its veracity and his need for it.

c. We receive God's grace by our obedience to the Truth.

    1.   "Seeing ye have purified your souls in obeying the truth through the Spirit unto unfeigned love of the brethren, see that ye love one another with a pure heart fervently: Being born again, not of corruptible seed, but of incorruptible, by the word of God, which liveth and abideth for ever." I Pet. 1:22,23

    2.   "Of his own will begat he us with the word of truth, that we should be a kind of first fruits of his creatures...Wherefore lay apart all filthiness and superfluity of naughtiness, and receive with meekness the engrafted word, which is able to save your souls." Js. 1:18,21

    3.   "For after that in the wisdom of God the world by wisdom knew not God, it pleased God by the

foolishness of preaching to save them that believe...For though ye have ten thousand instructors in Christ, yet have ye not many fathers: for in Christ Jesus I have begotten you through the gospel." I Cor. 1:21; 4:15

4. The message of these passages: The new birth is brought about by God at the point of OUR OBEDIENCE to His revealed message!

d. The Word is **all sufficient** to accomplish our salvation.

1. "All scripture is given by inspiration of God, and is profitable for doctrine, for reproof, for correction, for instruction in righteousness: That the man of God may be perfect, thoroughly furnished unto all good works!" II Tim. 3:16,17

a. The inspired Word of God will make us complete in God's sight.

b. It equips us for every opportunity we face!

2. "According as his divine power hath given unto us all things that pertain unto life and godliness, through the knowledge of him

that hath called us to glory and virtue." II Pet. 1:3

    a. God has given to man everything he needs to deal with every situation that he faces in life and how to be everything God wants him to be.

    b. How did He give us that direction? Through His Son.

3. "For I am not ashamed of the gospel of Christ: for it is the power of God unto salvation to every one that believeth: to the Jew first, and also to the Greek." Rom. 1:16

    a. The power of God to salvation is NOT an instantaneous operation of the Holy Spirit upon our hearts.

    b. That power is the Gospel of Christ!

e. Man DOES have **responsibility** in salvation; he can choose to **accept** or **reject** God.

1. Joshua knew man had choice!

    a. "Choose you this day whom ye will serve." Josh. 24:15

    b. Joshua presented the choice to Israel to serve either the gods of the Amorites or Almighty God.

   c. He chose to serve the Lord.

2. Jesus told his disciples, "If any man will come after me, let him deny himself, and take up his cross and follow me. For whosoever will save his life shall lose it: and whosoever will lose his life for my sake shall find it." Mt. 16:24,25

   a. The word "will" in these verses suggests "desire" or "want."

   b. Man has to chose to be saved.

3. "Behold, I stand at the door, and knock: if any man hear my voice, and open the door, I will come in to him, and will sup with him, and he with me." Rev. 3:20

   a. Jesus pictures Himself as desiring to come into the heart of man.

   b. Picture your heart as having a door.

   c. Where is the door knob? It is on the inside.

   d. Where is Jesus standing? On the outside.

   e. Who has to open the door? Man does!

    f. Calvinism pictures Jesus on the outside of man's heart; the man is unable to open the door to allow Him in. Therefore, Jesus just kicks the door open and comes into the heart!

        1. How does the word "rape" make you feel? It is so outrageous, so vicious, so wrong.

        2. In reality, Calvinism is "spiritual rape!"

4. God's grace is glorious; however, it is resistible.

5. A good illustration of grace being resistible is company rebates.

    a. Do companies have to give us rebates? No.

    b. The rebate is in reality their mercy toward the customer.

    c. The company's "grace" is the money they refund to you!

    d. Suppose a vacuum cleaner company offers you a $15 rebate if you buy their product.

    e. They are not going to force the $15 upon you — it IS resistible.

    f. To receive the $15, you have to meet the requirements. You must buy the product, send in the original receipt along with a filled out form. Some companies may require you to send in a stamped, self-addressed envelope. If you do not meet the requirements, you do not receive the rebate.

E. Perseverance of the saints!
   1. Two passages are often cited to try to support this position.
      a. Jn. 10:27-29
         1. "Neither shall any man pluck them out of my hand." Verse 28
         2. "No man is able to pluck them out of my Father's hand." Verse 29
      b. Rom. 8:35-39
         1. NOTHING can separate the Christian from the love of Christ.
         2. Christians can be more than conquerors in Christ.
         3. These passages certainly affirm that no one can **force** us to leave Christ; however, they DO NOT address the question, "Can we **choose** to leave Christ and His love?"

   2. Scripture affirms the possibility that man CAN fall!
      a. "Wherefore let him that thinketh he standeth take heed lest he fall." I Cor. 10:12

b. II Pet. 2:20-22
1. Christians have escaped the pollution of the world — sin.
2. They escaped sin through the knowledge of the Lord and Savior Jesus Christ.
3. Tragically, Christians can become entangled in sin again and be overcome.
4. It would have been better if such unfaithful brethren had never heard the Gospel than after hearing it to turn from it and return back into sin.

c. Paul cautions the Galatians against allowing false teachers to demand that they adopt practices of the Law of Moses like circumcision. If they did adopt such laws, they would fall from grace. Gal. 5:4

d. Jesus stated that every branch in Him that was fruitless would be cut off. Jn. 15:1-6

e. All of the verses that urge faithfulness emphasize that man can fall from grace!
1. Heb. 2:1-4; 3:12,13; 4:1
2. Imagine that it was impossible for you to have a car wreck.
a. You go to get into your automobile and I say, "Be

careful and do not have a wreck."

b. If it were impossible for you to wreck, what would you think? He must be crazy!

3. Imagine how it makes God look when over and over we are told "Be faithful" if it were impossible to fall from grace.
   a. God would seem totally foolish!
   b. He is cautioning us about a real danger — we CAN fall.

Conclusion:

A. You may wonder, "Why study this difficult topic?"
   1. It is one of the leading **false** concepts in religion today!
   2. Calvinism is extremely dangerous! It affects one's:
      a. View about **man** and his nature.
      b. View toward **Scripture**.
         1. The Calvinist will see the Word as not being very important.
         2. He is much more concerned about an experience.
      c. View toward **Deity** and Their working in our lives.
      d. View toward **salvation** and how it occurs.

e. View about everyday **decisions** because he believes that the Holy Spirit directs these decisions.

3. One who accepts ANY one of the five points of Calvinism will end up accepting a false theology!

B. The Bible declares God's love for you and His longing for you to be saved! In order for you to receive that grace, you must **obey** Him. You can make that choice in future lessons as we will see His Will in order that you might know how to choose to obey Him.

What Is The Bible?

Introduction to the Lesson:

A. Remind the student of the tie between the first five lessons and this lesson.

1. Lesson 1 emphasized that we can know that God exists. We saw the nature of Biblical knowledge and faith.

2. In Lessons 2-4 we learned about God, Christ and the Holy Spirit — the three Divine Beings of the Godhead!

3. In the last lesson we saw the relationship between the Godhead and mankind.
   a. Deity has made salvation available.
      1. God, the Father designed the plan.
      2. Christ came to earth, died and thereby created the plan.
      3. The Holy Spirit revealed the plan and confirmed it by supernatural gifts.
   b. The important questions are, "Has Deity made grace available and do They determine who is saved and when he is saved?" or "Has Deity made grace available and must man respond in faith to receive the saving benefits of that grace?"
   c. We learned that Deity has provided the grace. Man learns about that

grace in the revealed message of inspiration. We then have the privilege either to submit to God in order to receive that grace or to reject His Will and be excluded from that saving grace.

4. Once we realize that we must choose to obey God, the next question is: "Where do I learn about His Will so I can make that choice either to obey or reject Him?"

5. We learn about God's Will in the Bible, THE BOOK.

6. I promised you that this lesson will be less complicated than the last lesson. Hopefully you will find this to be very accurate.

B. It is imperative for the student to understand the importance of the Bible for man today.

C. As teachers, we must emphasize the importance of authority in spiritual matters and how that authority affects our lives.

I. The Bible — a Book Given by Inspiration of the Holy Spirit!

Goals To Accomplish As You Teach This Topic:

- Help the student grasp the significance of Biblical inspiration.
- Understand the trustworthiness of the Bible.

Struggles That The Student Might Have With This Topic:

- Confusing the typical definition of "inspiration" with God's definition of Biblical interpretation.
- Accepting that every word is chosen by God and is very important.

A. "Inspiration"
  1. We studied this word previously as we discussed the work of the Holy Spirit.

  2. "Inspired" means "**God-breathed.**"

  3. This emphasizes the source of the message — God in Heaven Himself!

B. Scriptures that teach this truth are:
  1. "All scripture is given by inspiration of God." II Tim. 3:16

  2. "Holy men of God spake as they were moved by the Holy Ghost." II Pet. 1:21

  3. "But we have the mind of Christ." I Cor. 2:16

C. The very **words** of the writers were inspired. I Cor. 2:13

1. These words were not words from the wisdom of man.

2. The specific words were chosen by the Holy Spirit from the author's vocabulary in order to carefully articulate in words the spiritual truths exactly as God wanted them revealed.

D. This emphasizes the importance of the Bible and its trustworthiness.

II. The Bible — the Power of the Word!

Goals To Accomplish As You Teach This Topic:

- Convince the student of the awesome power of the inspired Word.
- Emphasize that faith is man's response to the revealed message.
- Explain that the Word convicts our hearts, and that it shows us how to have spiritual life in Christ.

Struggles That The Student Might Have With This Topic:

- Accepting that God's power to save is in the Word. This is especially true for the student who has been taught Calvinistic "irrestistible grace."
- Being convinced that he needs to devote himself to reading and studying that Word so it will impact upon his life.

A. The Gospel is the **power** of **God** unto salvation.

   1. "For I am not ashamed of the gospel of Christ: for it is the power of God unto salvation to every one that believeth; to the Jew first, and also to the Greek." Rom. 1:16

   2. The message that will convict and convert hearts is the glorious Gospel of God's love, Christ's love as seen in His Incarnation, rejection and Crucifixion, and the love of the Holy Spirit in making known these glorious truths by inspiration!

B. God chose **preaching** of the Gospel to bring men to salvation.

   1. "It pleased God by the foolishness of preaching to save them that believe." I Cor. 1:21

   2. God determined to use a preached message as the way to touch the hearts of sinful men.

   3. The message is not foolish; however, it is seen as foolishness by men who glory in their own wisdom.

   4. Men may mock at the idea of a Divine Being coming to Earth and enduring the horrors of persecution, rejection, and Crucifixion. However, that Incarnation

and Death are CRUCIAL to man's salvation.

C. Faith comes by **hearing** that Word.
1. "So then faith cometh by hearing, and hearing by the word of God." Rom. 10:17

2. This emphasizes the importance of your having determination and drive to know that Word!

3. Without knowing that Word, we cannot come to saving faith!

D. We are **begotten** (brought to spiritual birth) by the Gospel!
1. "Of his own will begat he us with the word of truth," Js. 1:18

2. "Being born again, not of corruptible seed, but of incorruptible, by the word of God, which liveth and abideth for ever." I Pet. 1:23

3. God chose the Word to convict sinful man and to be the means by which we are brought to life.

4. This Word reveals unto man how to submit to Christ so we can receive the saving power of Christ's Blood to save us from our sin.

E. The Word is the **sword** of the Spirit.

    1. "And take the helmet of salvation, and the word of the Spirit, which is the word of God:" Eph. 6:17

    2. The Word is His sword to cut us to the heart, to convince us that Jesus is our only hope, and to show us the way to salvation.

III. The Bible — Its Significance for Man's Life!

Goals To Accomplish As You Teach This Topic:

- Explain that the Words of Jesus and the Words of the Bible are the Words of God, the Father.
- Encourage the student to realize that the Father has given us direction for every situation in life and has given us the guidance to be everything He expects us to be.
- Help the student see that God has explained to us in the Bible who we really are, what sin is and how much He wants us to be saved.

Struggles That The Student Might Have With This Topic:

- Being convinced that the Bible is so all inclusive.
- Realizing that if he follows the Bible, he can KNOW that his life is pleasing to God.

A. The revelation of the Bible and the teaching of Christ give us the **Will** or teaching of the **Father**.

    1. "Then answered Jesus and said unto

them, Verily, verily, I say unto you, The Son can do nothing of himself, but what he seeth the Father do: for what things soever he doeth, these also doeth the Son likewise." Jn. 5:19

2. "Jesus answered them, and said, My doctrine is not mine, but his that sent me." Jn. 7:16

3. "For I have not spoken of myself; but the Father which sent me, he gave me a commandment, what I should say, and what I should speak. And I know that his commandment is life everlasting: whatsoever I speak therefore, even as the Father said unto me, so I speak." Jn. 12:49,50

4. Jesus emphatically declares that His message came directly from the Father.

5. They are in total agreement as Divine Beings!

6. When we read the Bible, we are receiving the very mind of God, the Father Himself!

B. God, the Father has given us **all** things pertaining to life and godliness through Christ.

1. "According as his divine power hath given unto us all things that pertain unto life and godliness, through the knowledge

of him that hath called us to glory and virtue." II Pet. 1:3

2. The Father has given us direction for how to deal with every situation in life and how to please Him. All that direction was given through the knowledge of Christ!

3. When we obey the teaching of Christ, we can be absolutely confident that we are pleasing the Father!

C. He has given us what we need to be **complete** spiritually.
  1. "All scripture is given by inspiration of God, and is profitable for doctrine, for reproof, for correction, for instruction in righteousness: That the man of God may be perfect, thoroughly furnished unto all good works." II Tim. 3:16,17

  2. The inspired message is profitable for:
     a. Doctrine — **teaching**
     b. Reproof — shows us where we are **wrong**
     c. Correction — gets us back on the **right** track
     d. Instruction in righteousness — shows us the proper way to treat our **fellowman** .

  3. Its purpose — that the man of God may be:

      a. Complete — perfect (KJV); everything God wants us to be.

      b. Thoroughly furnished — given the directions God wants us to have for the true purpose for our lives, and equipped with all we need to be successful in dealing with every situation we face.

4. Thus, the inspired Scriptures give us all the guidance we need to be completely pleasing to our Father!

D. The Bible relates to us:

  1. What man is.

      a. Gen. 1:26,27

      b. Man is a spiritual being, different from all the rest of the creation!

      c. That eternal spirit, that which is made in the image of God, is what makes us different from all the rest of the creation.

  2. What sin is.

      a. Sin is transgressing (breaking or violating) God's law. I Jn. 3:4

      b. Passages like Galatians 5:19-21 specifically identify sinful actions.

  3. God's intense desire for man to be saved!

      a. "Search the scriptures; for in them ye think ye have eternal life: and they are they which testify of me.

And ye will not come to me, that ye might have life." Jn. 5:39,40

b. "And many other signs truly did Jesus in the presence of his disciples, which are not written in this book: But these are written, that ye might believe that Jesus is the Christ, the Son of God; and that believing ye might have life through his name." Jn. 20:30,31

c. The very purpose of the Scriptures is to convince us that Jesus is the true Messiah and that we can only have spiritual life by believing in and obeying Him.

IV. The Bible Will Be Our Judge!

Goals To Accomplish As You Teach This Topic:

- Convince the student that the Bible is more than just a good book.
- Help the student grasp that the Bible is God's standard of judgment for our lives.
- Explain that man is held responsible in God's sight for sins of omission and commission.

Struggles That The Student Might Have With This Topic:

- Overcoming the prevalent world view that makes man his own standard and that denies that there is any objective standard by which man is to live or by which he will be judged.
- Accepting the Bible as God's Divine standard by which all will be judged.

A. "He that rejecteth me, and receiveth not my words, hath one that judgeth him: the word that I have spoken, the same shall judge him in the last day." Jn. 12:48

    1. One who rejects Christ will be judged.

    2. The standard of that judgment: the Words of Christ Himself!

B. "Therefore we ought to give the more earnest heed to the things which we have heard, lest at any time we should let them slip. For if the word spoken by angels was steadfast, and every transgression and disobedience received a just recompense of reward; How shall we escape, if we neglect so great salvation; which at the first began to be spoken by the Lord, and was confirmed unto us by them that heard him." Heb. 2:1-3

    1. Paul urges the Jewish brethren to be dead serious about having sincere respect for the Gospel of Christ.

    2. He reminds them of God's expectations of Jews under the Law of Moses.

    3. That message was spoken by ANGELS, messengers from God to the Jews.

    4. Even under that Law, transgressions (sins of commission) and disobedience (sins of omission) were justly punished.

    5. How could people today possibly convince

themselves that the message delivered from the Father by HIS DIVINE SON and confirmed by supernatural signs would have fewer expectations or be of less importance?

6. It is amazing that many today have convinced themselves that God does not really expect obedience today!

7. This passage clearly shows us that God expects obedience; man will be judged for disobedience!

C. "And I saw the dead, small and great, stand before God; and the books were opened: and another book was opened, which is the book of life: and the dead were judged out of those things which were written in the books, according to their works." Rev. 20:2

1. Every person will be judged on the Day of Judgment.

2. The books that are opened are the Laws God has given to men under different dispensations — Patriarchal, Mosaic, and Christian.

3. The book of life is God's record of our lives while here on Earth.

4. Men will be judged as their lives are laid alongside the Law of God that was the standard for their lives.

V. Implications of These Truths!

Goals To Accomplish As You Teach This Topic:

- Caution the student about statements that may sound honorable but that in reality are denials of Biblical inspiration.
- Convince the student that the Bible IS the Word of God.
- Develop respect in the student that will imitate the respect Jesus had for the inspired Word.

A. The Bible is NOT to be read like any book of **human** origin — like a fairy tale, an autobiography, or a novel!

B. The Bible does NOT:
   1. JUST **contain** the Word of God!
      a. If I told you today that the Bible "contains" the Word of God, what would you think about that statement?
      b. Most people think that sounds like a very noble assertion.
      c. However, many theologians who declare that the Bible "contains" the Word of God mean that the Word of God is in the Bible, but not all of it is God's Word.
      d. Therefore, the reader must decide for himself what is God's Word and what is not the Word of God!
      e. The danger of such thinking:

       1. People begin with the presupposition that the whole Bible is not inspired of God.

       2. Many will try to abridge the Bible. Examples are the "Reader's Digest Bible" and the "Olive Pell Bible."

2. JUST **become** the Word of God!

   a. Those who make this assertion claim that the Bible is really a dead letter.

   b. It does not become the Word of God only when enlivened by the Holy Spirit in the heart of a sinner; neither does it become the Word of God only at the moment when a sinner applies that Word to his life.

C. The Bible **IS** the Word of God!

   1. It is God's Word if everyone in the world rejects it!

   2. It is God's Word no matter whether people like it or hate it!

D. We must become like Jesus who surely believed in the **authority** of the Scriptures!

   1. Jesus believed the stories and teachings of the Old Testament.

   2. He lived under that Law perfectly. Gal. 4:4,5; I Pet. 2:22

   3. Whatever His Father told Him to do, He

did, even if it meant dying on the Cross when He had the power to call ten thousand angels to deliver Him!

E. Our challenge:
   1. **Respect** the Bible as it is, the **Word of God**!
      a. This was the attitude of the people at Thessalonica.
      b. "When ye received the word of God which ye heard of us, ye received it not as the word of men, but as it is in truth, the word of God," I Thess. 2:13
      c. In a day and time in which the Bible is losing respect, you and I must hold it in the same esteem as these godly Christians!

   2. **Study** it (be diligent) to know it so you can be approved by the Lord! II Tim. 2:15

   3. "**Speak** where the Bible speaks and be **silent** where the Bible is silent.
      a. We must desire to obey the Will of the Lord, and it alone!
      b. We should be determined to follow it completely, not adding to it nor taking away from the Bible!
         1. Do not add to it nor take away from it! Rev. 22:18,19
         2. Do not think of man above what

is written. Never exalt a man above the Word because you like him nor exalt his opinions above that Word. I Cor. 4:6

4. **Search** the Scriptures to see if these things are so! Ac. 17:11
   a. This is a commendation of the dedication of the Berean Christians.
   b. "These were more noble than those in Thessalonica, in that they received the word with all readiness of mind, and searched the Scriptures daily, whether those things were so."
   c. We should long for God's pure Truths! We should compare everything we hear with what the Bible says, making sure it is His Will and not a man's ideas.

Conclusion:

A. In this lesson we have seen WHERE we learn of God's saving grace.

B. Now we know where to turn to find how to choose to obey Him and to receive salvation from our sins.

C. We should rejoice that God has given us personal choice!

D. In the next lesson we will study the

questions, "Where do we find the Will of Christ?" and "What Law are we under today?"

E. This will assist us in knowing exactly what Christ's Will is for us today!

The New Covenant Of Christ!

Introduction to the Lesson:

A. In the last lesson we emphasized the importance of the Bible.

B. The Godhead has extended the offer of salvation to sinful man; the Bible reveals Their offer of grace and calls upon man to respond to that grace by faithful obedience!

C. This lesson is CRITICAL for proper understanding of the Bible!
   1. It will help the student to know where to go in the Bible to find God's Will for his life today.
   2. It will assist the student to answer for himself so many questions that cause great confusion to Bible students.
   3. It will help him to know that the New Testament is the Law for mankind today.

D. Begin by pointing out that once we have studied God, Christ, the Holy Spirit, Calvinism, and the Bible, we MUST understand what LAW we are to obey.

E. Question: Have you ever wondered why

there is an Old Testament and a New Testament in the Bible?

I. The OLD Testament!

Goals To Accomplish As You Teach This Topic:

- Identify the first two dispensations introduced in the Old Testament Scriptures.
- Briefly describe the purpose and duration of the "Patriarchal Age."
- Emphasize the true purpose of the Old Testament Scriptures – God's providence in bringing the Hebrew Nation (Jews) into existence and in using them to bring the Messiah into the world.
- Show God's plan for the Law of Moses to be temporary, His promise of a New Law, and when the Law of Moses was abrogated.
- Expound upon the inadequacy of the Law of Moses.
- Answer an often asked question by students, "Why is the Old Testament still in the Bible?"

Struggles That The Student Might Have With This Topic:

- Overcoming past presuppositions or teachings by which he believes that God expects one to live by all the teachings of the Bible – Old Testament and New Testament.
- Accepting that the Law of Moses was never intended to last forever. Many have been taught that God removed the "Ceremonial Law" but not the "Moral Law."

Teaching Tools:

- Chart #6

A. What is the "Patriarchal Age?"
1. The word "patriarch" means "father."

2. The "Patriarchal Age" was the time when God spoke to the oldest male in each family.
   a. The patriarch had the obligation to pass on God's message to his family.
   b. This dispensation included the days of Adam, Noah, Job, Abraham, Isaac, Jacob, Joseph, Israel in Egypt, and Moses until Mount Sinai.

3. It was in effect from Creation (Adam) through Moses (receiving the Ten Commandments at Mount Sinai) for all people. It continued for all Gentiles until the house of Cornelius in Acts 10. See Chart #6.
   a. This chart shows God's Laws for mankind through the ages.
   b. Observe the different dispensations.
      1. Patriarchal
         a. From Creation to Mt. Sinai for all mankind.
         b. From Mt. Sinai until the house of Cornelius for all Gentiles.
      2. Mosaic
         a. For the Jews only.
         b. From Mt. Sinai until the Death of Jesus on the Cross.
      3. Christian

      a. For the Jews only for the first eight or nine years.

      b. Then for Jews and Gentiles.

      c. This is consistent with Christ's commands to the Apostles. "Ye shall be witnesses unto me both in Jerusalem, and in Judea, and in Samaria, and unto the uttermost part of the earth." Ac. 1:8

      d. This is exactly what the Bible declared in Rom. 1:16 "for the Jew first and also for the Greek."

B. What was the purpose of the Old Testament?

    1. It is a history of the **Hebrew** people.

      a. The Old Testament was never intended to be a history of all the nations of the world!

      b. It is a history of the Jews being selected to be God's special people — He selected them to bring the **Messiah** into the world.

          1. God made a promise to **Abraham**. Gen. 12:1-3

             a. God promised to give Abraham's descendants a land.

             b. Another promise was that his descendants would grow into a great nation.

c. The third promise: "In thee shall all nations of the earth be blessed."

1. Genesis 22:18 quotes the promise as, "And in thy seed shall all the nations of the earth be blessed."

2. This may appear to suggest that the Hebrew nation will be a blessing to the whole world and a nation above all other nations.

3. Paul, by inspiration of the Holy Spirit, clearly interprets this promise in Galatians 3:16. He declares that this promise refers to ONE descendant of Abraham, the Messiah, CHRIST!

2. The **record keeping** of the Hebrews would be SO beneficial in proving that Jesus was the **Messiah**!

a. Have you ever started to read the New Testament and given up almost as quickly as you started because of all the names listed in Matthew 1?

   b. Or do you just skip those names because they are too hard to pronounce?

   c. What is the purpose of the genealogies in Matthew 1 and Luke 3?

     1. Matthew gives the legal genealogy — through Joseph.

     2. Luke gives the literal genealogy — through Mary.

     3. The purpose of these genealogies — to prove that Jesus IS the promised Messiah, the Son of God!

 c. The Law of Moses was given to the Hebrews.

   1. Have you ever asked, "To whom did God give the Law of Moses?"

   2. Turn to Exodus 19:1-6; 20:1,2.

     a. Observe throughout chapter 19 to whom God is speaking — "children of Israel," "Israel," and "House of Jacob."

     b. This was three months after Israel had been delivered from Egyptian bondage.

     c. Now read Exodus 20:1,2. "And God spake all these

words, saying, I am the Lord thy God, which have brought thee out of the land of Egypt, out of the house of bondage."

    1. Whom did God bring out of Egypt? Israel!

    2. Notice in the next verse He begins to speak unto them the "Ten Commandments."

    3. To what nation is God speaking? Israel!

    4. That Law was only given TO THE JEWS, NOT TO ALL NATIONS!

  3. The **Ten Commandments** was the foundation of the Law of Moses. Ex. 20:3-17

2. To show man his need for a **Savior**!

  a. Gal. 3:19

  b. It was given to convince man that he could not live perfectly, that he needed a Savior, and that the promised Messiah was his only hope.

  c. It was a tutor or schoolmaster to bring man to Christ. It showed man he could not be saved without Jesus, the Messiah! Gal. 3:24

C. For what length of time was the Law of Moses to last?

1. It was **NEVER** intended to last forever!
    a. Gal. 3:19,16
        1. It was only to last "till the seed should come to whom the promise was made;" Verse 19
        2. Who is that seed? Christ! Verse 16
        3. How long was the Law of Moses, based upon the Ten Commandments, intended to last? Only until Christ came!
    b. It was removed at the **Cross** by **Christ** Himself!
        1. "Having abolished in his flesh the enmity, even the law of commandments contained in ordinances; for to make in himself of twain one new man, so making peace." Eph. 2:15
        2. Study the context of Ephesians 2:11-16.
            a. The Ephesians were Gentiles who were uncircumcised.
            b. The Israelites were Jews who had been circumcised.
            c. Christ came to bring peace to those who had been separated.
        3. Now look at the phrases of Ephesians 2:15.
            a. "Abolished" — "destroyed;" "done away with!"

      b. "In His flesh" — Christ! The other two Divine Beings never dwelt in flesh; this refers to the One who died on the cross!

      c. "Enmity" — "division"

      d. "Law of commandments" — Ten Commandments

   4. The message: Christ died on the Cross and destroyed the Ten Commandments which caused division between Jews and Gentiles because they were only for the Jews.

c. "Blotting out the handwriting of ordinances that was against us, which was contrary to us, and took it out of the way, nailing it to his cross." Col. 2:14

   1. Observe the phrases of this passage:

      a. "Blotting out" — "erasing;" " removing;" "destroying"

      b. "Handwriting of ordinances" — Ten Commandments. See Ex. 24:12; 31:18; 34:1,28; Deut. 4:13; 5:22; 9:10; 10:4

      c. "Took it out of the way, nailing it to his cross" — at His death on the Cross!

   2. Jesus removed the Ten Commandments at His Death.

     d. Why was the Law of Moses removed? So **all people** would be reunited under Christ.

2. Why the Law of Moses was not intended to last forever:

    a. God promised to give a **New** Law to Israel.

        1. I am going to read the prophecy in the Old Testament found in Jer. 31:31-34.

        2. Turn in your Bible to He. 8:8-12 and follow along as I read the prophecy given 600 years before Jesus came.

        3. Did you notice that the words are almost identical?

        4. Traits of the New Law:

            a. The Law of Moses was written upon stone; the New Law is to be written on hearts.

            b. When a child was born to the Jews under the Law of Moses, he was already a Jew at birth; later he had to be taught about God and the Law. By comparison, one is not a Christian today at birth. He must be taught the Law of Christ, and then, after knowing about God,

Christ and the plan for man's redemption, he must choose to obey it. Only then does he become a Christian.

c. Under the Law of Moses there was no forgiveness of sin. The glorious truth of the Gospel is that this New Law provides forgiveness of sins.

b. Complete **forgiveness** was not available under that Law! Heb. 10:1-4

1. Each year, on the Day of Atonement, the High Priest would make a sacrifice to God for his own sins and then another sacrifice for the sins of the people of Israel.

2. Truths about the Law of Moses:

a. It was only a "shadow" of the Law of Christ. It was not the great promised reality that God had planned for the world.

b. Those sacrifices could not make the sinners who approached God perfect.

c. The sins of Israel were remembered again by God on the Day of Atonement on the next year.

d. The blood of bulls and goats

was not accepted by God as an atonement for sin.

3. Why then do we have the Old Testament in the Bible?
   a. To give us a glimpse of God's preparation for redemption to come to the world.
      1. Throughout the Old Testament we see God's prophecies and providential working as He prepares to bring the Messiah into the world.
      2. We see His love, concern and determination for man to have a Savior!
   b. To prove to us that Jesus IS the promised Messiah !
      1. All of the prophecies about the Messiah in the Old Testament are critical in enabling us to be certain about the identity of the Savior.
      2. Jesus fulfills every prophecy — there is NO DOUBT that He is the Messiah, the Son of God!
   c. To be an example for mankind today.
      1. "For whatsoever things were written aforetime were written for our learning, that we through patience and comfort of the

scriptures might have hope."
Rom. 15:4

   a. We learn about the existence of the world — it came about by creation! Gen. 1:1

   b. We understand the nature of man — he is made in the image of God! Gen. 1:26,27

   c. We learn about Satan's determination to lead man into sin. Gen. 3:1-21

   d. We grasp how God feels about the sacredness of human life. Gen. 4:1-8

2. I Cor. 10:6,11

   a. "Now these things were our examples, to the intent we should not lust after evil things, as they also lusted."

   b. "Now all these things happened unto them for ensamples: and they were written for our admonition, upon whom the ends of the world are come."

   c. Truths from these verses:

      1. The fearful and unbelieving Jews who had been delivered from Egypt but died in the wilderness are examples to Christians of the

importance of remaining faithful.

2. The destruction of idolaters, fornicators and murmurers among the Jews is an example to Christians today that God will still punish sinners among His people.

II. The NEW Testament!

Goals To Accomplish As You Teach This Topic:

- Show that Christ's Law is for all people of all nations.
- Enable the student to see when the Law of Christ came into effect.
- Explain the serious spiritual consequences of trying to submit to both the Law of Moses and the Law of Christ simultaneously.
- Help the student see the glorious privileges of salvation now available.

Struggles That The Student Might Have With This Topic:

- Accepting the fact that the entire Law of Moses, Ceremonial and Moral Laws, were nailed to the cross.
- Comprehending the implications and consequences of seeking to obey Old Testament Laws today.

Teaching Tools:

- Chart #6

A. Christ has one **Law** for **all** men today!
1. He is the Mediator of the **New Testament**!

a. "And for this cause he is the mediator of the new testament, that by means of death, for the redemption of the transgressions that were under the first testament, they which are called might receive the promise of eternal inheritance." Heb. 9:15

b. Truths from this text:
   1. Christ is the Mediator, the One who can help restore us to the Father.
   2. He brought the New Testament as the New Law for mankind to obey.
   3. His Death on the Cross provided redemption that reached BACKWARD for all the faithful Jews under the first covenant (the Law of Moses) and FORWARD for all those on this side of the Cross who submit to the Gospel's call. (Note Chart #6 again to illustrate this point).

2. His Law came into effect when He **died** !
   a. "For where a testament is, there must also of necessity be the death of the testator. For a testament is of force after men are dead: otherwise, it is of no strength at all while the testator liveth." Heb. 9:16,17

b. Where have you heard the word "testament" used in everyday life?
1. Many have a "Last Will and Testament."
2. When does a "will" come into effect? It becomes valid at the death of the testator.
3. That "will" has no validity until the death of the testator.
c. Considerations about Christ's Will and Testament.
1. His Will came into effect when He died.
2. Thus, the teachings of Jesus recorded in Matthew, Mark, Luke and John were to come into effect when He died; they are His "Will."

B. The Jews had been **delivered** from that Law.
1. "But now we are delivered from the law, that being dead wherein we were held; that we should serve in newness of spirit, and not in the oldness of the letter. What shall we say then? Is the law sin? God forbid. Nay, I had not known sin, but by the law: for I had not known lust, except the law had said, Thou shalt not covet." Rom. 7:6,7

2. Truths from this text:

a. The Jews had been delivered from the Law of Moses — it was nailed to the Cross; it was no longer in effect!

b. The Law of Moses had died; the Jews were now free from it! Note the discussion of marriage in verses 2-4 that illustrates this fact.

c. What Law had died?
   1. The Law that said, "Thou shalt not covet."
   2. What Law is that? The Ten Commandments!
   3. Observe that God is NOT discussing the "Ceremonial Law;" He is discussing the "Moral Law" — the Ten Commandments!

C. The danger of attempting to serve both the Law of Moses and the Law of Christ at the same time is shown.
   1. Rom. 7:2-4
      a. Paul uses the illustration of marriage to explain that the Jews have been freed from the Law of Moses.
      b. Why does he use the woman in the illustration? He is explaining the concept of the Jewish Christian being married to the Law of Moses; later, becoming the bride of Christ.
      c. Truths about marriage:
         1. A woman is married to her

husband only as long as he lives.

2. If she leaves her living husband and marries another man, she will be in adultery.

d. The spiritual application:

1. The Jews were no longer married to the Law of Moses — it died when Christ died on the Cross.

2. Christ brought death to the Law of Moses.

3. That Law died in order that the Jews might be married to the risen Christ.

4. To attempt to serve both Laws simultaneously would put one in the position of committing SPIRITUAL adultery!

2. When one tries to take principles from the Law of **Moses** and bind them on men today, he places himself in spiritual trouble!

a. "For I testify again to every man that is circumcised, that he is debtor to do the whole law. Christ is become of no effect unto you, whosoever of you are justified by the law; ye are fallen from grace." Gal. 5:3,4

b. Judaizing teachers were trying to convince these Gentile Christians that they were obligated to keep both the Law of Moses and the Law of

Christ simultaneously.

c. These teachers tried to force these Christians to submit to circumcision, saying that if they did not, they would be displeasing to God.

d. Paul warns these Christians to realize that if they strive to return to the Law of Moses, they will fall from grace. They will be guilty of spiritual adultery and will be lost!

D. There are wonderful privileges under the Law of Christ!

1. We have a greater spokesman than **Moses**! Heb. 3:1 - 4:13

2. We have a greater High Priest than **Aaron**! Heb. 4:14 - 10:18

3. We have the privilege to be people of **faith** in Christ! Heb. 10:19 - 13:25

E. Why is understanding this truth SO vital?

1. Heb. 2:1-4

a. God kept His promises to punish disobeyers of the Law given through angels and prophets.

b. Be ABSOLUTELY sure that He will keep His promises and punish those who reject the Word spoken by Christ!

c. We MUST be anxious to obey the Law of Christ.

    2. His sacrifice made available **forgiveness** for ANY who will become true believers!

        a. "Neither by the blood of goats and calves, but by his own blood he entered in once into the holy place, having obtained eternal redemption for us." Heb. 9:12

        b. Under His Law, "Their sins and iniquities will I remember no more."

           1. Heb. 8:1

           2. Heb. 10:17

Conclusion:

  A. What does all of this mean for ME?

      1. I do not live under the Law of **Moses** today!

      2. I live under the Law of **Christ**!

      3. I can have **complete** forgiveness of my sins! Thank God!

  B. Why is this understanding SO VITAL to us?

      1. We know where to turn to answer the question, "What must I do to be **saved**?" (This will be addressed in Lessons 9 and 10.)

      2. We know where to turn to learn how to **worship** God. (This will be addressed in Lesson 12.)

      3. We learn how to live the Christian **life**.

        a. Mt. 5:21,22

        1. The Law of Moses commanded "Thou shalt not kill."

        2. Jesus commands us to avoid being angry toward our brother without a cause.

        3. Jesus requires Christians to control the thoughts that lead to the sinful actions!

    b. Mt. 5:27,28

        1. The Law of Moses commanded "Thou shalt not commit adultery."

        2. Jesus commands men to avoid lusting in their heart — having sexual desires for a woman when the man has no right to have her.

        3. Jesus requires Christians to control the thoughts that lead to adultery.

    c. Christian living will be addressed in more detail in Lesson 13.

D. We find answers to questions that are SO troubling to men today:

    1. Thief on the Cross.

        a. Many wonder why he was not commanded to be baptized.

        b. What Law was in effect when the thief asked Jesus for forgiveness? The Law of Moses!

        c. How do we know? The Law of Moses

ended when Jesus died on the Cross!
d.   Why was the thief not baptized? The
Law of Christ was not in effect at
that point.

2.   Sabbath Day.
a.   Many wonder if Christians should
worship on the Sabbath Day.
b.   What Law commanded worship on
the Sabbath? The Law of Moses gave
that command in the Ten
Commandments. Ex. 20:8
c.   If we followed the Ten Commandments today, on what day
would we have to worship?
Saturday.
d.   The New Testament shows that the
Christians worshipped on the first
day of the week, the Lord's Day or
Sunday.
e.   These facts proves that we are not
under the Ten Commandments
today!

3.   Tithing.
a.   The Law of Moses commanded giving
a tithe or ten percent.
b.   Christ requires Christians to give
from their heart, examining how they
have been prospered and then giving
accordingly. I Cor. 16:2

E.   Realizing that we live under the Law of

Christ found in the New Testament, we must challenge ourselves to study it, know it and live by it!

F. In the next lesson, we will see how God defines sin, note its consequences, and examine how we have sinned in our own lives and need a Savior!

Conviction Of Sin!

Introduction to the Lesson:

   A. Knowing that God exists, understanding who the members of the Godhead are, knowing that one has choice, realizing that the choice can only be known by studying the inspired Word, and being aware that the New Testament is our spiritual Law are critical facts that must be known.

   B. However, these facts are of no benefit unless we grasp our own personal need for these truths in our own lives.

   C. The purpose of this lesson is to make us aware of what sin really is, to see how God feels about sin, to understand specific actions that are declared by God to be sins, to see the eternal consequences of sin, and to come face to face with our own sinfulness and need for a Savior. Just as an alcoholic must realize that he has a problem before he will change, a sinner must see his sin problem before he will seek a Savior.

I. What IS Sin?

Goals To Accomplish As You Teach This Topic:

- Cause the student to compare the view that many people have about sin with God's clear explanation

of what sin truly is.
- Explain that sin is a violation of God's will.
- Discuss two types of sins, commission and omission.

Struggles That The Student Might Have With This Topic:
- Overcoming false views that he might have about sin.
- Accepting that violating God's Law is so serious.

A. How does the world view sin today?
  1. A generality.
     a. Many want preachers to harshly condemn "sin" from the pulpit, as long as the preachers use the word "sin."
     b. However, some of those same people will "get their feathers ruffled" in a hurry if he identifies specific actions as being sin.
     c. As long as the preacher speaks in generalities, people do not feel guilty and are very pleased with the preacher.

  2. A misnomer.
     a. The word "misnomer" means "an incorrect designation."
     b. Today, God's designations for sin are viewed as too harsh and judgmental; therefore, these actions are NOW given different designations.
        1. Fornication — "premarital sex."
        2. Adultery — "an affair," "fooling

around," "remarriage."

3. Murder — "unwanted fetal tissue," "abortion," "Pro-choice."

4. Homosexuality — "alternate lifestyle."

3. A BIG sin!

   a. Most actions are viewed as "no big deal."

   b. Only the most vicious actions are seen as sin; the problem is that many even question if murder is really all that horrible.

4. A violation of another person's choice.

   a. Many identify sin as "a non-consensual act."

   b. Thus, one person forcing his desires upon another, particularly in the sexual realm, would be viewed as sin.

   c. Under this definition, rape would be a sin. Consensual homosexuality, adultery or fornication would be seen as acceptable action.

5. A mystical concept.

   a. Some view sin as "vague speculation," "an obscure action."

   b. These people do not view sin as specific violations of God's Laws.

6. Some seem to totally deny that sin exists.

   a. Amoral libertines espouse the idea that one is free from self-restraint and that there is NO action that is sinful.

b. Such persons believe "anything goes," and simply ignore any discussion of sin.

B. God's explanation of sin.
 1. It is **transgression** or lawlessness.
    a. "Whosoever committeth sin transgresseth also the law: for sin is the transgression of the law." I Jn. 3:4
    b. "Transgression" — "stepping across the line."
       1. God specifically identifies which actions are sinful.
       2. Sin is violating that law.
       3. It is "stepping across that line" by doing what God commanded us not to do.
    c. "Lawlessness" — "refusing to submit to or be regulated by law."
       1. It is an attitude of heart that refuses to listen to God.
       2. It is a refusal to subject one's self to God's Law that is in effect.

 2. All **unrighteousness** is sin.
    a. "All unrighteousness is sin:" I Jn. 5:17
    b. "Unrighteousness" is being unjust and dishonest with my fellowman.

3. "For if the word spoken by angels was stedfast, and every transgression and disobedience received a just recompence of reward." Heb. 2:2
   a. In this passage, Paul identifies two types of sinful actions.
   b. The types of sins:
      1. "Transgression" — sin of **commission** ·
         a. Stepping across the line in disobeying God.
         b. If God says, "Do not lie," He has laid a line in the sand and told us not to step across it.
         c. If we lie, we have transgressed that law.
      2. "Disobedience" — sin of **omission** ·
         a. This is a refusal to obey a command of the Lord.
         b. He has commanded man to worship Him; refusal to worship Him is, therefore, sin.

II. How Does GOD Feel About Sin?

Goals To Accomplish As You Teach This Topic:
- Show why God despises sin.
- Emphasize the impact that sin has upon man's relationship with God.

- Explain that when we sin against man, we also sin against God.

Struggles That The Student Might Have With This Topic:
- Grasping that sin is SO horrible!
- Understanding the consequences of our own sins.
- Realizing that all sin is in reality reproach against God.

A. God regards sin as an **abomination**!

   1. "These six things doth the Lord hate: yea, seven are an abomination unto him." Pr. 6:16-19

   2. This passage then lists seven sins that God despises.

   3. The word "abomination" is such a strong word! It denotes something that God absolutely abhors, detests, despises, or hates!

   4. This passage gives us great insight into the difference of perspectives that God and men have toward sin.

     a. God sees sin as totally despicable!

     b. Man looks at some of the seven "abominable sins" as being quite insignificant. For example, pride, lying and sowing discord are viewed as quite harmless.

     c. Some today even question the horrible nature of murder.

    d. God is absolutely clear about how He detests all sin.

    e. Why would He be so harsh against sin? Note the next three points.

B. Sin **separates** man from his God!
1. God explained to the people of Judah why their nation is about to fall: "Behold, the Lord's hand is not shortened, that it cannot save; neither his ear heavy, that it cannot hear: But your iniquities have separated between you and your God, and your sins have hid his face from you, that he will not hear." Is. 59:1,2

    a. God had not changed, nor had He moved.

    b. The sins of the people of Judah separated them from Him; therefore, He would not hear their cries.

2. "For the wages of sin is death;" Rom. 6:23

    a. When you work hard all week, what do you expect to receive?

        1. WAGES!

        2. Why? Because you earned it.

    b. God affirms in this passage that sin produces spiritual death — separation from God!

    c. All men will ultimately choose to disobey God's commands in their lives; when they do, they have sinned!

1. "For all have sinned, and come short of the glory of God." Rom. 3:23
2. "All" refers to Jews and Gentiles.

d. Because of our sin, we have earned separation from God. We have earned a home in Hell! We have already condemned ourselves. Jn. 3:18

C. Against WHOM do we sin?
1. Obviously, we sin against our **fellowman**.

2. However, ALL sin is in reality against **God** Himself!
   a. Against thee, thee only, have I sinned, and done this evil in thy sight:" Ps. 51:4
      1. David had committed adultery with Bathsheba and in an attempt to cover the subsequent pregnancy, David devised a plan whereby her husband, Uriah, would be murdered. II Sa. 11
      2. After Nathan, the prophet, convicted him of sin, David was filled with remorse. II Sa. 12
      3. David realized that every sin is in essence against the God of Heaven!
   b. "I have sinned against the Lord." II Sa. 12:13

3. NOTE: Because GOD is the one sinned against, **GOD** ALONE has the right to set the terms for forgiveness!
   a. Amazingly, people often convince themselves that they can set their own terms for how to be forgiven of their sins.
   b. This is as absurd as thinking that a convict can set his own terms of punishment!
   c. We must realize that ONLY GOD can set those terms of forgiveness; we will study these terms of pardon in future lessons.

D. How dangerous is sin? Why would God consider sin to be so severe?
   1. It is SO **deceitful**!
      a. It offers pleasure. Heb. 11:25
      b. Even the godly can become envious. Ps. 73:2-7
      c. Sin convinces man that it is acceptable: "Everybody is doing it!"
      d. It convinces man that it can be hidden even from God!
         1. Neither Adam and Eve, Gen. 3:10,11; Cain, Gen. 4:10; Achan, Josh. 7; nor Jonah could hide their sins from God!
         2. Truly, "be sure your sin will find you out." Nu. 32:23

2. It is SO deadening!
   a. Sin takes away man's feeling; it numbs his conscience.
   b. "Having their conscience seared with a hot iron." I Tim. 4:2
   c. "They were not at all ashamed, neither could they blush:" Jer. 6:15

3. It is SO degrading!
   a. Sin does NOT build up; rather, it starts man on a downward slide that just goes deeper and deeper into wickedness.
   b. It enslaves. Men become "servants [slaves] of sin." Rom. 6:17

4. It is SO destructive!
   a. Man may deny its sting; that will NOT take away its devastation.
   b. It destroys our relationship with God and brings eternal separation from Him!

III. What Is Sin?

Goals To Accomplish As You Teach This Topic:

- Study four passages in the New Testament where God identifies long lists of sin.
- Specifically identify actions that are sinful.
- Help the student clarify some of those difficult to pronounce and seldom understood sinful actions.

Struggles That The Student Might Have With This Topic:
- Accepting that some actions truly are sinful.
- Rejecting the world's acceptance of so many of these abominable actions.

A. Gal. 5:19-21
1. **Adultery** (In KJV and NKJV)
   a. Sexual unfaithfulness of a married person to his or her spouse.
   b. An illicit relationship or marriage of a married person with someone other than his/her "lawful" spouse.
   c. A person who is allowed to be married legally (in accordance to the laws of the land), may be an "adulterous" spouse in God's sight. A "lawful" spouse is one acceptable in GOD'S sight. Rom. 7:2,3; Mt. 5:32; 19:9

2. **Fornication**
   a. The Greek word "πορνεία" (porneia) is defined as "any illicit sexual intercourse."
   b. This word is a very broad and inclusive word. It might be described as a pie that is cut into many pieces.
   c. Pieces of that pie would include pre-marital sexual intercourse, adultery, incest, homosexuality, lesbianism, and bestiality.

3. **Uncleanness**
   a. This is NOT being dirty or having body odor.
   b. It is "moral impurity."
   c. This sin involves having impure motives in our hearts.

4. **Lasciviousness**
   a. Most cannot pronounce this word, let alone try to define it.
   b. Newer translations that supposedly make the Scriptures easier to understand translate this word as "licentiousness." Most people cannot pronounce or define this word either.
   c. Lasciviousness is "anything that tends to, leads to or that is involved in the promotion of lust."
   d. But what is "lust?" It is the enticement of a person to desire another when he has no right in God's sight to be with that person.
   e. Other lexical definitions of this word include:
      1. "Indecent bodily movements."
      2. "Unchaste handling of males and females."[29]

5. **Idolatry**
   a. This may involve worship of a statue, but it is much more inclusive.
   b. It is putting anything before God!

6. **Witchcraft**

   a. Other translations have the word **"sorcery."**

   b. The Greek word "φαρμακεία" (pharmakia) means "worship of the devil and demons coupled with hallucinating drug abuse."

7. **Hatred**

   a. This is passionate animosity.

   b. The strong dislike is coupled with ill will within one's heart toward the one who is hated.

8. **Variance**

   a. This is being contentious.

   b. Because of discontent, one causes struggles and rivalry between people.

9. Emulations (**Jealousies**)

   a. Jealousy is milder than envy and covetousness.

   b. Jealousy is resentment because of another's attainments.

10. **Wrath**

   a. It is violent anger or rage.

   b. This includes sudden outbursts of anger.

11. **Strife**

   a. Selfish ambition.

   b. Constant, competitive rivalry.

12. **Seditions**
    a. Divisions.
    b. Disagreeable attitudes and actions that lead to disruption, discontent and division.

13. **Heresies**
    a. Divisions caused by false doctrines.
    b. Sects and denominations.

14. **Envy**
    a. Grudging desire.
    b. Having a longing desire for another's possessions or position.
    c. Envy is stronger than jealousy which is the resentment of another's attainments; envy focuses on that person's attainments with a desire to have them.

15. **Murder**
    a. Intentional, willful taking of another's life.
    b. Premeditated killing.
    c. This is not condemning self-defense.

16. **Drunkenness**
    a. Intoxication.
    b. Given to the drinking of intoxicating beverages.

17. **Revellings**
    a. Wild, drunken parties.
    b. "Partying."

B. I Cor. 6:9,10 (We will only define the new words in this list.)
1. **Effeminate**
   a. A passive partner in sodomy.
   b. A submissive homosexual.

2. **Abusers** of themselves with mankind
   a. Sodomites.
   b. Aggressive homosexuals.

3. **Thieves**
   a. Those who steal the belongings of others.
   b. They have no respect for another's ownership of possessions.

4. **Covetous**
   a. Lust for another's possessions to the point of doing wrong to take his possessions.
   b. It is much stronger than jealousy (the resentment of another's attainments), and envy (grudging desire to have the attainments of another).
   c. Covetousness is the willingness to do wrong to take his possession.
   d. An illustration: you may own a really nice car (maybe a Mercedes or a Lexus) but not understand its maintenance or operation. Realizing this, and being covetous for your car, I might take off one or two spark plug wires without your knowledge.

Then I would try to convince you that your car is "a piece of junk." Subsequently, I would offer you a ridiculously low price for the car. If you trusted me and sold it to me, I would then have your car, reattach the plug wires, and gloat about how I conned you!

e. God defines "covetousness" as idolatry! Col. 3:5

f. In reality, your car has become my idol! I want it much more than I want to be obedient to God.

5. **Revilers**
   a. Those who speak reproachfully.
   b. Attempting to destroy another's reputation by words.

6. **Extortioners**
   a. Using pressure to seize and carry off another's possessions.
   b. Extortion is acting like a vicious predator who sees another's property as a piece of meat to grab and take.

C. Col. 3:5,8,9 (We will only define the new words in this list.)
   1. Inordinate **affections**
      a. Unnatural desire.
      b. **Passions** that are not normal.
      c. An example: bestiality.

2. **Evil** concupiscence
   a. **Desire** or lust for forbidden things.
   b. **Longing** in one's heart for things that are wrong.

3. **Anger**
   a. Strong displeasure.
   b. Inflammed excitement or displeasure, usually because of being insulted or being offended.

4. **Blasphemy**
   a. **Slander**.
   b. Speech that defames the majesty of God, Christ, and sacred things.
   c. Also, this involves slander of a man's good reputation.

5. **Filthy Communication**
   a. Cursing.
   b. Dirty jokes, suggestive, and improper language.

6. **Lying**
   a. Being a deceiver.
   b. Not telling the truth.

D. Rev. 21:8 (We will only define the new words in this list.)
   1. **Fearful**
      a. Timid.
      b. Cowardly.

2. **Unbelieving**
   a. One who rejects faith in Christ.
   b. A disbeliever.

3. **Abominable**
   a. A detestable person.
   b. One defiled with abominations.

IV. The Seriousness of Such Sins?

Goals To Accomplish As You Teach This Topic:
- Show God's abominable hatred of sin.
- Explain the eternal consequences one faces if he continues to live in sin and does not find God's answer for justification.

Struggles That The Student Might Have With This Topic:
- Believing that the sins in his life might damn his soul to an eternal Hell!
- Developing the attitude toward sin in his mind that God has toward it.

A. "They which do such things shall not inherit the kingdom of God." Gal. 5:21

B. "Know ye not that the unrighteous shall not inherit the kingdom of God?" I Cor. 6:10

C. "For which things' sake the wrath of God cometh on the children of disobedience." Col. 3:6

D. "Shall have their part in the lake which burneth with fire and brimstone: which is the second death." Rev. 21:8

V. Personal Thought Questions and Evaluation!

Goals To Accomplish As You Teach This Topic:

- Help the student come to see his own sinfulness and personal need for salvation.
- If the student has made a past commitment to God, cause him to see how he sinned BEFORE he made a commitment and how he has sinned SINCE.
- Cause the student to have a longing for Christ and His Blood to justify him from his sins.

Struggles That The Student Might Have With This Topic:

- Refusing to look at the sins of his life.
- Rationalizing and attempting to convince himself that his own sin is not so serious.
- Facing his own sin and being overwhelmed with feelings of guilt and remorse.

Struggles TEACHERS Might Have With This Topic:

- Wanting to omit this part of the lesson because we may feel uneasy and find this unpleasant.
- Being uncomfortable about guiding the student to come face to face with his sins.
- Trying to comfort one who is overwhelmed with grief and guilt. Rather, we must allow the student to have tears and cry. Be quiet and allow one's heart to be convicted. This will lead to repentance!

A. Have you sinned against God?

   1. Explain to the student that you are not attempting to be his "priest" to whom he must come for confessional.

   2. Rather, as a teacher, you want to lovingly guide the student to see himself as God already sees him.

   3. Urge the student to look at the above list of sins we have studied and answer this question, "Have you sinned against God?"

     a. God tells us that we ALL have sinned!

       1. "For all have sinned, and come short of the glory of God;" Rom. 3:23

       2. John reminded Christians that all have sinned in the past! "If we say that we have not sinned, we make him a liar, and his word is not in us." I Jn. 1:10

       3. As a teacher, you may help the student to be freer to look at his own sins if you will explain to him that you too have sinned. Give an example such as a time you lied or stole something.

     b. Ask the student to identify in his own mind or write on a piece of paper (that he alone will see) how he has sinned against God.

    4. How has sin affected your relationship with God? How has it affected your life?

B. How do you think God feels about your sinning against Him?

    1. He designed us to be creatures who love and praise Him.

    2. Imagine how badly it hurts Him when we choose to reject Him.

C. How do YOU feel about sinning against your God?

    1. Does it "break your heart?"

    2. How do you feel about God viewing you as a "sinner?"

D. What have you earned because you have sinned?

    1. Remember, "For the wages of sin is death;" Rom. 6:23

    2. Sinners have separated themselves from God!

    3. Sinners are lost in sin!

    4. Sinners have earned a home in Hell!

E. Is it important to you to be forgiven?

F. Do you REALLY want to go to Heaven?

G. Where can you POSSIBLY find an answer for your sins?

   1. THERE IS HOPE FOR YOU!

      a. "For the wages of sin is death;" Rom. 6:23 If that is all of the message of the Bible, we are totally without hope, DOOMED to eternal separation from God in Hell!

      b. Thankfully, the verse continues, "but the gift of God is eternal life through Jesus Christ our Lord."

   2. ONLY IN CHRIST can you find an answer for your sin!

      a. "For God so loved the world, that he gave his only begotten Son, that whosoever believeth in him should not perish, but have everlasting life." Jn. 3:16

      b. "I am the way, the truth, and the life: no man cometh unto the Father, but by me." Jn. 14:6

      c. "Neither is there salvation in any other: for there is none other name under heaven given among men, whereby we must be saved." Ac. 4:12

   3. Christ died for YOUR sins!

      a. Is. 53:4-6

         1. As the student reads this passage, ask him to emphasize the personal pronouns.

         2. "Surely he hath borne OUR

griefs, and carried OUR sorrows, yet we did esteem him stricken, smitten of God, and afflicted. But he was wounded for OUR transgressions, he was bruised for OUR iniquities: the chastisement of OUR peace was upon him; and with his stripes WE are healed. All WE like sheep have gone astray; WE have turned every one to HIS OWN way; and the Lord hath laid on him the iniquity of US ALL."

b. "So Christ was once offered to bear the sins of many; and unto them that look for him shall he appear the second time without sin unto salvation." Heb. 9:28

4. Christ can be your propitiation (appeasement of God's wrath) and advocate!

a. "My little children, these things write I unto you, that ye sin not. And if any man sin, we have an advocate with the Father, Jesus Christ the righteous: And he is the propitiation for our sins: and not for ours only, but also for the sins of the whole world." I Jn. 2:1,2

b. He is sinful man's appeasement of God's wrath.

c. He is the pleader or Lawyer who pleads to the Father for Christians when they sin. He wants you to be saved; then He wants you to be successful!

H. Again, please remember — YOUR SINS put Christ on the Cross; you need HIS BLOOD and its power to EVER get back to a right relationship with your God!

1. Between now and the next lesson, please continue to focus upon the fact that you have sinned and that you need a Savior.

2. In the following lessons we will learn how to receive the benefits of His Blood and to be cleansed so that we might be justified in God's sight!

Faith, Repentance, And Confession

Introduction to the Lesson:

A. Previously we have studied about God, Christ, and the Holy Spirit, and we have learned that God has given us the privilege of choosing if we wish to receive His grace. We learn about that choice in the Bible; the New Testament is the Law under which He presents the terms whereby we can receive that grace.

B. In the last lesson, we saw how God feels about sin, identified specific sins, and learned the consequences of our sins.

C. Then you were asked to look into your own life, to be convicted of your own sin, and to realize your own need for Christ!

D. In this lesson, we begin to see ALL of God's plans come together.

E. Our goal is to find out how to be saved!
   1. Realizing you have sinned and how deadly your sin is in God's sight, how can you KNOW that you have been forgiven?

---

2. The important question for every sinner is, "What must I do to be saved?"

    a. This was the question of the Jews on the Day of Pentecost.

        1. Those responsible for Jesus' Crucifixion were convicted of their sin and convinced that Jesus was the promised Messiah. Ac. 2:37

        2. They cried out, "Men and brethren, what **shall** we do?"

    b. This was the same question asked by the jailer of Philippi.

        1. Ac. 16:30

        2. The circumstances of this question are as follows:

            a. Paul and Silas had been arrested for casting the demon out of the girl who followed them daily.

            b. Men were using her to "pad their pocketbooks" as they promoted her as a soothsayer.

            c. Therefore, these men brought Paul and Silas before the magistrates accusing them of teaching unlawful customs.

            d. Thus, Paul and Silas were beaten and thrown in jail.

            e. At midnight, Paul and Silas

were singing praises to God and praying. I wonder how many of us would be feeling sorry for ourselves or bemoaning the fact that we were being mistreated because we were Christians.

f. A strong earthquake shook the city of Philippi so severely that the foundations of the jail were shaken, the doors were thrown ajar, and the bands that held the prisoners were broken.

g. The jailer, knowing his charge to keep the prisoners secure and suspecting that they had escaped, planned to commit suicide rather than be convicted for not keeping them secure.

h. Paul quickly informed the jailer that he and Silas were still there — they were so honorable that they refused to flee.

i. The jailer was overwhelmed by their honor, faith and security in the midst of such a terrifying earthquake.

j. Thus, he was desperate to know the source of their

confidence and hope.

3. He asked, "Sirs, what must I do to be saved?"

3. As you faced your sins in the last lesson, hopefully you are eagerly asking, "What must I do to be saved?"

4. Let us eagerly begin to find God's answer for our sins!

I. Faith in Christ!

Goals To Accomplish As You Teach This Topic:

- Help the student understand what is encompassed in faith.
- Remove from his mind that faith is mere "mental assent" that Jesus is the Son of God.
- Emphasize the trust and confidence of true faith.
- Show that true faith involves obedience to Christ's teachings.

Struggles That The Student Might Have With This Topic:

- Realizing the all-encompassing nature of faith.
- Overcoming the shallow concept of faith that suggests it is mere acknowledgement of the truths about Jesus.

A. God expects mankind to believe in Christ!

1. "For God so loved the world, that he gave his only begotten Son, that whosoever believeth in him should not perish, but have everlasting life." Jn. 3:16

2. "He that believeth on the Son hath everlasting life: and he that believeth not the Son shall not see life; but the wrath of God abideth on him." Jn. 3:36

3. The jailer of Acts 16:31 was told to "believe on the Lord Jesus Christ, and thou shalt be saved, and thy house."

4. Thus, we can see that God expects man to believe in Christ.

B. But WHAT IS faith?
1. This is the critical question.

2. There are SO MANY misunderstandings about what is involved in faith in Christ.

3. Ideas held by many:
   a. Speculation.
      1. Such people view faith as mere conjecture.
      2. This concept involves theorizing about what might be true.
      3. There is NO certainty in speculation.
      4. THIS IS NOT BIBLE FAITH!
   b. Probability.
      1. Those who hold this view try to determine if there is greater evidence on the side of believing or not believing.
      2. Thus, if he decides there is a 51% probability that Jesus might be

God's Son, he will believe in Jesus; if he thinks the greater probability is on the side of disbelief, he will not believe.

3. There is NO certainty in probability.

4. THIS IS NOT BIBLE FAITH!

c. Existential "leap in the dark."

1. The existentialist believes that one has very few pieces of evidence; the evidence does not really support his convictions, but he merely CHOOSES to believe.

2. He suggests that one simply leaps from one or two facts to belief in Christ.

3. I liken this concept of faith to:
   a. Belief in "Santa Claus."
   b. Belief in the "Tooth Fairy."

4. There is no real support for one to believe in the reality of such beings, he just chooses to believe!

5. There is NO certainty in existentialism!

6. THIS IS NOT BIBLE FAITH!

4. What is Bible Faith?
   a. Hebrews 11:1
      1. "Substance of things hoped for."
         a. "Substance" — foundation; assurance; guarantee.

   b. "Things hoped for" — what
       you EXPECT to happen.
2. "The evidence of things not seen."
   a. "Evidence"   —   proof;
       persuasion.
   b. It is the conviction of the
       reality even of the unseen.
3. There IS certainty in genuine
    faith!
b. True faith is confidence based upon
    evidence.
   1. We KNOW that God can be
       trusted.
   2. He cannot and does not lie. Tit.
       1:2
   3. It is a confidence that when HE
       speaks, man must listen and
       obey.
c. Faith is trust in Christ as THE ONE
    who can save me from my sin against
    God.
   1. Faith begins with the realization
       that I am a sinner.
   2. It continues with the realization
       of the horribleness of sin.
   3. Faith also involves the
       realization that I MUST find an
       answer for my sin.
   4. It also includes a longing for a
       Savior.
   5. Faith acknowledges that God
       HAS promised me that Jesus is

the Savior I need and my ONLY **answer** for salvation.

    6. It culminates with my **obedience** to Christ.

  d. Genuine faith involves man's **loving response** to the love of Deity.

    1. "If ye love me, keep my commandments." Jn. 14:15

    2. "But God be thanked, that ye were the servants of sin, but ye have obeyed from the heart that form of doctrine which was delivered you." Rom. 6:17

    3. Observe that genuine faith emphasizes obedience.

    4. How is faith attained?

      a. "So then faith cometh by **hearing** and hearing by the word of God." Rom. 10:17

      b. Faith is MAN'S response to God's Word and **promises** Rom. 10:9,10. He promises faithful men salvation.

C. The imperativeness of faith in Christ.

  1. "I said therefore unto you, that ye shall die in your sins: for if ye believe not that I am he, ye shall die in your sins." Jn. 8:24

  2. "But without faith it is impossible to please him: for he that cometh to God

must believe that he is, and that he is a rewarder of them that diligently seek him." Heb. 11:6

3. "The just shall live by faith." Gal. 3:11

4. These verses unequivocally show that faith in Christ is absolutely necessary as a sinner seeks salvation.

D. Is salvation attained at the point of mere mental assent? By faith only?
  1. Many have a false concept about faith.
    a. Some consider "belief" not to be as strong as "faith."
    b. However, "faith" and "belief" are the SAME word in the original Greek language "πιστεύω" (pisteuo).
    c. If man is saved at the point of mere mental assent, then the demons will also be saved.
      1. James chastised those who claimed to have faith but refused to obey the Lord.
      2. "Thou believest that there is one God; thou doest well: the devils also believe, and tremble." Js. 2:19
        a. The demons often confessed that Jesus was the Christ, the Son of God.
          1. "Let us alone; what have we to do with thee, thou

Jesus of Nazareth? art thou come to destroy us? I know thee who thou art, the Holy One of God." Mk. 1:24

2. "What have we to do with thee, Jesus, thou Son of God?" Mt. 8:29

b. Obviously these demons had "mental assent" and confessed the truth about Jesus; yet, they were the demons of the Devil!

3. James continues by clearly stating that "faith **only**" will not save! "Ye see then how that by works a man is justified, and not by faith only." Js. 2:24

2. True Bible faith is living, vibrant, responsive **obedience**!

E. Questions about your faith and response to Christ!

Purpose Of These Questions:

- Urge the student to conduct serious self evaluation of his past commitment to Christ, if he has made a commitment.
- Assist the student to identify what he has been taught and obeyed, then, to compare what he has done with what Christ teaches one must do in order to be saved.

Struggles That The Student Might Have With This Topic:

- Remembering exactly when and what he did in making a commitment in the past.
- Answering objectively – he may want to give answers that will please the teacher or answers that will assure him that he truly obeyed God when he made his commitment.

Cautions To Teachers:

- Explain to the student the purpose of these questions: they are to assist the student in evaluating if he has truly obeyed Christ and has been forgiven.
- Allow the student time to answer these questions on his sheet.
- Then have him to review his answers so you can hear his answers.
- WRITE DOWN his answers on a separate sheet of paper and keep them to assist you in understanding the points you will need to emphasize in future lessons. DO NOT COMMENT ABOUT THE ANSWERS AT THIS TIME!
- I have had some students who later in our study changed answers after learning that what they had been taught and obeyed was contradictory to what the Bible taught. I do not think this is an attempt to be dishonest, rather, it shows the student's desire to have certainty about his salvation.

1. Have you ever made a commitment to Jesus?
    a. If the student answers "no" to this question, he does not need to proceed to other questions.
    b. If he answers "yes," he needs to proceed.

2. If so, how old were you?
   a. If the student is not sure of his age, have him to give an estimate.
   b. The age at which this commitment was made will later help the student see if he truly understood the consequences of sin and was mature enough to make that decision for himself.

3. Did you make a confession at the time of your commitment?
   a. Many students will answer "no!" These are students in churches whose theology is based upon the false doctrine of "original sin."
   b. Others will answer "yes!"

4. If so, what did you confess?
   a. The purpose of this question is to have the student to specifically identify his confession.
   b. Here are some answers you may expect:
      1. Some were asked to confess their past sins.
      2. Others confessed their belief in a denominational tenet.
      3. Others confessed their belief that Jesus is the Son of God.

5. Have you been baptized?
   a. If the student answers "no," there

will be no need to answer the rest of the questions.

   b. If he answers "yes," he needs to answer the remaining questions.

6. If so, how were you baptized?
   a. Some were immersed.
   b. Many were sprinkled or had water poured upon their heads.

7. Were you baptized before or after making a commitment?
   a. Those who were sprinkled as infants will answer "before."
   b. Those who were taught later in life and then were baptized will answer "after."

8. If you were baptized AFTER your commitment, how long after the commitment was it until you were baptized?
   a. The answers you will hear in response to this question will be so varied.
   b. I have heard answers from "immediately" to "two and one-half years!"

9. If you have been baptized, for what purpose were you baptized?
   a. The purpose of this question is to urge the student to evaluate the reason for which he was baptized.

    b. In Lesson 10 we will see the significance of purpose in relationship to the act of baptism.

10. Was it your understanding that you were saved BEFORE or AFTER your baptism?

    a. Many who have been immersed have been taught that their salvation was received before their baptism. These are students who have been taught Calvinistic theology.

    b. Others will answer "after!"

II. Repentance!

Goals To Accomplish As You Teach This Topic:

- Give the student a proper understanding of the subject of repentance.
- Help the student see the impact of true repentance upon one's heart.
- Encourage him to evaluate how repentance will affect his own life in relationship to sin.

Struggles That The Student Might Have With This Topic:

- Overcoming incorrect concepts about repentance.
- Coming to a clear definition and understanding of repentance.

A. Repentance is a **command** of God!

    1. "I tell you, Nay: but, except ye repent, ye shall all likewise perish." Lk. 13:3

  2. "And the times of this ignorance God winked at; but now commandeth all men everywhere to repent." Ac. 17:30

B. But WHAT IS repentance?
  1. "Repent ye therefore, and be converted," Ac. 3:19
    a. "Converted" — changed.
    b. Use illustrations such as a gas stove having its orifice changed to convert it from burning natural gas to burning bottled gas.
      1. These orifices have different size holes in them.
      2. The bottled gas orifice is much smaller that the natural gas orifice.
      3. If a person uses a natural gas orifice in a stove connected to bottled gas, he will have a huge explosion.

  2. One of the clearest explanations of repentance is found in the following passage: "For godly sorrow produces repentance to salvation, not to be regretted; but the sorrow of the world produces death." II Cor. 7:10 (NKJV)
    a. The King James translation is very confusing in this text.
      1. The word "repentance" is used twice in the KJV.

2. The second instance where the KJV uses "repented" is translated "regretted" by the NKJV and other translations.

3. This is the correct translation.

b. Explanation of this text:

1. This verse contrasts two kinds of sorrow — **godly** sorrow and **worldly** sorrow.

2. Study of godly sorrow:

a. It leads to **repentance**.

b. Repentance is a change of mind that leads to a change of **action**.

c. It is a change that one will NEVER regret because it leads to his salvation.

3. Study of the sorrow of the world:

a. It is being sorry that you were **caught**.

1. This is explained by the story of the little boy whose mother told him not to eat the newly baked cookies that she had placed in the cookie jar. However, the aroma permeated the house and the little boy just could not contain himself.

2. Many adults have the same feelings when they

are caught speeding.
They may not be sorry
for speeding, just sorry
that they were caught.
b. This type of sorrow is not
something that you TRULY
mean from the heart.

C. Examples of repentance:
1. The parable of the son asked to work in
his father's **vineyard**.
a. Mt. 21:28-32
b. A father had two sons whom he
asked to work in his vineyard.
c. The second son promised to go, but
did not keep his word.
d. The first son angrily said that he
would not go to work; later he
REPENTED and WENT TO WORK.

2. **Zacchaeus**.
a. Zacchaeus was a tax collector.
b. These men were hated by their own
countrymen because they were seen
as thieves and traitors.
1. They had to collect a set amount
of money that the Roman
government had determined. If
they charged the people more,
they could keep it. Thus, they
charged exorbitant rates in order
to become wealthy themselves.

2. The Jews saw these men as traitors who had sold out to the Roman government.

   c. After Zacchaeus met Jesus and had Him come to his house, he repented of his sins. He promised to give half of all his possessions to the poor, and to restore money fourfold to those whom he had extorted. Lk. 19:8

   d. After his repentance, Jesus said, "This day is salvation come to this house." Lk. 19:9

D. How will TRUE repentance affect your sins?
1. Take one sin such as lying.

2. If you repent, how will genuine repentance affect your life? Obviously it will cause you to be ashamed of that lying and to quit the lying.

III. Confession!

Goals To Accomplish As You Teach This Topic:
- Explain to the student what is to be confessed.
- Help him grasp the depth of the confession that Jesus is the Christ.

Struggles That The Student Might Have With This Topic:
- Just amazement at how this differs from what he has been taught.

A. God **commands** confession of our faith.

    1. He said, "Whosoever therefore shall confess me before men, him will I confess also before my Father which is in heaven. But whosoever shall deny me before men, him will I also deny before my Father which is in heaven." Mt. 10:32,33

       a. Note WHAT is confessed.

       b. We DO NOT confess our sins as we seek to become God's child — HE KNOWS WE ARE SINNERS!

         1. I believe it is in God's wisdom that He did not ask us to confess our sins before men.

         2. Many Christians would be so unforgiving and would think of the sins every time they saw the person.

         3. Too, would we have to confess EVERY SIN in order to be forgiven?

           a. One lady very seriously asked me that question in a Bible study years ago.

           b. I responded, "Could you NAME EVERY SIN you every committed?"

       c. Thank God that our confession is "Jesus is the **Christ**, the **Son** of **God**!"

2. "That if thou shalt confess with thy mouth the Lord Jesus, and shalt believe in thine heart that God hath raised him from the dead, thou shalt be saved. For with the heart man believeth unto righteousness; and with the mouth confession is made unto salvation." Rom. 10:9,10

B. An example of this simple, yet profound, confession is seen in Scripture. Ac. 8:37
   1. He was a **eunuch** of Ethiopia.
      a. He was the treasurer for Candace, the queen of Ethiopia.
      b. He was a Jew who had come to Jerusalem to worship.
      c. On his return home, he was reading the Messianic prophecy of Isaiah 53; however, he did not understand about whom the prophecy was talking.
      d. Philip taught him about Jesus.

   2. When the eunuch was convinced, he confessed, "I believe that Jesus Christ is the Son of God."

C. Profession is SO important!
   1. The **demons** OFTEN confessed that Jesus was the Son of God. Mk. 1:24

   2. Yet, it is NOT the point of **salvation**!

Conclusion:

A. A sinner desiring salvation must hear the Gospel, believe in Jesus as the One who can save him, repent of his sins, and confess his faith in Christ.

B. These commands (faith, repentance and confession) are not one time acts. These actions must continue the REST OF OUR LIVES!

1. One who becomes a Christian will NEVER stop believing in Jesus and trusting His commands and promises.

2. One who becomes a Christian will NEVER stop repenting of sin. He will sin and must be penitent before he can be forgiven.

3. One who becomes a Christian will NEVER stop confessing his faith in Christ. He will do that by his vocal profession and by his life profession as long as he lives on the earth.

C. In the next lesson we will see WHEN and HOW God says our sins can be removed by the Blood of Jesus Christ.

D. HOW EXCITING — God has given us the knowledge whereby, when we obey, we CAN be forgiven.

What Does The Bible Teach About Baptism?

Introduction to the Lesson:

A. This lesson is extremely detailed and thorough.

    1. I have planned this lesson to answer many of the most often asked questions by students.

    2. Students will learn so much about this terribly misunderstood topic in this one lesson.

    3. There are many stories that I could relate to you about students who were convinced that baptism was not necessary for salvation before this lesson, who were totally convinced of its necessity by the end of this lesson.

    4. Teach this lesson thoroughly and try not to deviate from it.

B. In our last lesson we began to answer the question, "What must I do to be saved?"

    1. This question comes from a convicted heart knowing, "I AM LOST!"

    2. Such a heart is determined to find an answer for sin and its guilt.

C. Commands we have already studied:
1. Faith in Christ.

2. Repentance of sin.

3. Confession of our faith in Christ.

D. In the last lesson I suggested that in this lesson we would:
1. See WHEN and HOW God says our sins can be removed by the Blood of Christ.

2. Come to know that we CAN be forgiven and be assured of that fact.

3. Be challenged to evaluate our faith. Remember, faith is the conviction that leads to obedience.

I. Is Baptism REALLY Necessary or Essential to Salvation?

Goals To Accomplish As You Teach This Topic:

- Show the student many of the passages that discuss baptism in the Scriptures.
- Explain that the Bible teaches that baptism is absolutely essential to man's salvation from sin.

Struggles That The Student Might Have With This Topic:

- Overcoming previous teaching that has taught him that baptism has nothing to do with salvation.
- Seeing baptism as an act of faith, not an attempt to earn our salvation.

Teaching Tools:
- Two items that you can lay on the table to illustrate the commands mentioned in each passage. I have used a salt shaker and pepper shaker, two books, two spoons, or two pens or pencils.
- A pen, pencil, or another item to represent salvation.

A. How would YOU answer that question?
  1. Allow the student to answer based upon his present understanding.

  2. Have him to write down his answer.

  3. Do not comment upon his answer.

B. Let's see how GOD answers this question.
  1. "And he said unto them, Go ye into all the world, and preach the gospel to every creature. He that believeth and is baptized shall be saved; but he that believeth not shall be damned." Mk.16:15,16
    a. This passage records Jesus giving the Great Commission to the Apostles immediately preceding His Ascension.
    b. What two commands does He tell the Apostles to require of sinful men?
      1. Believe.
      2. Be baptized.
      3. I place two items on the table to represent belief and baptism.
    c. When did Jesus say one will be saved?

1. I then use the ink pen or other item that represents salvation.

2. Did Jesus place salvation before belief? After belief but before baptism?

3. When did Jesus say one will be saved? **After you believe and are baptized**.

4. When will a sinner's sins be removed? **After you believe and are baptized**.

5. Please notice two observations about these questions:

   a. The above two questions are designed to help the student to begin to understand that salvation and remission of sins occur at the same time. This is so important for those who believe they are saved before baptism, but are baptized "for the remission of sins."

   b. Notice that in the answers both belief and baptism are mentioned. It is critical that we never separate baptism from belief. This helps the student realize that we are never emphasizing just baptism alone.

2. "Then Peter said unto them, Repent, and
    be baptized every one of you in the name
    of Jesus Christ for the remission of sins,
    and ye shall receive the gift of the Holy
    Ghost." Ac. 2:38
    a. This passage records the preaching
        of Peter and the Apostles on the Day
        of Pentecost, the first day the
        salvation of the Gospel was offered!
    b. The multitude included the very
        crucifiers of Jesus.
    c. What two commands did Peter give
        to these sinners?
        1. Repent.
        2. Be baptized.
        3. Again, I place two items on the
            table to represent repentance
            and baptism.
    d. When did Peter tell the crucifiers of
        Jesus they would have remission of
        sins?
        1. Again, I use an ink pen or
            another item to represent
            remission of sins.
        2. Did the Apostles offer salvation
            to these crucifiers of Christ
            before repentance? After
            repentance and before baptism?
            Or after repentance and
            baptism?
        3. Obviously, it was **after
            repentance and baptism**.

   e. When would they be saved?

     1. They would be saved **after repentance and baptism**.

     2. Why have both these questions been asked? Again, this is to meet the same problem mentioned under Mark 16:15,16. So many have been taught that salvation occurs before baptism, but that baptism is for the purpose of remission of sins.

     3. Mark 16 and Acts 2 clearly emphasize that these two terms are used to explain the same action — God's removing the sinner's sins.

 3. "And now why tarriest thou? arise, and be baptized, and wash away thy sins, calling on the name of the Lord." Ac. 22:16

   a. This passage records the teaching of Ananias to the penitent Saul of Tarsus, later known as the Apostle Paul.

   b. Paul was on the way to Damascus to persecute Christians.

   c. The Lord appeared to Saul on the road, convicted him of his sin, and sent him into Damascus to learn what he must do to be saved. Verse 10

    d. Paul was led into the city and for three days was in deep contrition, embarrassed that he had been fighting against the Will of God. Ac. 9:9

    e. The Lord sent Ananias to teach this penitent sinner how to be forgiven from his sins.

    f. What two commands did Ananias give Saul?

        1. Arise.

        2. Be baptized.

        3. Again, I place two items on the table to represent these two commands.

    g. When did Ananias tell Paul his sins would be washed away? **After he arose and was baptized**.

    h. When was Paul saved? **After he arose and was baptized**.

4. "Then Philip opened his mouth, and began at the same scripture, and preached unto him Jesus. And as they went on their way, they came unto a certain water: and the eunuch said, See, here is water; what doth hinder me to be baptized? And Philip said, If thou believest with all thine heart, thou mayest. And he answered and said, I believe that Jesus Christ is the Son of God. And he commanded the chariot to

stand still: and they went down both into the water, both Philip, and the eunuch; and he baptized him. And when they were come up out of the water, the Spirit of the Lord caught away Philip, that the eunuch saw him no more: and he went on his way rejoicing." Ac. 8:35-39

a. This passage is pregnant with information.

b. The eunuch, treasurer for Candace, the queen of Ethiopia, was a Jew who had been to Jerusalem to worship at the temple. On his return, he was reading Isaiah 53 but did not understand about whom this prophecy referred.

c. Philip was sent by the Spirit to teach this searching man.

d. Whom did Philip preach to the eunuch? **Jesus**.

e. What was the NEXT THING about which the Eunuch asked him? **Baptism**.

f. If I preach Christ, about what MUST I tell people? **Baptism**.

g. What was the element of baptism? **Water**.

h. What was the "good confession?" "**I believe that Jesus Christ is the Son of God.**"

i. What was the action of baptism? **Going down into the water,** coming out of the water; immersion.

j. When did the eunuch rejoice? **After he came up out of the water.**

k. When was the Eunuch saved? **After he believed, confessed, and was baptized.**

5. "Know ye not, that so many of us as were baptized into Jesus Christ were baptized into his death? Therefore we are buried with him by baptism into death: that like as Christ was raised up from the dead by the glory of the Father, even so we also should walk in newness of life." Rom. 6:3,4

a. Here Paul discusses how he and the Romans became Christians.

b. When does one get INTO Jesus Christ? **When he is baptized.**

c. When do we contact His Blood? **At baptism.**

d. What is the action of baptism? **Immersion; a burial.**

e. When do we die to sin? **At baptism.**

f. When do we walk in newness of life? **After baptism.**

C. When does God say one is saved? **After belief, repentance, confession and baptism.**

D. God **OBVIOUSLY** declares baptism to be **ESSENTIAL** to salvation!

    1. Observe the consistency in all these passages.

    2. Christ commanded, the Apostles taught, Saul, the eunuch and the Romans all obeyed the SAME plan of salvation.

II. What Is the Action (Mode) of Baptism?

Goals To Accomplish As You Teach This Topic:
- Show that New Testament baptism is an immersion.
- Explain this truth by looking at the English text and the Greek words.

Struggles That The Student Might Have With This Topic:
- Accepting that immersion is the ONLY mode of baptism.
- Realizing that one who has submitted to another mode has not obeyed God.

A. This is an often discussed question.

B. What are some modes of "baptism" you have heard mentioned?

    1. **Sprinkling**.

    2. **Pouring**.

    3. **Immersion**.

C. What does the Bible teach?

    1. John the Baptizer, the forerunner of the Christ who taught and baptized Jews, baptized at Aenon because there was **much water** there! Jn. 3:23

    2. Baptism is a **burial**. Rom. 6:4

    3. When one is baptized he goes "**down** into" the water and comes up "**out of**" the water. Ac. 8:38,39

    4. Only immersion would fit these descriptions!

D. Greek words verify this conclusion.

Greek Word	**Transliteration**	**Definition**
1. " ῥαντίζω "	"Rantize"	"I sprinkle"
2. " χέω "	"Chee"	"I pour"
3. " βαπτίζω "	"Baptize"	"I immerse"

    4. The above chart is explained as follows:
      a. The Greek words are in the left column.
      b. The second column is transliteration — using the equivalent English letters that correspond to the Greek letters.
      c. The third column is the true

definition, what the word truly means.

    d. Thus, the Greek words prove that New Testament baptism MUST BE immersion.

III. What Is the Purpose of Baptism?

Goals To Accomplish As You Teach This Topic:

- Urge the student to understand that there is ONLY ONE purpose for acceptable baptism – for SALVATION.
- Explain that purpose has always made a difference in God's sight!
- Show that there is a Biblical example of purpose making a difference in baptism.

Struggles That The Student Might Have With This Topic:

- Overcoming the popular position that as long as one is baptized, purpose is not important.
- Realizing that his own baptism might have been done for the wrong reason.
- Admitting that one who was baptized for an improper reason is still in his sin, even if he feels secure spiritually.

    A. Return to Romans 6:3,4.

        1. It looks **backward** to the Death, Burial and Resurrection of Jesus Christ.

        2. It looks **inward** at my OWN sin and need to die, to be buried as a man of sin, and to be raised as a child of God.

3. It looks **forward** to my desire to be with Christ forever.

B. Observations about baptism from the texts we have studied:
1. It is the point of **salvation!** Mk. 16:15,16

2. It is the point of **remission of sins!** Ac. 2:38

3. **Atonement**.
   a. God's wrath against the sinner's sin has now been appeased.
   b. The Blood of Christ has reconciled him with his God.

4. **Reconciliation** — reunited to a harmonious relationship with God.

C. Truths about purpose.
1. Purpose makes the difference whether God accepts an action or not.
   a. In the use of His **name**.
      1. "Thou shalt not take the name of the Lord thy God in vain;" Ex. 20:7
      2. The Jews believed that the name of Jehovah was so holy that they could not speak the word.
      3. This passage is NOT condemning using God's name.
      4. It is declaring that when the Jews used His name, it was to

be used in a holy, reverent way.

5. THE POINT: PURPOSE MAKES THE DIFFERENCE in the use of God's name!

b. In killing an **animal** for sacrifice or personal food.

1. Dt. 12:10-15

2. God is speaking to the children of the Jews who had been delivered from Egypt, but because of rebellion, had died in the wilderness during the forty years of wandering.

3. In this text, God gives commands for these Jews who are about to enter the Promised Land.

4. God would set up a place where the Jews were to offer their tithes and sacrifices. Verse 11

5. Animals that were to be sacrificed to God were only to be killed at this appointed place — we know that this was to occur at the Temple in Jerusalem. Verses 11-14

6. If a Jew was hungry, he could kill an animal in the land of any of the twelve tribes. It did not matter if he was ceremonially clean or unclean. Verse 15

7. THE POINT: PURPOSE MADE THE DIFFERENCE in the use

of the animal that was killed!

c. In taking the bread and fruit of the vine of the **Lord's Supper**.

   1. I Cor. 11:18-34

   2. In this text, Paul is chastising the Corinthians for the abuse of the Lord's Supper.

   3. They had adopted the idolatrous practice of the rich coming to worship first, the poor worshipping separately later. Verses 21,22

   4. Some were not giving consideration to the Body of Christ as they took this feast. Verse 29

   5. Because of the misuse of the Lord's Supper, some were spiritually sick, and some had died spiritually. Verse 30

   6. THE POINT: PURPOSE MAKES THE DIFFERENCE in partaking the Lord's Supper!

2. Purpose makes the difference in baptism!

  a. Read Acts 19:1-6.

   1. Apollos, a dynamic and intelligent preacher, came to Ephesus and taught in the synagogue. 18:24-27

   2. However, there was one serious problem; he taught about Jesus, yet combined that teaching with

the baptism of John. 18:25

3. When Paul came to Ephesus, he met twelve men who had been baptized by Apollos. 19:7

4. Paul asked them if they received the Holy Ghost (miraculous gifts) when they were baptized.

5. These men had not heard that the Holy Ghost had been given.

6. Immediately Paul realized something was wrong.

7. He asked them about their previous baptism.

8. They stated that they were baptized of John's baptism.

9. Immediately, Paul commanded them to be baptized in the name of the Lord Jesus.

10. Afterward, he laid his hands on them and they received spiritual gifts.

b. Comparisons of the baptism that John taught and the baptism that Jesus commanded.

John's	**Jesus'**
1. Ordained by God. Mt. 21:24	1. Ordained by God.
2. Immersion.	2. Immersion.

3. In water.	3. In water.
4. Preceded by repentance. Mk. 1:4; Mt. 3:2,8	4. Preceded by repentance.
5. For remission of sins! (Salvation) Mk. 1:4	5. For remission of sins! (Salvation)
6. In view of a COMING Messiah	6. In view of an ALREADY come Messiah!
7. No accompanying supernatural gifts.	7. Accompanying supernational gifts.

    c.   The point: An improper purpose for baptism makes it invalid in God's sight!

    d.   If one has been baptized thinking he/she has ALREADY been saved before that baptism, was that person baptized just exactly the way God said do it? **NO!**

    e.   I remind you, GOD is the One who extends forgiveness, NOT the sinner!

IV. Important Questions Often Asked About This Topic!

Goals To Accomplish As You Teach This Topic:

- Explain why seemingly different answers are given to the question, "What must I do to be saved?"
- Help the student understand the true meaning of passages that seem to say that one is saved by faith.
- Answer the often asked question about the thief on the cross and why he was not baptized.
- Examine infant "baptism" to see if it is acceptable to God.
- Show that Holy Spirit baptism is NOT baptism for salvation.
- Urge the student to evaluate his previous baptism and spiritual condition.

Struggles That The Student Might Have With This Topic:

- Grasping why different answers are given to those asking about salvation.
- Seeing the context of passages often used to suggest that salvation is by faith only, and understanding that faith includes baptism.
- Evaluating his own baptism and dealing with the reality that he may have felt secure and saved while still being in his sin.

A. Why are different answers given in the texts we studied?

    1. This IS a very difficult problem in the minds of many sincere students.

        a. The student may observe, "Some passages say 'believe and be baptized;' some say 'repent and be baptized;' some say 'believe;' and some say 'be baptizcd.' This is all SO CONFUSING! Am I allowed to choose which method I want?"

b. Teachers must be understanding and patient in assisting the student to grasp the consistency of these passages.

2. Examples of those different answers:

a.	Mk. 16:15,16	Believe		Be Baptized
b.	Ac. 2:38		Repent	Be Baptized
c.	Ac. 22:16			Be Baptized

3. Illustration of travel and getting different answers:

a. Use an illustration of traveling from where you are to a distant city.

b. Here is the example I use since I live in Evansville, IN. Suppose we are on a trip from Evansville to Louisville, KY.

1. If I ask at a gas station in Evansville, "How far is it to Louisville?", the answer would be, "About 125 miles."

2. If I travel up I-164 to Elberfeld, IN, I would receive an answer, "About 110 miles."

3. After traveling to Dale, IN, and asking the distance to Louisville, I would be told, "About 75 miles."

4. At Corydon, IN, I might ask again. The answer here would be, "30 miles."

5. I might just pull off the interstate and say, "These Hoosiers! Every time you ask them a simple question, you get a different answer."

   c. Why are different answers given? I am at different **points** on the trip to Louisville.

4. Why are different answers given to the question, "What must I do to be saved?"

   a. People are at different **points** on the path to finding salvation.

   b. One who has never heard is told to believe and be baptized.

   c. A person who already believes is told to repent and be baptized.

   d. The sinner seeking salvation who already believes and has repented is simply told to be baptized.

B. What about passages that state one is saved by faith?

1. Again, this is an excellent question.

   a. It is obvious why the student might ask this question.

   b. Calvinistic preachers and teachers have always emphasized that salvation is attained by faith; they are so derogatory toward baptism.

2. Ac. 16:30-33
   a. This is the story about the Philippian **jailer** and Paul and Silas being held in his jail.
   b. After an earthquake came, and the jailer saw Paul and Silas' calmness in such a terrifying event, he asked them, "Sirs, what must I do to be saved?" Verse 30
   c. Their response was, "**Believe** on the Lord Jesus Christ, and thou shalt be saved, and thy house." Verse 31
   d. We may ask, "Now does that not say, 'Believe and you will be saved?'"
   e. Let's read the rest of the context.
      1. They spake unto him the **Word** of the Lord. Verse 32
      2. What would you expect that to include?
         a. What had Jesus commanded to be taught to all people in the whole world?
         b. Obviously we would expect the Word of the Lord to include **baptism**.
      3. The jailer then took Paul and Silas the same hour of the night (midnight, Verse 25) and washed their stripes. This is an

indication of what? **Repentance**.

4. Then notice — "And was **baptized**, he and all his, straightway." Verse 33

f. Note the consistency of this story with the other passages about salvation.

3. Gal. 3:26,27

a. Verse 26 seems to say that one is a child of God by **faith**.

b. Note these points:

1. Ye **ARE** the children of God.
   a. What tense is this verb?
   b. **Present** tense.

2. Why are they the children of God?
   a. "For as many of you as HAVE BEEN BAPTIZED into Christ have put on Christ." Verse 27
   b. What tense is this verb phrase? **Past** tense.

3. WHY are the Galatians NOW Christians? Because of their previous **baptism** INTO Christ.

4. The point of emphasis on faith is that man must come to confidence in Christ so he trusts Christ for his salvation by obeying Christ. That is what is known as "calling on the name of the Lord." Ac. 22:16. Sinful man is saved at the point

of his baptism; he lives the rest of his life in faith in Christ.

C. What about the thief on the Cross? He was not baptized.
1. Again, this is a correct observation.
   a. I always appreciate students asking such questions.
   b. This shows me that the student is seriously thinking and earnestly trying to "put it all together."
   c. He wants to find answers to all his questions and confusions.

2. At this point in a study, this is such an easy question. The student will answer it himself as you ask him three simple questions.

3. One MUST ask, "What Law was then in effect?"
   a. "When did CHRIST'S Law come into effect? After His Death.
   b. When did Jesus say to the thief, "Today shalt thou be with me in paradise?" Lk. 23:43 Before His Death.
   c. What Law was in effect then? The Law of Moses.

D. What about babies being baptized?
1. What action usually occurs in "baptism" of babies? Sprinkling.

2. Why are babies NOT acceptable candidates for baptism?
   a. They have NOT **sinned**!
   b. They cannot **believe** that Christ can save them from their sin!
   c. They cannot **repent** of their own sins!
   d. They cannot **confess** their faith in Jesus!

3. Therefore, babies are NOT candidates for baptism!

E. Is New Testament baptism Holy Spirit baptism?
   1. Holy Spirit baptism only occurred twice.
      a. At the entrance of JEWS into the Church. A.D. 33. Ac. 2
      b. At the entrance of GENTILES into the Church. A.D. 41. Ac 10

   2. By A.D. 63, Paul affirms that there is NOW only ONE acceptable baptism in God's sight. Eph. 4:4

   3. Peter, who commanded baptism on the Day of Pentecost, forever settles the matter. He says New Testament baptism is **water** baptism. I Pet. 3:20-22
      a. God used the waters of the Flood to save Noah and his family.
      b. In like manner, God chose the waters of baptism to be the way in which

He would extend salvation to man through the Blood of Jesus Christ.

c. Baptism is NOT to remove dirt or filth from our body. If we need a bath, get a wash cloth, soap, and water.

d. Baptism is a command of Christ. Any sincere person who knows that Christ commanded baptism will immediately do so because he wants to have a clean conscience.

e. The event that gave power to baptism was the Resurrection of Christ. His Blood became the saving power by His Resurrection! Rom. 1:4

f. He is now the reigning Lord.

VI. Personal Evaluation!

Goals To Accomplish In This Section:

- Show the unbaptized student that salvation IS AVAILABLE to him.
- Urge the previously baptized person to evaluate his baptism; was it pleasing to Christ? Was he truly saved?

Struggles That The Student Might Have With This Topic:

- Admitting that his previous baptism is unacceptable in the sight of God.
- Admitting that he is in sin and would be lost in Hell if he died.

Cautions To Teachers:

- Practice the Golden Rule! Ask yourself how you would want one to treat you if you had just realized that your precious spiritual security was invalid.
- Do not PUSH for the student to be baptized now. Some will want to be baptized immediately; others will want time to think.
- You do want the student to "count the cost" by understanding that he will be baptized into the Church of Christ, not a denomination. Also, he needs to understand worship, Church organization, and Christian living.

A. Urge the student to evaluate his OWN spiritual condition.

    1. Are you still in your sin?

        a. You CAN be forgiven!

        b. Understand we are NOT emphasizing baptism alone but baptism preceded by faith, repentance, and confession.

        c. Think about this: God WANTS you to be saved and has given you His plan!

        d. You can choose that salvation.

    2. Have you BEEN baptized?

        a. For what purpose were you baptized?

           1. As a teacher you already know what the student answered in the last lesson.

           2. Make sure you have reviewed those answers before this lesson.

      3. Lovingly help the student be consistent with his previous understanding, even though this can be very painful as he realizes that his soul is in jeopardy.

  b. Have you been baptized JUST EXACTLY the way God said do it?

      1. Here we must remind the student of the ONE purpose for baptism — SALVATION!

      2. If he was baptized for any other reason, he submitted to a baptism that is NOT the Lord's baptism.

      3. Again, remind him of the twelve men at Ephesus.

3. If you TRULY believe in Christ, what will you determine to do?

  a. True faith relies totally upon Christ.

  b. If you truly believe, NOTHING will stop you from obeying Him so you can KNOW that you are saved!

The Church In God's Plan Of Redemption!

Introduction to the Lesson:

   A. This lesson is critical for the student who earnestly seeks to please Christ.

   B. The last lesson, on the subject of baptism, addressed an extremely controversial topic. This lesson is perhaps equally difficult for the student to grasp.

      1. The word "church" means so many different things to different people.

      2. Most students will probably think that "one church is as good as another."

      3. That is the product of the ecumenical philosophy that prevails in the religious world today.

      4. Be thorough and patient as you teach this lesson. Make sure the student grasps the glory and exclusivity of the Church established by Christ.

   C. In the previous study, we saw Christ's teaching about baptism.

      1. Baptism is the point where we get INTO Christ.

2. Baptism is where we contact the saving Blood of Christ.

D. What does baptism do for us? Where does it place us?
   1. It places us among the saved. Mk. 16:15,16

   2. It makes us NEW creatures. II Cor. 5:17

   3. It makes us Christians. Tit. 2:14; I Pet. 2:9; Gal. 3:26,27

   4. We become those whose names are written in Heaven! Heb. 12:22,23

   5. It adds us to the Church. Ac. 2:47

I. What IS the Church?

Goals To Accomplish As You Teach This Topic:

- Show different ways the word "church" is used in Scripture.
- Contrast God's revelation of the Church with the typical view the world has.
- Raise the student's appreciation of the privilege of being a Christian, a member of the Church.
- Help the student realize that the Church was planned by God in eternity, it was prophesied throughout the Old Testament and came into being on the Day of Pentecost after Christ's Resurrection.
- See the glory of the Church magnified in the titles assigned to it!

Struggles That The Student Might Have With This Topic:

- Seeing the Church as those called out of sin to submit to Christ.
- Accepting that he could EVER be a priest or a saint in God's sight.
- Understanding that the Church is Christ's Kingdom.
- Grasping that the Church was always in the eternal plan of God.

A. About what do you think when you hear the word "church?"

1. **Building**.

2. **Denomination**.

3. How do these definitions compare with what the Bible teaches about "the Church?"

B. CHRISTIANS are called "the Church!"

1. The word "church" comes from the Greek word " ἐκκλησία' (ekklasia) which means "the **called** out."

   a. This word is used in a general sense of any group of people called to assemble. The angry mob that assembled to oppose Paul in Ephesus is described as an "ἐκκλησία" (ekklasia) Ac. 19:32

   b. The technical spiritual application refers to Christians.

2. Christians are those who heard the

Lord's call, left the world, and came to Christ.

3. Terms Christians are called.
   a. **Saints**.
      1. Could you ever imagine yourself being a saint?
         a. This may seem absurd because of the concept of sainthood seen today in religion.
         b. A saint is seen as one who is so virtuous, seemingly far above the common person.
         c. It is interesting to notice that in many religions one is not exalted to sainthood until centuries after his or her death. By that time, anyone who knew his or her faults is dead and no one can criticize the saint.
      2. ALL Christians are called "saints" in the Bible!
      3. "To all that be in Rome, beloved of God, called to be saints:" Rom. 1:7
      4. This word comes from the Greek word "ἅγιος" (hagios), that is translated "holy," and "sanctified."
      5. It does not refer merely to "moral

purity;" rather, it refers to those "set apart to serve God." Obviously moral purity will be an important aspect of their sanctified life.

6. The moment one is baptized, he is set apart from sin and is a new creature in Christ — a "saint!"

b. **Disciples.**

1. "And upon the first day of the week, when the disciples came together to break bread, Paul preached unto them, ready to depart on the morrow; and continued his speech until midnight." Ac. 20:7

2. The word "disciple" means a "follower" of Christ.

3. All Christians are to be His followers or disciples.

c. **Priests.**

1. Can you in your wildest dreams imagine yourself being a priest?

2. When you think of a priest, what comes to your mind? A Catholic priest?

3. In God's sight, ALL CHRIST- IANS are "priests!"

4. "Ye also, as lively stones, are built up a spiritual house, an holy priesthood, to offer up

spiritual sacrifices, acceptable to God by Jesus Christ...But ye are a chosen generation, a royal priesthood, an holy nation, a peculiar people; that ye should show forth the praises of him who hath called you out of darkness into his marvelous light:" I Pet. 2:5,9

5. Christians are called "priests" because God accepts their worship and hears their prayers and pleas for forgiveness.

6. How beautiful! You can talk directly to God, you can confess your sins to Him, and you can ask Him to forgive you without going through any man!

d. **Brethren**.

1. Every saved person is a part of God's family!

2. We are "brothers and sisters" in Christ.

3. We are to care deeply for each other.

4. "Brethren, if a man be overtaken in a fault, ye which are spiritual, restore such an one in the spirit of meekness; considering thyself, lest thou also be tempted." Gal. 6:1

e. **Children** of God.
   1. Can you imagine yourself being called a "child of God?"
   2. Every saved person has been given spiritual life by God!
   3. "Beloved, now we are the sons of God, and it doth not yet appear what we shall be: but we know that, when he shall appear, we shall be like him; for we shall see him as he is." I Jn. 3:2
   4. "For ye are all the children of God by faith in Christ Jesus." Gal. 3:26
   5. Christians are SO loved; we are "God's children!"

f. **Christians**.
   1. What does the word "Christian" mean?
   2. All my life I have heard the word "Christian" defined as "Christ-like."
      a. However, many are Christ-like at times who in reality are so evil.
      b. The Devil is like Christ in the sense that he quotes scripture. Mt. 4:6
   3. The word "Christian" means "one who belongs to Christ."
      a. It is like the word "American"

that means "one who belongs to America."

b. When do we belong to Christ? At baptism that is preceded by hearing the Gospel, faith, repentance and confession.

4. The word "Christian" is only used three times in the Bible.

a. "And when he had found him, he brought him unto Antioch. And it came to pass, that a whole year they assembled themselves with the church, and taught much people. And the disciples were called Christians first in Antioch." Ac. 11:26

b. "Then Agrippa said unto Paul, Almost thou persuadest me to be a Christian." Ac. 26:28

c. "Yet if any man suffer as a Christian, let him not be ashamed; but let him glorify God on this behalf." I Pet. 4:16

4. Thus, individual Christians who are called out of the world by the Gospel are known as "the Church."

C. A GROUP OF CHRISTIANS in a **locality**!
1. "The church of God which is at Corinth." I Cor. 1:2

2. "The church which was at Jerusalem;" Ac. 8:1

3. "The church that was at Antioch." Ac. 13:1

4. Seven churches of Asia. Rev. 2,3

5. These were congregations of Christians in each community.

D. The UNIVERSAL BODY of Christ!
1. The Church was for ALL people of ALL nations!
   a. "And it shall come to pass in the last days, that the mountain of the Lord's house shall be established in the top of the mountains, and shall be exalted above the hills; and all nations shall flow unto it. And many people shall go and say, Come ye, and let us go up to the mountain of the Lord, to the house of the God of Jacob; and he will teach us of his ways, and we will walk in his paths: for out of Zion shall go forth the law, and the word of the Lord from Jerusalem." Is. 2:2,3
      1. This would come into being in the "last days" — the Christian

dispensation.

2. The Church would be established in Jerusalem.

3. It would be for people of all nations.

4. The Gospel would first be preached in Jerusalem and then go from there to the rest of the world.

b. "Go ye therefore, and teach all nations, baptizing them in the name of the Father, and of the Son, and of the Holy Ghost: Teaching them to observe all things whatsoever I have commanded you: and, lo, I am with you alway, even unto the end of the world. Amen." Mt. 28:19,20

1. The Gospel was to be preached to people in all nations.

2. Any who will be baptized belong to the Church of Christ!

2. ALL are invited to enter the Church through obedience. "And the Spirit and the bride say, Come. And let him that heareth say, Come. And let him that is athirst come. And whosoever will, let him take the water of life freely." Rev. 22:17

a. Anyone who will hear the Gospel and obey it will be a member of the Lord's Church.

b. God has made grace available; we must choose to enter His Church.

E. An **INSTITUTION** ordained by God and purchased by or belonging to Christ!
  1. It is an institution!
     a. Jesus declared, "I will build **my** church; and the gates of hell [Hades] shall not prevail against it." Mt. 16:18
        1. Jesus, during His earthly ministry, promised that He would build His Church.
        2. Hades itself would not deter His fulfilling the plan of the Father to establish His Church.
     b. Once the church was established, He is described as the head of His Church!
        1. "For the husband is the head of the wife, even as Christ is the head of the **church**." Eph. 5:23
        2. It exists; He is its head.
     c. Just as the home is a Divine institution of God, the Church is too!
     d. Man did not plan it nor bring it into being; Deity did!

  2. It was planned by God in **eternity**!
     a. The book of Ephesians reveals the glory of the Church.
     b. "To the intent that now unto the principalities and powers in heavenly places might be known by the church the manifold wisdom of God,

According to the eternal purpose which he purposed in Christ Jesus our Lord." Eph. 3:10,11

c. By the Church, God wanted to show His wisdom in His plan to save mankind.

   1. We have already seen some of His wisdom as He gave every man a choice to hear the Gospel and to obey it.

   2. Another example of His wisdom is seen as Christ commanded that baptism was to be an immmersion in water — an element that covers two-thirds of the face of the Earth and without which man cannot live. Obviously, He wanted to make it extremely easy for man to submit to baptism.

   3. Other examples of God's wisdom will be seen in the remainder of our lessons.

3. It was prophesied before it came into being!

   a. In the Old Testament.

      1. Dan. 2:21-45

         a. Nebuchadnezzar had a dream of a huge image.

         b. He had no idea that God was giving a picture of future nations.

      c. Four consecutive world empires were identified.

         1. Babylon.

         2. Medo-Persian.

         3. Greek.

         4. Roman.

      d. In the days of the fourth empire, God would establish a **Kingdom** that would NEVER be destroyed. Verse 44

  2. Christ's Law would go forth from **Jerusalem**.

      a. "And it shall come to pass in the last days, that the mountain of the Lord's house shall be established in the top of the mountains, and shall be exalted above the hills; and all nations shall flow unto it. And many people shall go and say, Come ye, and let us go up to the mountain of the Lord, to the house of the God of Jacob; and he will teach us of his ways, and we will walk in his paths: for out of Zion shall go forth the law, and the word of the Lord from Jerusalem. And he shall judge among the nations, and shall rebuke many people: and they shall beat their swords into plowshares, and their spears into pruninghooks: nation shall not lift up sword against nation, neither shall they learn war any more." Is. 2:2-4

b. Truths from this text:

1. The Messiah's Law will usher in the last dispensation, the Christian Age.

2. This Law will be for people of all nations.

3. It would first be taught in Jerusalem.

4. It would cause those who were formerly enemies to be at peace as they become brethren.

b. It was also prophesied during Christ's life on Earth.

1. It was "**at hand**."

a. What does "at hand" mean?

1. Is the year 2,200 "at hand?" Obviously not! We will not be here to see it.

2. If you have a dentist's appointment next week,

is that "at hand?" You know it is!

b. John the Baptizer prophesied this truth: "In those days came John the Baptist, preaching in the wilderness of Judea, And saying, Repent ye: for the kingdom of heaven is at hand." Mt. 3:1,2

c. Jesus made the same prophecy: "The time is fulfilled, and the kingdom of God is at hand: repent ye, and believe the gospel." Mk. 1:15

d. Jesus commanded the Apostles to prophesy the same truth, "And as ye go, preach, saying, The kingdom of heaven is at hand." Mt. 10:7

2. Some standing with and talking to Jesus would see the Church or Kingdom come with **power**!

a. "Verily I say unto you, That there be some of them that stand here, which shall not taste of death, till they have seen the kingdom of God come with power." Mk. 9:1

b. This is one of the amazing prophecies about the

establishment of the Church or Kingdom.

c. Jesus affirmed that it would come into existence in the lifetime of some of those people to whom He was speaking.

d. There are only two logical conclusions from this prophecy:

    1. Either, the Kingdom DID COME in the first century as Jesus prophesied;

    2. OR, the Kingdom HAS NOT COME and some of those people still have to be alive today and are over 2,000 years old.

        a. With technology today, we would definitely know if such people were living anywhere in the world.

        b. People of such age simply do not exist today!

    3. The only conclusion is that Christ's Kingdom DID come into existence in the first century!

4. The Church came into being with supernatural power!

   a. This had been prophesied in the Old Testament.

     1. Joel the prophet foretold of this event about 800 years before it occurred.

     2. "And it shall come to pass afterward, that I will pour out my spirit upon all flesh; and your sons and your daughters shall prophesy, your old men shall dream dreams, your young men shall see visions: And also upon the servants and upon the handmaids in those days will I pour out my spirit. And I will shew wonders in the heavens and in the earth, blood, and fire, and pillars of smoke. The sun shall be turned into darkness, and the moon into blood, before the great and the terrible day of the Lord come. And it shall come to pass, that whosoever shall call on the name of the Lord shall be delivered:" Joel 2:28-32

      a. God promised supernatural gifts would accompany the institution of the Lord's Kingdom, the Church.

      b. Its arrival would bring about a cataclysmic event.

         1. The statements about the sun and moon may immediately focus our minds upon the end of the world.

         2. However, this is an example of Old Testament Jewish apocalyptic literature. Compare Is. 13:10; 24:19-23; Ezek. 32:6-10; 38:20

         3. It was used to describe the fall of great world powers.

         4. Here, God is foretelling the end of Judaism and the Law of Moses.

         5. These events would occur when the Gospel call was extended to the world.

    b. Jesus prophesied to the Apostles that they were going to receive that power in Jerusalem.

        1. This was just before His Ascension into Heaven.

        2. "But ye shall receive power, after that the Holy Ghost is come upon you: and ye shall be witnesses unto me both in Jerusalem, and

in all Judea, and in Samaria, and unto the uttermost part of the earth." Ac. 1:8

    3. This was going to happen in just a few days (in fact, it occurred 10 days later).

  c. They did receive that power.

    1. It was on the Day of Pentecost.

    2. "And when the day of Pentecost was fully come, they were all with one accord in one place. And suddenly there came a sound from heaven as of a rushing mighty wind, and it filled all the house where they were sitting. And there appeared unto them cloven tongues like as of fire, and it sat upon each of them. And they were all filled with the Holy Ghost, and began to speak with other tongues, as the Spirit gave them utterance." Ac. 2:1-4

    3. This power came upon the Apostles. Ac. 1:26; 2:1,13,15,37; 11:15

  d. Compare Joel 2:28-32 with Acts 2:16-21. Peter, by inspiration, declares that Joel's prophecy has just come to pass.

5. Christians were **in** the Church in the first century!

a. "I John, who also am your brother, and companion in tribulation, and in the kingdom and patience of Jesus Christ, was in the isle that is called Patmos, for the word of God, and for the testimony of Jesus Christ." Rev. 1:9

b. "Who hath delivered us from the power of darkness, and hath translated us into the kingdom of his dear Son:" Col. 1:13

c. One can only be IN a building if it exists; one could only be IN the Church if it was already in existence!

6. This God-ordained, Christ-purchased institution is:

   a. "The **Church**."

      1. "The called out!"

      2. Mt. 16:18; Ac. 2:47

   b. "The Church of **Christ**." Rom. 16:16

   c. "The Church of **God**." I Cor. 1:2; Ac. 20:28

   d. "The **Blood-bought** Body of Christ."

      1. "The church of God, which he purchased with his own blood." Ac. 20:28

      2. This is why Christ's plan of salvation is SO important.

         a. It is when we are redeemed by Christ's Blood.

      b. Obeying it, God adds us to the Church. Ac. 2:47

  3. "Body of Christ" — It is His **spiritual** Body.

  4. Christ is the **head** of His Body.

      a. "And hath put all things under his feet, and gave him to be the head over all things to the church, Which is his body, the fullness of him that filleth all in all." Eph. 1:22,23

      b. "For the husband is the head of the wife, even as Christ is the head of the church:" Eph. 5:22-25

      c. "And he is the head of the body, the church: who is the beginning, the first-born from the dead; that in all things he might have the pre-eminence." Col. 1:18

  e. **Kingdom** of God. Mt. 16:16-18; Col. 1:13

  f. The home of the **saved**.

      1. "Christ is the head of the church: and he is the savior of the body." Eph. 5:23

      2. When saved, one is added to the Church by Christ Himself. Ac. 2:47

3. "Neither is there salvation in any other: for there is none other name under heaven given among men, whereby we must be saved." Ac. 4:12

g. The **bride** of Christ.

1. "Wherefore, my brethren, ye also are become dead to the law by the body of Christ; that ye should be married to another, even to him who is raised from the dead, that we should bring forth fruit unto God." Rom. 7:4

2. "Come hither, I will show thee the bride, the Lamb's wife." Rev. 21:9

h. Where **ALL** spiritual blessings are found.

1. "Blessed be the God and Father of our Lord Jesus Christ, who hath blessed us with all spiritual blessings in heavenly places in Christ." Eph. 1:3

2. The message of the book of Ephesians is the glory of the Church.

3. Draw a circle to represent the Church. All spiritual blessings are "In Christ." What truth does this show us? There are NO spiritual blessings outside of the Church.

II. The New Testament Church Is NOT a Denomination!

Goals To Accomplish As You Teach This Topic:
- Emphasize that Christ built only ONE Church.
- Contrast the Lord's Church with denominations.
- Explain that God hates denominationalism.
- Show how denominations come into being.
- Describe the attitude that causes people to begin denominations.
- Convince the student that all baptized believers will be added to the Lord's Church, never to a denomination.

Struggles That The Student Might Have With This Topic:
- Accepting that there is only ONE Church in God's sight!
- Realizing that God detests denominationalism.
- Grasping the difference in the Lord's Church and denominations.
- Overcoming the idea that one "church" is as good as another.

A. Christ built **ONE** Church!
   1. "I will build MY church." Mt. 16:18

   2. "There is ONE body." Eph. 4:4
     a. What is the Body?
      1. The Church.
      2. See chapter 1:22,23 "and gave him to be the head over all things to the church, which is his body."
      3. "And he is the head of the body,

the church:" Col. 1:18

b. There is ONE Church in God's sight as surely as there is ONE **God**, ONE **Christ**, and ONE Holy Spirit.

B. God HATES denominationalism!
1. What IS a denomination?
    a. Definition:
        1. Division of religion; a sect.
        2. It is a division brought about because of teaching something contradictory to the original Truths of God's Word.
        3. If the Truth of God's Word were taught, there would be no division!
        4. The world uses the word "sect" as a derogatory term applied to any religion it sees as "non-traditional." This is why the Lord's Church was called a "sect" in the first century (Ac. 24:14; 28:22), and the same charges are made against It today throughout the world.
    b. One word to help in the understanding of the word "denomination" is "denominator."
        1. In a fraction, the bottom number is called the "denominator."
        2. Why is it called a "denominator?"
        3. It is a divider.

2. The Lord's Church is NOT a denomination; It is ALL the **saved**!

   a. All those whom Christ saves, He adds to His Church!

   b. Those who obey men's teachings are added by men to their denominations which CANNOT provide salvation to any man.

3. Christ identifies denominationalism as **SIN**!

   a. In Gal. 5:19-21 Paul identifies sins that will cause one to lose the opportunity of going to Heaven.

   b. One of those sins is "heresies." This word means "false teachings that lead to division in religion; denominations."

4. Why are there so many different religions today?

   a. God prophesied that denominationalism was going to occur.

      1. II Thess. 2:3-12

      2. This passage emphasizes the following facts:

         a. There will come a falling away from the Truth and the institution of denominationalism before the Lord returns.

         b. The underlying principle that promotes the rise of

   denominationalism: man
exalts himself as God in his
own life.

 c. The source of denomi-
nationalism is Satan who
tempts man to leave Christ
and exalt his own ways. This
is the same attitude that
Satan promoted to Eve in the
Garden of Eden.

 d. God will allow man to believe
a lie and be lost because He
made us as beings of choice.

b. Paul foretold teachings that would
be the basis of denominational
dogma.

 1. I Tim. 4:1-4

 2. The Holy Spirit affirmed that
people would leave the faith and
teach false doctrines.

 3. Examples of those doctrines:

  a. Exalting celibacy and
binding it upon men.

  b. Forbidding the eating of
certain types of foods.

 4. Interestingly, many Catholic
students readily identify with
these teachings because of their
prevalence in the Catholic
Church.

c. People began to exalt **men**.

 1. Their ideas became of greater

importance than God's ways.

2. If the teachings of men and God contradicted, men's ways were valued above God's teachings.

d. People began to **change** God's Will.

1. Church government.

a. One elder was exalted above the others and called the "bishop."

b. Ultimately this led to the hierarchy of Roman Catholicism.

2. Sprinkling for baptism.

3. Holy days.

4. Purgatory.

5. Instrumental music.

6. Exalting of celibacy.

7. Abstaining from eating certain foods.

III. How Can I Know If I Am in the Lord's Church?

Goals To Accomplish As You Teach This Topic:

- Note the identifying marks of the Lord's Church that we have already studied.
- Urge the student to focus on the previously studied identifying marks.

Struggles That The Student Might Have With This Topic:

- Admitting that the church of which he is a part is

not the Lord's Church.
* Accepting that Christ's Church is the ONLY Church.

A. The importance of identifying marks.
   1. All of us understand this concept and use it every day.

   2. I usually use the example of finding my van in a parking lot.
      a. I have a 1984 Chevrolet Beauville diesel van.
      b. If I walked out of the church building or a mall and there were a thousand vans, I could identify MY van.
      c. How could I do that?
         1. My van is a Chevrolet. That would exclude all Fords, et. al.
         2. My van is a 1984. A new van would not be mine.
         3. My van is blue and white. Those of different color are not my van.
         4. My van has Indiana license plates; Vanderburgh County's prefix is 82. Any van from another state or another county would not be mine.
         5. I could identify the items inside my van.
         6. The vehicle identification number would surely prove that it is my van.

     d. All of these identifying marks prove that "This is MY van!"

3. Another example: baseball.

    a. We know the identifying marks of baseball.

       1. It is a game that uses a ball and a bat.

       2. The pitcher's mound is sixty feet, six inches from home plate.

       3. Four balls is a walk; three strikes is an out.

       4. It is played on a diamond shaped field with four bases.

    b. Suppose I took this game and taught my friends in Michigan and in Belarus where the weather is very cold in the winter.

       1. Because of the cold weather, we start playing the game on an ice hockey rink.

       2. Instead of using balls and bat, we use hockey sticks and pucks.

       3. Instead of having four bases and scoring a home run by touching all four bases, a home run is scored by knocking the hockey puck into the hockey net.

       4. If I taught my friends and they taught their children for generations that this was baseball, they would think they were playing baseball.

        5. Is that really baseball? Obviously not!

c. Suppose that in the year A.D. 4,000, someone is digging under an abandoned shed and finds a metal box. He is hoping to find a stash of money. When he opens the box, the first thing he sees is a very old book entitled "The Rules for Baseball" dated, 1998.

    1. This book describes the game of baseball.

    2. It talks about a diamond shaped field, balls and a bat, four balls is a walk, and three strikes is an out.

    3. He scratches his head and says, "That is the craziest game I ever heard."

d. Could he play real baseball again?

    1. CERTAINLY!

    2 How? By following the rule book!

e. The application:

    1. Two thousand years ago, Christ gave us the rule book for His Church.

    2. In the past two thousand years, man has altered Christ's teaching in every possible way.

    3. Yet, they still call their denomination or sect, "church."

4. When changes are made to the Lord's Church, what is the result? A denomination or sect in God's sight! Is the result the true Church? ABSOLUTELY NOT!

5. How can we today be a part of the the Church that Christ established? Simply follow His rule book, the New Testament!

C. Identifying marks of the Lord's Church!
   1. The New Testament Law is followed.

   2. The headship of Christ is respected.

   3. Christ's plan of salvation is obeyed.

   4. It worships as Christ authorizes (We will study worship in the next lesson.).

   5. It is organized as God reveals His plan of Church organization (Lesson 13).

D. Using these identifying marks, you can KNOW if the church you have been attending is the Church which Christ extablished or a denomination.

E. You can also KNOW when you are a part of THE LORD'S Church!

Conclusion:

    A. Being saved from our sins is SO vital to each of us!

    B. However, we must understand that one cannot have Christ without the Church — when saved, He adds us to His Church!

    C. Our goal must be to become Christians, and then determine to find those who are fellow Christians and teach, worship and live as Christ commands.

God-Ordained Worship!

Introduction to the Lesson:

    A. I encourage the teacher of this lesson to observe the approach to this study.

        1. The goal of this lesson is to help the student understand WHO is to be worshipped, the proper ATTITUDE of the worshipper, and GOD-AUTHORIZED worship.

        2. I make no attempt in this lesson to argue against every false practice that may be used in worship such as instrumental music, using wine on the Lord's Table, practicing "closed" communion.

        3. I have not tried to give all the arguments that those who use instrumental music have made to attempt to justify its use in worship. In this lesson I am simply trying to emphasize the Will of God.

        4. My goal in this lesson is to show the student what CHRIST has authorized! By this point in a study, the student should be thoroughly convinced that he must obey just the Will of Christ in everything.

        5. If he is convinced of Christ's authority, you will not have to argue against false teachings or practices; just teach him

Christ's commands.

6. Obviously, if the student asks questions about the possibility of these false practices, you will need to address them lovingly, but candidly.

B. Once one finds God's answer for salvation and is added to the Lord's Church, he must immediately seek to worship as God directs.

C. The identifying marks of the New Testament Church certainly involve proper worship.

D. Thus, what IS God's Will about worship?

E. What is your concept of worship?

I. God Wants to be Worshipped!

A. "God is a spirit: and they that worship him must worship him in spirit and in truth." Jn. 4:24

B. Acceptable worship must be characterized by two traits. It must be in:
1. Spirit.

2. Truth.

II. What IS Worship in Spirit?

Goals To Accomplish As You Teach This Topic:
- Emphasize the importance of proper attitude as one worships.
- Explain that worship is not for man's entertainment, it is man giving praise and adoration to God.

Struggles That The Student Might Have With This Topic:
- Overcoming today's emphasis on entertainment as worship.
- Realizing that wrong attitude will nullify the acceptability of our worship.

A. Worship "in spirit" refers to our ATTITUDE as we worship!

B. Why do many people attend a worship service?
1. Habit.
2. Social gathering.
3. Place to hear recent news.

C. What IS worship?
1. The word means:
   a. Kiss toward.
   b. Bow before.
   c. Showing adoration to One greater than we are and humbling ourselves before His greatness.

2. Worship is an act that pays honor to God.
   a. Worship is not just an attitude of heart.
   b. It is action.

3. Worship is NOT a "spectator concept!"
   a. Many view worship as entertainment.
   b. Thus, they are constantly asking, "What will I get?" "Am I being entertained?"
   c. The result of this type of thinking: there is a constant need for something more sensational to LIVEN UP their worship.

4. Worship is what YOU give!
   a. It is an outpouring of your love to God.
   b. It is glorifying your God.
   c. Many scriptures clearly affirm that worship is what YOU GIVE.
      1. "GIVE unto the Lord the glory due unto his name; worship the Lord in the beauty of holiness." Ps. 29:2
      2. "I will GIVE thee thanks in the great congregation: I will praise thee among much people." Ps. 35:18
      3. "Unto thee, O God, do we GIVE thanks, unto thee do we GIVE

thanks: for that thy name is near thy wondrous works declare." Ps. 75:1

4. "It is a good thing to GIVE thanks unto the Lord, and to sing praises unto thy name, O most High:" Ps. 92:1

5. "Oh GIVE thanks unto the Lord; call upon his name: make known his deeds among the people." Ps. 105:1

6. "Praise ye the Lord. O GIVE thanks unto the Lord; for he is good: for his mercy endureth for ever." Ps. 106:1

5. Examples of unacceptable worship because the attitude was not right:
   a. The Pharisee who "prayed thus with himself." Lk. 18:9-14
      1. He gloried that he was better than others and praised himself for his service to God. His worship was rejected by God.
      2. By contrast, the publican was so ashamed of his sin that he could not even look upward toward Heaven. His worship was accepted by God.
   b. Israel.
      1. Am. 5:21-24.
      2. God rejected their worship

because they were so wicked in their daily lives. Verses 10-12

3. They practiced authorized acts of worship; yet, the worship was rejected because of their sinful hearts.

c. The **Corinthians** taking the Lord's Supper.

1. They were making distinctions between the rich and poor as they took the Supper.

a. Adopting practices of idolatrous temples, the rich would worship and leave, then the poor would worship.

b. I Cor. 11:17-22, 33

2. Many were not focusing on Christ's Body and His Death on the Cross as they ate the unleavened bread and took the fruit of the vine. Verses 27-29

3. The result: many were spiritually sick; some had even died spiritually. Verse 30

III. What IS Worship in Truth?

Goals To Accomplish As You Teach This Topic:

- Explain that God expects man to worship as HE directs.

- Give examples of those who were condemned because of worshipping in error.
- Emphasize God's commands of acceptable worship in the Church.
- Show how God feels about innovations to His pattern of worship.

Struggles That The Student Might Have With This Topic:

- Realizing that God expects man to worship Him as He directs.
- Understanding that the Lord's Supper is to be observed every Sunday.
- Accepting that singing is the only authorized type of music in worship commanded by Christ.
- Seeing the seriousness of innovations in worship, that they make our worship unacceptable to God!

A. Acceptable worship involves our emotion, but it must also be combined with offering that worship in truth (as God has directed).

B. Examples where God was displeased with worship that did not follow His commands.
   1. Cain.
      a. Gen. 4:1-8
      b. During the days of the Patriarchal and Mosaic Ages, God commanded that the blood of animals be offered for man's sins.
      c. Abel, Cain's brother, offered a firstling lamb as required by God.
      d. Cain, a farmer, brought the best of his crops and offered it to God.

      e.   God immediately rejected that sacrifice.

      f.   Why? It was not offered in faith.

          1. He. 11:4

          2. Abel offered his sacrifice BY FAITH; he did exactly what God commanded. Therefore, his worship was accepted by God.

2.   Israel with the **golden calf**.

      a.   This story is recorded in Exodus 32.

      b.   Moses had gone into the mountain to receive the Ten Commandments which God would write on the two tables of stone.

      c.   The people became despondent and accused Moses of taking them into the wilderness and leaving them.

      d.   They demanded that Aaron build them idols that they could worship.

      e.   Aaron made them a golden calf and placed an altar before it.

      f.   The people began to practice idolatrous worship.

      g.   God was enraged because He had condemned idolatrous worship earlier. Ex. 20:3-5

      h.   When Moses returned and saw this heathen worship, he broke the two tables of stone.

      i.   Three thousand unrepentant idolaters were killed that day! Ex. 32:28

3. **Nadab** and **Abihu**. Lev. 10:1-7
   a. These men were sons of Aaron.
   b. They offered "strange fire" upon the altar.
   c. God immediately sent fire and consumed them.
   d. He slew them because of using unauthorized fire on the altar.
   e. Someone might say, "Well, fire is fire no matter where one gets it."
   f. However, God had commanded them to obtain fire from one certain spot.
   g. The point: God expects men to follow HIS Laws about worship; if man does not obey, his worship will be rejected!

4. **King Saul.**
   a. Offering a **sacrifice**.
      1. After Samuel anointed Saul king of Israel, he told Saul to go down to Gilgal and wait for seven days. Samuel would come to Gilgal to offer sacrifices. I Sa. 10:8
      2. As the seventh day neared an end, Samuel was nowhere in sight. Saul, becoming impatient, decided he would offer the sacrifices himself. I Sa. 13:8,9
      3. As soon as Saul made the sacrifices, Samuel arrived and asked, "What have you done?" Verse 11 "You have acted

foolishly!" Verse 13 "Your kingdom will not continue." Verse 14

    4. Saul sinned because he was not a priest. Only the priests could offer sacrifices to God.

  b. Capturing **animals** for sacrifice. I Sa. 15

    1. God told Saul to utterly destroy the Amalekites.

    2. Saul disobeyed; he spared king Agag, and the best of the animals, claiming that he would offer them to God in worship.

    3. Samuel accused Saul of the sins of rebellion and stubbornness and told Saul, "to obey is better than sacrifice;"

5. **Jeroboam** changing the place of worship in Israel. I Ki. 12:27-29

  a. God ordained that all the Israelites were to come to the Temple in Jerusalem to worship.

  b. After Jeroboam led ten tribes away from the nation, he was deeply concerned about the people returning to Jerusalem to worship.

  c. Therefore, he set up two calves in Dan and Bethel and told the people they did not have to return to Jerusalem to worship.

    d. This brought God's condemnation upon him.

C. Traits of worship in truth.
1. God **alone** must be worshipped.
   a. "Thou shalt worship the Lord thy God, and him only shalt thou serve." Mt. 4:10
   b. "Worship God." Rev. 19:10; 22:8,9
   c. Worship of any idol is sinful. Ex. 20:4-6; Ac. 17:22,23

2. Worshipping as He has **commanded**.
   a. It involves collective worship **WHEN** He directs — on the **first** day of the week.
      1. In the Old Testament, Israel worshipped on the Sabbath Day, Saturday. Ex. 20:8-11
      2. Christians in the New Testament Church worshipped on the first day of the week — Sunday.
         a. "And upon the first day of the week, when the disciples came together to break bread,..." Ac. 20:7
         b. "Upon the first day of the week let every one of you lay by him in store, as God hath prospered him, that there be no gatherings when I come." I Cor. 16:2

      c.   Why did they worship on Sunday? This is in honor of Christ and His being our resurrected Savior. Sunday is the "Lord's Day." Rev. 1:10

  3. To forsake or nonchalantly miss worship opportunities is SINFUL! "Not forsaking the assembling of ourselves together, as the manner of some is;" Heb. 10:25

b. Communion or the Lord's Supper.

  1. Passages addressing this feast: Mt. 26:26-29; Lk. 22:19,20; I Cor. 11:23-29

  2. What two items were to be taken in this feast?

      a. Unleavened bread.

      b. Fruit of the vine.

  3. Why were these items taken?

      a. The bread represents Christ's Body.

      b. The fruit of the vine represents His Blood.

c. Prayer.

  1. Scriptures:

      a. "Pray without ceasing." I Thess. 5:17

      b. "And they continued stedfastly in the apostles' doctrine and fellowship, and in breaking of bread, and in prayers." Ac. 2:42

2. Christians have the blessed privilege of carrying every thought, wish, and desire before the Throne in Heaven.

   a. "Let us therefore come boldly unto the throne of grace, that we may obtain mercy, and find grace to help in time of need." Heb. 4:16

   b. Imagine the power of Christians praying collectively.

d. Bible study and preaching.

1. When Paul came to Troas, he met with the Christians on the first day of the week.

2. He preached God's Word to them.

3. Opening the Bible and hearing the truths of God's Word preached is God speaking to us through the Word.

e. Giving.

1. Passages:

   a. "Now concerning the collection for the saints, as I have given order to the churches of Galatia, even so do ye. Upon the first day of the week let every one of you lay by him in store, as God hath prospered him, that there be no gatherings when I come." I Cor. 16:1,2

1. Paul is urging the Corinthians to make contributions so they can assist their Judean brethren who are in a famine.

2. They are to give on the first day of the week.

3. They are to give as God has prospered them.

b. "But this I say, He which soweth sparingly shall reap also sparingly; and he which soweth bountifully shall reap also bountifully. Every man according as he purposeth in his heart, so let him give; not grudgingly, or of necessity: for God loveth a cheerful giver." II Cor. 9:6,7

1. God has not required a set amount of money that Christians should give.

2. Rather, he urges Christians to purpose and give as they have been blessed.

3. God accepts gifts given by cheerful givers. He does not accept gifts

given grudgingly or out
of a feeling of necessity.
2. God has always required His
people to give back to Him of our
blessings.
3. Our giving supports the work of
the Church and preaching of the
Gospel.

f. Singing.
1. There are nine verses in the New
Testament that mention music
in worship.
a. Mt. 26:30
b. Ac. 16:25
c. Rom. 15:9
d. I Cor. 14:15
e. Js. 5:13
f. Heb. 2:12
g. Heb. 13:15
h. "Speaking to yourselves in
psalms and hymns and
spiritual songs, singing and
making melody in your heart
to the Lord;" Eph. 5:19
i. "Let the word of Christ dwell
in you richly in all wisdom;
teaching and admonishing
one another in psalms and
hymns and spiritual songs,
singing with grace in your
hearts to the Lord." Col. 3:16

2. Note the purposes of this singing:
   a. **Speaking**.
   b. **Teaching**.
   c. **Admonishing**.
3. What are we to sing?
   a. **Psalms** — scriptures used as songs.
   b. **Hymns** — songs of praise to Deity.
   c. **Spiritual songs** — songs that have true Biblical content or encouragement.
4. What is the command of the New Testament about music in worship? **Sing**!
5. Man has NO right to add any other type of **music** than what God has authorized!
6. People who visit the services of the Churches of Christ will often say, "You are the people who do not have music." I always respond, "We certainly do have music! We sing! We have a cappella (unaccompanied) music. We just do not use instrumental music."

3. These traits are not only God-ordered, but **history** verifies that these were the practices of worship that the Christians observed in the first century.

4. How does God feel about innovations to His order of worship?
   a. He calls it "ignorant" worship.
      1. "Whom therefore ye ignorantly worship, him declare I unto you." Ac. 17:23
      2. "Ignorant" worship is worship that is not God-ordained and God-instituted.
   b. He calls it "will" worship.
      1. "Will" worship occurs when man worships as HE desires, not as God commands!
      2. Paul mentioned those who were encouraging the Colossians to practice asceticism (the idea that one will become spiritual through self-denial and self-torture), to worship angels, and to return to the requirements of the Law of Moses.
         a. These people were practicing worship that they felt was pleasing to God and that they saw as uplifting and rewarding.
         b. Paul condemned such innovations: "Which things have indeed a shew of wisdom in will worship, and humility, and neglecting of the body; not in any honour

to the satisfying of the flesh."
Col. 2:23

   c. He declares worship using innovations to be "vain" worship.

      1. "This people draweth nigh unto me with their mouth, and honoureth me with their lips; but their heart is far from me. But in vain they do worship me, teaching for doctrines the commandments of men." Mt. 15:8,9

      2. "Vain" means "empty," "worthless," "totally unacceptable in God's sight."

5. Examples of innovations men have brought into worship.
   a. Instrumental music.
   b. Counting beads.
   c. Burning candles.
   d. Burning incense.
   e. Washing hands or feet.
   f. Worshipping icons.

Conclusion:

A. Remember the greatness of God, His authority and His right to tell man how He is to be worshipped.

B. Remember we must worship "in spirit" and "in truth."

Church Organization And Christian Living

Introduction to the Lesson:

A. In this lesson, we will emphasize organization of the Church as designed by God.

   1. The organization designed by Christ will be examined.

   2. The wisdom of that organization will be seen.

B. We will also examine the lifestyle that Christ expects Christians to live each day.

C. Once one finds the answer for salvation, he must continue to be concerned that he is in the Lord's Church.

D. Let us look at two more identifying traits.
   1. Church organization.

   2. Christian living.

I. Church Organization.

Goals To Accomplish As You Teach This Topic:

• Exalt Christ as the ONLY head of the Church!

- Explain God-ordained organization of the local congregations – elders, deacons, and ministers.
- Emphasize the importance of each member in the Church.
- Show the wisdom of God in planning the Church with each local congregation being an autonomous entity subject only to Christ Himself.

Struggles That The Student Might Have With This Topic:

- Accepting that the organization of the Church could be SO simple.
- Overcoming the denominational idea of local, state, national, and international hierarchy.
- Understanding Biblical terminology as God uses it for the leaders of the Church.

A. Christ is the head of His Church.
1. Scriptures that teach this truth:
   a. "And hath put all things under his feet, and gave him to be the head over all things to the church, Which is his body, the fulness of him that filleth all in all." Eph. 1:22,23
   b. "And he is the head of the body, the church: who is the beginning, the firstborn from the dead; that in all things he might have the preeminence." Col. 1:18

2. Why is this important?
   a. He has ALL authority over the Church!
      1. "And Jesus came and spake unto them, saying, All power

[authority] is given unto me in heaven and in earth." Mt. 28:18

2. His Laws are respected above ALL else!

b. His Will directs members in all facets of life and in decisions that are made.

B. Elders oversee each local congregation.
1. There was always to be a plurality of Elders.
   a. Paul told Titus, "For this cause left I thee in Crete, that thou shouldest set in order the things that are wanting, and ordain elders in every city, as I had appointed thee:" Tit. 1:5
   b. Paul addressed the plurality of Elders at Philippi, "Paul and Timotheus, the servants of Jesus Christ, to all the saints in Christ Jesus which are at Philippi, with the bishops and deacons:" Phil. 1:1
   c. WHY would God ordain a plurality of Elders? So that no one man will become a dictator and impose his own wishes upon the congregation!
2. The qualifications of Elders are given in Scripture.
   a. I Tim. 3:1-7
   b. Tit. 1:5-11

    c.   The word "Elder" or "Presbyter" suggests they are to be **mature** in the faith.

    d.   An Elder must be:
1. A man.
2. One who desires to serve the Lord's people.
3. The husband of one wife.
4. He must be a man of godliness and with a good reputation.
5. He must know the Word and be able to teach it.
6. He must have children who are Christians and who respect their father.
7. He must be a mature Christian.
8. He must be able to defend the Truth against false teachers.

3. Their work.
    a.   Ac. 20:28-30
    b.   I Pet. 5:1-3
    c.   They are:
1. "Overseers" or "Bishops" — they oversee the work of that congregation.
2. "Shepherds" or "Pastors" — they see that the flock is fed spiritually.

    d.   These words DO NOT refer to the preacher; rather, they refer to the "Elders" or "Overseers" of the congregation.

    e.   They are to see that the congregation remains true to Christ's Word and faithful to Him.

4.   They have authority only in the local congregation.

    a.   Each congregation is governed by its own Elders.

    b.   There are NO earthly headquarters.

    c.   Why do you think God gave them authority in just their local congregation?

        1.   So numerous congregations will not be led away from the Truth.

        2.   For the care of local Christians in THAT congregation.

C.   Deacons assist the Elders.

1.   They are special servants of the Elders.

2.   The qualifications of a Deacon are listed in I Timothy 3:8-13.

    a.   He is to be a faithful Christian.

    b.   He is to be a married man; the husband of one wife.

    c.   His children must be well-disciplined.

    d.   He is to be dependable.

D.   Ministers or Evangelists preach the Word.

1. "Who then is Paul, and who is Apollos, but ministers by whom ye believed, even as the Lord gave to every man?" I Cor. 3:5

2. Ministers are under the authority of the Elders in the congregation; however, they do have authority.
   a. "Preach the word; be instant in season, out of season; reprove, rebuke, exhort, with all longsuffering and doctrine." II Tim. 4:2
   b. Ministers are to preach the Word when the people LIKE the message and when they DO NOT LIKE IT!
   c. They are to point out error and to encourage brethren to greater devotion to God.

3. Ministers are NOT:
   a. "Pastors" — Elders are!
      1. Ac. 20:28
      2. If a minister meets the qualifications of an Elder, he could be an Elder also if chosen by the brethren.
   b. "Reverend" — GOD IS!
      1. "Holy and reverend is his name." Ps. 111:9
      2. This is the ONLY TIME in scripture that the word "reverend" is used and it refers to God.

4. Why do you think God established the Church with Ministers under the authority of Elders?

    a. **They do not have total authority in the Church.**

    b. **This provides a system of checks and balances in the Church.**

E. Members.

  1. All members make up the Body of Christ.

  2. We are ALL:

    a. **Christians** (those who belong to Christ).

      1. "And the disciples were called Christians first in Antioch." Ac. 11:26

      2. "Then Agrippa said unto Paul, Almost thou persuadest me to be a Christian." Ac. 26:28

      3. "Yet if any man suffer as a Christian, let him not be ashamed; but let him glorify God on this behalf." I Pet. 4:16

    b. **Saints** (those set apart from sin to serve God).

      1. "To all that be in Rome, beloved of God, called to be saints: Grace to you and peace from God our Father, and the Lord Jesus Christ." Rom. 1:7

      2. "Unto the church of God which

is at Corinth, to them that are sanctified in Christ Jesus, called to be saints, with all that in every place call upon the name of Jesus Christ our Lord, both their's and our's:" I Cor. 1:2

3. "Paul and Timotheus, the servants of Jesus Christ, to all the saints in Christ Jesus which are at Philippi, with the bishops and deacons:" Phil. 1:1

c. **Brethren**.

1. "Brethren, if a man be overtaken in a fault, ye which are spiritual, restore such an one in the spirit of meekness; considering thyself, lest thou also be tempted." Gal. 6:1

2. Christians are brothers and sisters in Christ.

d. **Sons** of God.

1. "But when the fulness of time was come, God sent forth his Son, made of a woman, made under the law, To redeem them that were under the law, that we might receive the adoption of sons." Gal. 4:4,5

2. "For ye are all the children of God by faith in Christ Jesus." Gal. 3:26

3. "Behold, what manner of love the Father hath bestowed upon us, that we should be called the sons of God," I Jn. 3:1

4. Imagine: YOU can be a "child of God!"

e. Priests.

1. "Ye also, as lively stones, are built up a spiritual house, an holy priesthood, to offer up spiritual sacrifices, acceptable to God by Jesus Christ." I Pet. 2:5

2. "But ye are a chosen generation, a royal priesthood, an holy nation, a peculiar people; that ye should shew forth the praises of him who hath called you out of darkness into his marvellous light:" I Pet. 2:9

3. Christians can offer acceptable worship to God and can personally appeal to Him for forgiveness. All of this is available because of Christ's Death and His Blood's power in the lives of those who have been baptized for salvation.

F. Why is Church organization important?

1. God ordained it!

2. Change in the organization of the Church

will lead to many other **changes**.

   a.   The first major change in the Church when established by God was in Church organization.

      1.   One Elder in the local congregation was exalted to "the bishop."

      2.   This led to the "bishops" in nearby communities meeting to make decisions for "their congregations."

      3.   Later, one of these "bishops" was exalted as the most important "bishop."

      4.   This ultimately culminated in the organization known today as "Catholic Church hierarchy" with the Pope as its head.

   b.   That one change led to making alterations in Christ's commands about worship, sprinkling for baptism, introduction of instrumental music, and all types of human traditions becoming doctrine.

   c.   Through the centuries, this led to more and more denominations based upon human tradition instead of the Word of Christ!

3.   How does God feel about changing His Word?

   a.   "For I testify unto every man that

heareth the words of the prophecy of this book, If any man shall add unto these things, God shall add unto him the plagues that are written in this book: And if any man shall take away from the words of the book of this prophecy, God shall take away his part out of the book of life, and out of the holy city, and from the things which are written in this book." Rev. 22:18,19

1. In your own words, what is the Lord telling those who read the Revelation?
2. "Do not add to my Word; do not take away from It."
3. "Just do what I say!"

b. "And these things, brethren, I have in a figure transferred to myself and to Apollos for your sakes; that ye might learn in us not to think of men above that which is written, that no one of you be puffed up for one against another." I Cor. 4:6

1. Against what is Paul cautioning the Corinthian brethren?
2. Never put the word of a man ABOVE the Word of God!
3. To say it differently, God's Word must always be exalted and accepted as the only standard in all religious matters.

c. "But though we, or an angel from heaven, preach any other gospel unto you than that which we have preached unto you, let him be accursed." Gal. 1:8

1. What is Paul's caution in this text?

2. Even if an Apostle or an angel taught anything contradictory to the Gospel, he would be accursed (condemned; viewed by God as "anathema").

3. God, thus, expects man to follow HIS Will!

II. Christian Living.

Goals To Accomplish As You Teach This Topic:

- Emphasize the importance of Christians living holy lives as they serve God.
- Show the life that Christians must avoid and the life they must live.
- Cause the student to desire to live with anticipation of Christ's second coming.
- Urge the student to see the importance of faithfulness as a Christian; and to realize that being faithful does not mean being perfect. He will continue to have God's grace available through the Blood of Christ.

Struggles That The Student Might Have With This Topic:

- Being convinced that he CAN LIVE an acceptable Christian life.

- Understanding that God's grace is always available for the faithful Christian.
- Realizing that faithfulness does not mean perfection!
- Accepting that one can fall from God's grace and be lost!

A. God requires Christians to live "holy" lives!
1. "According as he hath chosen us in him before the foundation of the world, that we should be holy and without blame before him in love:" Eph. 1:4
    a. God predestined that Christians (those "in Christ") would be people whose lives glorified Him and were separate and different from those who live in sin.
    b. Holy Christian living is JUST AS MUCH A PART OF GOD'S PLAN for the Church as His Law, terms of entrance, worship, and Church organization.

2. "But as he which hath called you is holy, so be ye holy in all manner of conversation; Because it is written, Be ye holy; for I am holy." I Pet. 1:15,16
    a. Our goal is to be like our Heavenly Father.
    b. This is a challenge to live like Him in our daily lives.

B. God also expects Christians to avoid
1. "Mortify therefore your members which

are upon the earth." Col. 3:5

    a. "Mortify" — what does this word mean?

    b. Perhaps the only word in English that we use that might help our understanding is the word "mortician." This is an "undertaker."

    c. The word means "put to death," "be separated from."

    d. God wants His people to separate themselves from sinful practices.

2. "But now ye also put off all these;" Col. 3:8

    a. What is the Lord's direction in this passage about sin?

    b. "Put off (rid) yourselves of all these."

C. Christians are to be living sacrifices to God.

1. "I beseech you therefore, brethren, by the mercies of God, that ye present your bodies a living sacrifice, holy, acceptable unto God, which is your reasonable service. And be not conformed to this world: but be ye transformed by the renewing of your mind, that ye may prove what is that good, and acceptable, and perfect, will of God." Rom. 12:1,2

2. Under the Old Testament, sacrifices were healthy and spotless animals that were slain on the altar; in the New Testament,

sacrifices are the everyday lives of LIVING Christians.

3. What is involved in being a "living sacrifice?"
   a. It involves being holy and living acceptably before God.
   b. It involves refusing to be conformed to the ways of the world.
   c. It involves transforming our thinking to the Will of God.

D. "For the grace of God that bringeth salvation hath appeared to all men, Teaching us that, denying ungodliness and worldly lusts, we should live soberly, righteously, and godly, in the present world; Looking for that blessed hope, and the glorious appearing of the great God and our Saviour Jesus Christ; Who gave himself for us, that he might redeem us from all iniquity, and purify unto himself a peculiar people, zealous of good works." Tit. 2:11-14

1. Christian living involves REJECTING:
   a. Ungodliness.
   b. Worldly lusts.

2. It involves CORRECT LIVING in this present world.
   a. Soberly — of sound mind; in control of your actions; temperate and modest.
   b. Righteously — treating your fellow

man as Christ would have you treat him; being just and fair.

c. Godly — reverent; having a proper attitude toward God; living as HE directs.

3. Why should a Christian live such a life?

a. Christians are looking for the return of Christ.

1. Nothing should excite the Christian more than seeing his Lord face to face!

2. It will provide the most wonderful time of praise to our Lord!

b. We know we have been redeemed!

1. We will have the privilege to give thanks to Christ for His sacrifice and for "buying us back" from sin.

2. He is the One who has given us spiritual life and hope.

c. We know to whom we belong.

1. The phrase in the KJV, "a peculiar people," gives such a false concept to Christians today.

2. We think of "peculiar" as "an oddball;" someone who is really "weird."

3. The word here rather means "a people of His own possession."

4. As Christians, we belong to Christ.

E. Christian living involves faithfulness as long as we live.
    1. We must be faithful unto death.
        a. "Be thou faithful unto death, and I will give thee a crown of life." Rev. 2:10
        b. Christians must continue to walk in trust and in devotion to their Lord.
        c. OBSERVATION: There is a GREAT difference between "being faithful" and "being sinlessly perfect!"
            1. One of the struggles many have as they eagerly consider becoming a Christian is: "But I do not know if I can do it. What if I sin after becoming a Christian?"
            2. Here are truths of great comfort and hope:
                a. God never demanded sinless perfection; He asked you to be faithful!
                    1. You CAN BE faithful; you WILL NEVER BE perfect!
                    2. A great illustration of this is marriage.
                        a. If, before we married, Vicky had asked me to be a "perfect husband," I would have quickly replied,

"I cannot do that; there is no use for us to marry."

b. However, Vicky had EVERY RIGHT to expect me to be faithful to her when we married, and I CAN DO THAT!

3. The same is true about God.

a. He never demanded perfection.

b. Rather, He requires Christians to be faithful to Him.

b. In writing TO CHRISTIANS in the book of I John, John declared, "If we say that we have no sin, we deceive ourselves, and the truth is not in us." I Jn. 1:8

1. God KNOWS that we will sin.

2. If that is true, how can Christians have hope?

a. "But if we walk in the light, as he is in the light, we have fellowship one with another, and the blood of Jesus Christ his Son cleanseth us from all sin." I Jn. 1:7

b. "If we confess our sins, he is faithful and just to forgive us our sins, and to cleanse us from all unrighteousness." I Jn 1:9

c. Thus, God declared that Christians will sin but have a way of forgiveness.

c. But several passages may cause some confusion.

1. Do not some passages say that Christians cannot sin?

a. "Whosoever abideth in him sinneth not: whosoever sinneth hath not seen him, neither known him." I Jn. 3:6

b. "Whosoever is born of God doth not commit sin; for his seed remaineth in him: and he cannot sin, because he is born of God." I Jn. 3:9

c. "We know that whosoever is born of God sinneth not; but he that is begotten of God keepeth himself, and that wicked one toucheth him not." I Jn 5:18

d. At first reading, these verses seem to emphatically state that a Christian CANNOT and MUST NOT sin!

e. However, in Chapter 1, John said Christians WOULD SIN and that the Blood of Christ will continue to cleanse us when we repent, confess our sins to Him and ask His forgiveness.

f. The answer to this seeming contradiction is that the Greek words translated "doth not sin" are in the present tense in the Greek language. These words mean that one in Christ will be determined to avoid sin and will never **continue** to live a life of sin. He has rejected that lifestyle and refuses to walk therein.

2. Do not other passages state that we should be perfect?

   a. "Be ye therefore perfect, even as your Father which is in heaven is perfect." Mt. 5:48

   b. Again, we must remember that John has earlier stated that we CANNOT live perfectly.

   c. The word "perfect" does not mean "sinless;" it means, "**mature**," "full-grown," "complete," "all that God wants you to be."

d. You **CAN BE** a faithful Christian!

   1. "There hath no temptation taken you but such as is common to man: but God is faithful, who

will not suffer you to be tempted above that ye are able; but will with the temptation also make a way to escape, that ye may be able to bear it." I Cor. 10:13

2. God truly wants you to be a Christian and to be **successful!** He wants you to be in **Heaven** with Him forever!

2. Does "be faithful" imply that a Christian can fall from God's grace and be lost? ABSOLUTELY!

   a. "For if after they have escaped the pollutions of the world through the knowledge of the Lord and Saviour Jesus Christ, they are again entangled therein, and overcome, the latter end is worse with them than the beginning. For it had been better for them not to have known the way of righteousness, than, after they have known it, to turn from the holy commandment delivered unto them. But it is happened unto them according to the true proverb, The dog is turned to his own vomit again; and the sow that was washed to her wallowing in the mire." II Pet. 2:20-22

      1. What is the "pollution of the world?" SIN!

      2. How can one escape sin?

Through the knowledge of Christ!

3. After escaping sin one can be entangled in it again AND OVERCOME!

4. He is in a worse condition spiritually after knowing the Truth and leaving it than before he ever heard the Word.

b. "But I keep under my body, and bring it into subjection: lest that by any means, when I have preached to others, I myself should be a castaway." I Cor. 9:27

1. Paul discusses his concern about his own spiritual life.

2. He continued to discipline and watch his own life even though he was preaching to others. Why? He did not want to be rejected by God himself.

c. "Wherefore let him that thinketh he standeth take heed lest he fall." I Cor. 10:12

1. A Christian must never become full of pride.

2. One who feels that he is totally secure is in danger of falling from the faith.

d. "Christ is become of no effect unto you, whosoever of you are justified by the law; ye are fallen from grace."

Gal. 5:4

1. If Christians were encouraged to attempt to obey requirements such as circumcision from the Old Testament Law in order to be justified before God, they would fall from the grace of God.

2. They would be severed from Christ.

e. Heb. 3:7-13

1. Paul is encouraging Christians to remain faithful to their Christian profession.

2. By the example of the fall of the Israelites in the wilderness, he urges Christians not to harden their heart.

3. He reminds these Christians that they can turn to unbelief and depart from the living God.

f. "For if we sin wilfully after that we have received the knowledge of the truth, there remaineth no more sacrifice for sins, But a certain fearful looking for of judgment and fiery indignation, which shall devour the adversaries." Heb. 10:26,27

1. What IS "willful sin?"

a. Knowing that something is wrong before you do it, is NOT "willful sin!"

b. NOT ONE of us could profess

innocence if that was the definition of "willful sin."

c. "Willful sin" is turning one's back on Christ and returning to another system of religion for justification.

d. In the book of Hebrews, the Jews who had become Christians were being encouraged by their family and friends to return to Judaism.

e. Their families were saying, "You need to leave this 'new-fangled religion' and return to the 'old, tried and true Law of Moses.'"

2. However, Paul informs them that to leave Christ is to leave the only sacrifice for sins; thus, it is to bring eternal damnation upon their souls!

3. Thus, our challenge is to determine to remain true to God so Heaven can be our home.

F. God promises to bless us if we live holy, faithful lives.
1. He promises His providential care.
a. "But seek ye first the kingdom of God, and his righteousness; and all

these things shall be added unto you." Mt. 6:33

    1. His call is for His people to put Him first!

    2. Then He promises to see that food, clothing and shelter will be provided for Christians.

  b. This has always been true for God's people.

    1. "I have been young, and now am old; yet have I not seen the righteous forsaken, nor his seed begging bread." Ps. 37:25

    2. David knew that God always had and would continue to care for His people.

2. There is NO NEED to **worry**; trust God and depend on Him.

  a. "Be careful for nothing; but in everything by prayer and supplication with thanksgiving let your requests be made known unto God." Phil. 4:6

  b. "Be careful for nothing" means "do not be anxious" or "do not worry." Rather, pray! Why? Because God hears you and is interested in you.

3. The Christian can live in GREAT CONFIDENCE no matter what life brings.

  a. Even in prison, Paul could say, "For

to me to live is Christ, and to die is **gain**." Phil. 1:21

b. David, with all the mistreatment and turmoil he faced in his life, could confidently say, "Yea, though I walk through the valley of the shadow of death, I will fear no evil: for thou art with me;" Ps. 23:4

c. We can confidently rely on Christ's promise of Heaven if we remain faithful to Him.

1. "Let not your heart be troubled: ye believe in God, believe also in me. In my Father's house are many mansions: if it were not so, I would have told you. I go to prepare a place for you. And if I go and prepare a place for you, I will come again, and receive you unto myself; that where I am, there ye may be also." Jn. 14:1-3

2. He is preparing a home in Heaven for all the faithful.

3. Are you anxious to become His child, and to remain faithful to Him so that Heaven can be your home?

4. He NEVER promised us a life void of problems; He DID promise us **strength** to make it through EVERY problem.

      a. "For which cause we faint not; but though our outward man perish, yet the inward man is renewed day by day." II Cor. 4:16

         1. Paul is discussing persecutions he received for teaching about Christ.

         2. These troubles only made him stronger as he kept his eyes on Heaven. Verses 17,18

      b. You CAN be faithful! "I can do all things through Christ which strengtheneth me." Phil. 4:13

G. Do you believe that God wants you to be a Christian, and that He truly wants you to be faithful and successful as a Christian?

    1. Notes to the teacher:

      a. In almost every study, the student is ready to become a Christian at this point.

      b. If you are uncertain, proceed immediately to the "personal evaluation."

    2. If the student expresses readiness to submit to Christ, rejoice with him and immediately take his confession and baptize him into Christ that he might be saved by Christ's Blood.

Personal Evaluation!

A.   Yes — No   Do You Realize You Have Sinned In Your Life?

B.   Yes — No   Does God Hate Sin?

C.   Yes — No   Has Sin Separated You From God?

D.   Yes — No   Does God Alone Have the Right to Tell You How to Be Saved?

E.   Yes — No   Do You Believe You Can Choose To Obey God?

F.   Yes — No   Do You Believe That Jesus is the One Who Died on the Cross and Shed His Blood for You and That He Can Save You From Your Sin?

G.   Yes — No   Have You Confessed That Faith?

H.   Yes — No   Have You Repented of Your Sins of Commission? Omission?

I.   Yes — No   Have You Been Baptized in Order to be Saved From Your Sins By the Blood of Christ?

J.   Yes — No   Now That You Know the Facts About Jesus, Do You KNOW Him as Your Savior?

K.   Yes — No   Are You a Member of The New Testament Church?

L.   Yes — No   Do You Worship as God Authorized Including Taking the Lord's Supper Every Sunday and Practicing A Cappella Singing?

M.   Yes — No   If You Were to Die Today, Would You Be Right With God and Ready to Enter Heaven?

N.   Yes — No   SHOULD You Obey God Now?

O.   Yes — No   WILL You Obey God Now?

Encouragements To The Teacher:

- You should not have to use this information very many times. Most students who study all thirteen lessons will be ready to commit their lives to Christ.
- If a student does delay and you must help him deal with his excuses, do not become despondent nor discouraged toward him.
- God has given you the answer to every excuse that the student might have. It is in His Word. Sometimes it may take us a long time to grasp the answer, but it IS in the Bible!
- Guard your own attitude as you assist the student with his excuses.
- Even if he does not respond at this time, try to leave the door open to continue to encourage him in the future.

I. Personal Attitude as You Assist the Student Who Has Excuses.

A. As a teacher, you should NEVER view helping the student as an attempt to win an argument. We are concerned about a SOUL being saved by Christ.

B. Always make sure that you allow the Word of God to convict the student's heart; you will only drive people away by being pushy.

C. However, persuasion IS biblical!
1. "Knowing therefore the terror of the Lord, we persuade men;" II Cor. 5:11

2. Peter on Pentecost persuaded the Jews. "And with many other words did he

testify and exhort, saying, Save yourselves from this untoward generation." Ac. 2:40

3. Paul used persuasion at Ephesus. "And he went into the synagogue, and spake boldly for the space of three months, disputing and persuading the things concerning the kingdom of God." Ac. 19:8

D. Let me urge you to cultivate and practice the attitude that others will appreciate and that God would want us to practice in evangelism and in ALL aspects of life.
1. The "Golden Rule."

2. "Therefore all things whatsoever ye would that men should do to you, do ye even so to them: for this is the law and the prophets." Mt. 7:12

II. Assisting Sinners to Work Through Their Excuses.
A. "I want to wait."
1. This might be necessary in order for one to make a commitment from the depths of his heart.

2. An effective way to touch the student's heart is to suggest that you set a future day on which he will obey the Lord.
a. Set a date one hundred years from today.

   1. Typically the answer will be, "Oh, no!"

   2. "Why not?"

   3. "I'll not be here then!"

   4. "True! Will you be here tomorrow?"

  b. How do you know you will be alive tomorrow? "Whereas ye know not what shall be on the morrrow. For what is your life? It is even a vapour, that appeareth for a little time, and then vanisheth away." Js. 4:14

  c. You WILL die; then you will face the judgment! "And as it is appointed unto men once to die, but after this the judgment:" Heb. 9:27

  d. NOW is the time to obey! "(For he saith, I have heard thee in a time accepted, and in the day of salvation have I succoured thee: behold, now is the accepted time; behold, now is the day of salvation.)" II Cor. 6:2

B. "I will condemn my family!"

  1. You will not condemn ANYONE!

   a. We condemn OURSELVES if we disobey God.

   b. "He that believeth on him is not condemned: but he that believeth not is condemned already, because he hath not believed in the name of the only begotten Son of God." Jn. 3:18

      c. You and I have NO authority to condemn anyone.

  2. If a family member did die in sin, he would be praying and pleading for you to obey God.

      a. The rich man of Luke 16 pled for his family still on Earth.

      b. "Then he said, I pray thee therefore, father, that thou wouldest send him to my father's house: For I have five brethren; that he may testify unto them, lest they also come into this place of torment." Lk. 16:27-28

  3. "He that loveth father or mother more than me is not worthy of me: and he that loveth son or daughter more than me is not worthy of me." Ma. 10:37

C. **"I just wish I could see a sign or have God speak to me and tell me I am right!"**

  1. The rich man begged Abraham to send one from the dead to convince his brothers to repent. Lk. 16:28

  2. "Abraham saith unto him, They have Moses and the prophets; let them hear them. And he said, Nay, father Abraham: but if one went unto them from the dead, they will repent. And he said unto him, If they hear not Moses and the prophets, neither will they be persuaded, though

one rose from the dead." Lk. 16:29-31

3. If one will not be convinced by the Word of God, he would not be convinced if Jesus stood before him and spoke to him.
   a. Most people just do not believe they would continue in unbelief if they could SEE Jesus or one from the dead.
   b. However, observe how people responded who saw Him in the first century.

D. "My conscience is OK! I feel all right!"
   1. It IS important that we can live with our conscience.

   2. However, conscience can be improperly taught; thus, it will feel secure even though it is wrong.

   3. "And Paul, earnestly beholding the council, said, Men and brethren, I have lived in all good conscience before God until this day." Ac. 23:1
      a. That included the time he held the coats of those who stoned Stephen. Ac. 7:58
      b. It also included the time he was on the road to Damascus to persecute Christians. Ac. 9:1-9

E. "I do not know enough!"

1. How much do you think you have to know?

2. Do you know you are lost? Do you know what Christ teaches you to do to be saved?

   a. The Jews on Pentecost knew a Messiah was coming; they knew they were in sin; however, they did not know that Jesus was the Messiah. When they learned He was the Savior, they obeyed. Ac. 2

   b. The eunuch, who studied the Old Testament, knew a Messiah was coming, but had not identified the Messiah. Ac. 8:30-39

3. Having studied the previous lessons, you do know enough.

F. "I am afraid of what people will say!"

1. "And fear not them which kill the body, but are not able to kill the soul: but rather fear him which is able to destroy both soul and body in hell." Mt. 10:28

2. "Yet if any man suffer as a Christian, let him not be ashamed; but let him glorify God on this behalf." I Pet. 4:16

G. "I am afraid I will not remain faithful."

1. Obviously, NONE of us know what the future holds.

2. However, would God ask you to do anything impossible? Is He not a loving, caring Father?

3. "I can do all things through Christ which strengtheneth me." Phil. 4:13

4. "There hath no temptation taken you but such as is common to man: but God is faithful, who will not suffer you to be tempted above that ye are able; but will with the temptation also make a way to escape, that ye may be able to bear it." I Cor. 10:13

5. Rom. 8:35-39 — NOTHING is powerful enough to separate you from the love of Christ! Only YOU can choose to leave Him!

H. "I want to ask my preacher!"

1. That is all right; however, compare what he tells you with what GOD says in the Bible.

2. I have had some students attempting to study with me and with a denominational preacher at the same time. They became SO confused. However, after being encouraged to get away from both of us and deal objectively with God's Word, they saw the Truth and left their error.

3. I have had some students who just could not accept that they might have been taught wrong. Together, we have called and questioned the preacher about what he taught.

4. The important thing to remember is, who will be your Judge? "He that rejecteth me, and receiveth not my words, hath one that judgeth him: the word that I have spoken, the same shall judge him in the last day." Jn. 12:48

I. "I feel that I am ALREADY saved."

1. Urge the student to compare his answers previously in the lesson on "Faith" with what God says.

2. "Therefore to him that knoweth to do good, and doeth it not, to him it is sin." Js. 4:17

3. You may disagree with God; however, please be careful.
   a. Rationalization is SO deadly in spiritual matters. You are talking about the destiny of your eternal soul.
   b. "For we dare not make ourselves of the number, or compare ourselves with some that commend themselves: but they measuring themselves by themselves, and comparing

themselves among themselves, are not wise. But we will not boast of things without our measure, but according to the measure of the rule which God hath distributed to us, a measure to reach even unto you." II Cor. 10:12,13

4. "And he said unto them, Ye are they which justify yourselves before men; but God knoweth your hearts: for that which is highly esteemed among men is abomination in the sight of God." Lk. 16:15

J. "It requires TOO much! It is TOO much to give up!"
1. Lk. 14:26-33
   a. In this text Jesus discusses commitment to Him.
   b. We must love Him more than family AND self.
   c. We must bear our cross.
   d. We must forsake all we have to be His.

2. Serving Him MUST be our first priority. Lk. 9:57-62

K. "I will obey Christ when the time is right!"
1. Do you TRULY believe you are lost?

2. Felix waited for a "convenient season;" yet, we have NO record that he ever found that convenient time.
   a. Paul taught this ruler and convicted him of his sin.
   b. "And as he reasoned of righteousness, temperance, and judgment to come, Felix trembled, and answered, Go thy way for this time; when I have a convenient season, I will call for thee." Ac. 24:25

L. "I do not believe all of this but I DO love Jesus!"
   1. If you love Jesus, what will you do? "If ye love me, keep my commandments." Jn. 14:15

   2. "And why call ye me, Lord, Lord, and do not the things which I say?" Lk. 6:46

   3. You only deceive yourself if you believe that you love Jesus, yet, refuse to obey Him.

M. "God will not punish me!"
   1. The Gospel is for all men. Those who refuse to obey will be punished. "He that believeth not shall be damned." Mk. 16:16

   2. "I tell you, Nay: but, except ye repent, ye shall all likewise perish." Lk. 13:3

3. "And to you who are troubled rest with us, when the Lord Jesus shall be revealed from heaven with his mighty angels, In flaming fire taking vengeance on them that know not God, and that obey not the gospel of our Lord Jesus Christ: Who shall be punished with everlasting destruction from the presence of the Lord, and from the glory of his power." II Thess. 1:7-9

N. "What if I cannot forgive?"
   1. "But if ye forgive not men their trespasses, neither will your Father forgive your trespasses." Mt. 6:15

   2. See the Parable of the Wicked Servant. Mt. 18:23-35
      a. This servant begged mercy of his master.
      b. Yet, this same servant refused to show mercy to one of his fellow servants who owed him very little.
      c. His master was furious because of his lack of mercy; the lord withdrew his compassion to the servant.
      d. This is an illustraton of how God expects man to forgive others if we desire HIS forgiveness.

   3. One question is extremely important here: "Is your struggle with forgiving or with forgetting?"

     a. Many equate "forgiving" with "forgetting."

     b. If they cannot forget, they feel evil and sinful.

     c. Forgetting is humanly IMPOSS-IBLE!

     d. God never asked you to forget; He asked you to forgive! That means you do not continue to count the person as liable for sin against you after he has repented and asked you to forgive him.

O. "I am TOO mean."

   1. You are not alone in that feeling; many struggle in trying to understand how God could forgive them.

   2. However, God will forgive any person who repents.

   3. Note who He forgave:
     a. The crucifiers of His Son. Ac. 2
     b. Paul, "the chief of sinners." I Tim. 1:15

   4. He explained His mission: "For the Son of man is come to seek and to save that which was lost." Lk. 19:10

P. "There are TOO many hypocrites in the Church!"

   1. If there is ONE, there are TOO many!

2. However, NEVER judge God by hypocrites.

3. Story of the pig farmer:
   a. A preacher frequently visited a pig farmer and urged him to become a Christian.
   b. One day the pig farmer said to the preacher, "Do not come back out here again and talk to me about coming to church. There are too many hypocrites in the church. I will never become a part of the church!"
   c. So the preacher left.
   d. A few weeks later, the preacher drove back out to the farm.
   e. As soon as the pig farmer saw the preacher, he was a little irate, expecting the preacher to "preach at him" about becoming a Christian.
   f. When the preacher got out of his car, much to the surprise of the pig farmer, he asked about buying a pig.
   g. The farmer took the preacher out to his barn and showed him all of his prize, fat hogs. They were well-bred and well-fed.
   h. However, the preacher asked if the farmer had any other pigs.
   i. The farmer replied, "Well, there are a few runts out back in a pen."
   j. The preacher said, "Let's go look at them."

k. In the pen were some pitiful and scrawny runts.

l. The preacher pointed to the least runt of all and said, "That's the one I want to buy."

m. The pig farmer said, "No way! I cannot let you pay for that runt; I'll give it to you."

n. So the preacher, with the runt under his arm, got in his car, started the engine, and pulled the gear shift down into drive.

o. He then reached over and rolled the window down and said to the pig farmer, "Oh, by the way, you know what I'm going to do with this runt? I'm going to town and tell people that this is the kind of pigs you raise."

p. THE MORAL OF THE STORY: You don't judge a pig farmer by his runts. And you do not judge God by half-hearted people who are not truly committed to Him.

   1. Judge the pig farmer by the prize hogs that he raises, not by a few runts.

   2. Judge God by those who are truly committed and whose lives have been eternally changed by that commitment!

4. May we never try to justify ourselves by other people. "Ye are they which justify yourselves before men; but God knoweth your hearts: for that which is highly esteemed among men is abomination in the sight of God." Lk. 16:15

5. "But after thy hardness and impenitent heart treasurest up unto thyself wrath against the day of wrath and revelation of the righteous judgment of God; Who will render to every man according to his deeds:" Rom. 2:5,6

6. Someone gave me an interesting quote once about hypocrites: "If there's a hypocrite standing between you and God, guess which one is closer to Him. Also, guess which one is farther away."

Q. "I believe God will save me even if I have not been baptized!"
1. Can you make that statement based UPON FAITH — based on Christ's Word?

2. Return to Mark 16:15,16 and other passages.

3. Illustration: What if one plans to buy an insurance policy? He gets the application, fills out a check, but forgets to mail it. If he dies that night, is he covered? CERTAINLY NOT!

4. What if one dies without having his sin forgiven by the Blood of Christ? Is his sin covered by the Blood of the Son?
   a. ABSOLUTELY NOT!
   b. Only those who truly know Christ as their Savior will have HIS forgiveness! "For I will be merciful to their unrighteousness, and their sins and their iniquities will I remember no more." Heb. 8:12

It Will Work! You Can Do It!

This strategy is being very effectively used by a number of Christians. You can do it too!

The following are **statements** by a number of my beloved brethren **concerning the doctrinal content and usage of these lessons**:

- "The greatest success today is probably coming from personal teaching and your material is a most effective tool. People converted by using your method will most likely stay converted because they will be taught the basics of the truth. You have developed topics that are essential to New Testament Christianity."

  E. Claude Gardner
  Preacher and President Emeritus
  of Freed-Hardeman University

- "Having reviewed your material I find it scriptural, challenging and a great guide to studying the Bible with others."

  James Meadows
  Director of East Tennessee School
  of Preaching and Missions

- "I appreciate very much the chance to look over your personal work material. It is the most thorough that I have ever seen. I can see why that when you take a person through it, they are ready to obey the gospel. As a matter of fact, they should know considerably more than many Christians seem to know even years later....If used, I think it will do a great job; and once it is out should be a real service to the brotherhood."

Clayton Winters
Minister, Erwin Church of Christ, Erwin, TN.

- "Stephen Rogers has written a powerful book that will be a valuable tool in personal evangelism. This book will also ground new Christians in the faith. It is a practical book of solid Biblical substance."

Tom Holland
Former Professor of Speech and Bible at Freed-Hardeman University and David Lipscomb University, former Minister at Crieve Hall Church of Christ, Nashville, TN. Presently engaged in Gospel Meetings and lecturing throughout the U.S

- "I was able to study the books which you have written. I enjoyed them very much. I feel like what you have prepared is something very useful for those who are teaching the gospel to others. The ideas in your books serve in making the process much less frightening to anyone who is reaching out to teach others. They are presented in a very understandable way."

Milton Sewell
President, Freed-Hardeman University

- "I have read carefully this splendid, Scriptural and scholarly material by Stephen Rogers. He does a good job in helping soul winners and those who are to be won for the Cause of Truth. There is some repetition in the material but this is good since repetition is the first law of learning and the mother of learning. The material is well arranged, gets to the fundamental heart of the gospel and is presented in an understandable manner. I commend it highly for soul winners and for those who seek to know the way of salvation, how they can become obedient to it and remain faithful to it the remnant of their days on earth."

> Robert R. Taylor, Jr.
> Author, Preacher for the Ripley Church of Christ, Ripley, TN

The following are **statements from Christians who have taught these materials:**

- "Over the past years, it has been my privilege to teach people the Bible in several different countries. I have used many different teaching aids and study guides to help me teach in a more meaningful way. I have even taken courses myself in how to teach people the Bible. When I first became acquainted with your lessons, I must admit I was reluctant to use them. I thought they were too long and covered many things that most really didn't need to know in the beginning. I was wrong.

I have found that your lessons for teaching people the Bible are so useful that even I learned from them when I first started using them. I presently use them with the aid of an interpreter because I am living and teaching the Bible in a foreign country. They are just as useful here as they are in the U.S. The thing I like most about them is the wide range of topics covered helps to promote a more complete understanding of God's plan of salvation. I can also tell you from personal experience that the thoroughness of these lessons has helped to prevent many problems that sometimes come because a new Christian did not completely understand some truths from God's Word.

I am anxiously awaiting your new book that incorporates your lessons. I hope you will decide to have it translated into Russian in the nearest future also."

Barry Green
Personal Evangelist and Missionary

- "Before one can ask the question, 'What must I do to be saved?', he must first ask the question, 'Who is God?'. As I continue to teach this series to a variety of students of differing ages and background both in the United States and overseas, the appeal is the universal appeal of God's grace as revealed in His eternal Word. These lessons deal with the privilege of 'choice' that God has given mankind. This simple, yet profound, lesson guide allows the teacher to begin the study and another teacher to do follow up lessons as is often necessary in the mission field. Emphasis is on the message and not the messenger."

Danny Weddle
Former Missionary, Elder at the Washington Avenue Church of Christ, Evansville, IN

• "I used to think that I was incapable of being able to teach anyone the Bible. This book has changed my thinking completely! I now KNOW I can teach others how to become Christians. This book is a very organized way to teach someone from beginning to end. They do not have to know anything about the Bible when they begin. The way the lessons are organized, they build upon each other, and basically by reading the scriptures, the person is guided through the Bible, almost teaching themselves.

I am no longer afraid to teach others, I KNOW I can and that I can have fun while I do it. Thank you Stephen Rogers, with all of my heart."

Jama Scherer
Member at Washington Avenue Church of Christ, taught on overseas mission trips, Evansville, IN

• These are good lessons. There will be a lot of people saved by using these lessons, I'm sure of that! They are easy to teach, easy to present and make it easy for a student to learn. These lessons make it easy for a person to see what condition he is in spiritually and he can see without a doubt what God expects of him if he wants to be saved in the end.

Len Kempf
Member of Washington Avenue Church
of Christ, personal worker, Mackey, IN

• "Your outline has helped me to teach others about the most important gift we could ever give ourselves, our salvation....It has helped me to show people a need for Christ in their lives....I am a much more confident person today than I was before....All you need is a Bible, this outline, and the desire to teach others."

Becky Barker
Member of Washington Avenue Church
of Christ, taught on overseas trips,
Evansville, IN

• "'Evangelism Made Simple' is exactly that — simple! I have incorporated my style with this material and I believe I have become a better personal work teacher.

This material coupled with God's Word is a powerful teaching material that thoroughly convicts the hearts of lost people. I have witnessed people, filling in the blanks, literally teach themselves with this material.

Not only is the material excellent for teaching lost souls, but it is excellent for the Christian to keep Himself attuned to the basics.

I am thankful to be able to use this material."
Neil Kempf
Member of Washington Avenue Church
of Christ, personal worker, Evansville,
IN

The following are **statements from those who have studied God's Word and become Christians by using the lessons, "The Gospel Made Simple — You <u>CAN</u> <u>KNOW</u> It!"**

- "The lessons, presented in the outline form developed, were like stepping stones to growing and understanding what the Bible holds for all of us. There were many emotional times during the studies when my old doctrine that I was taught was proven to be so very wrong. The proof was IN WRITING in front of me — the Bible.

  The studies were beneficial in helping me understand that I HAD to make a change in my life! They also helped me understand how important it was for me to make a change in my life and to make a commitment for the rest of my life.

  Christianity has totally changed my life, my behavior, my outlook on a spiritual future and has changed my family relationships."
  Karen Tanner
  44 year old, former Catholic

- "By using the outline and reading the Scriptures that correspond with each lesson, the study was not only easy to follow, but will serve as a great reference for future use."

Anthony Cox
39 year old, former Nazarene

• "You got me started on the good book, the Holy Bible....Every class got better than the last. I enjoyed the whole thirteen classes. After all my lessons, and when I thought I was ready and knew what the Bible was about, I was baptized....You cannot imagine how happy I was to be a Christian....I am going to be a good Christian....I am going to work for Christ's Church for the rest of my life."

Al Auteri
Former Catholic, 83 years old student

• "The thirteen lessons enable a person seeking the truth to form a solid building on the indestructible cornerstone, which is Jesus. Many people begin to read the Bible in search for the truth, some with the book of Genesis, some with Jesus' genealogy in the book of Matthew, but not many of them can understand the good news about salvation through 'system-less reading.'

Your lessons provide a student with full knowledge of the power of faith, God's nature, His love and grace, Jesus, the Holy Spirit, salvation offered to all people, and victory over sin.

Studying the word of God by means of these lessons helps to avoid many wrong opinions and mis-apprehensions, to come to know God through Jesus Christ with full understanding and faith driven by love, to enter this path and become a child of God through faith, repentance, confession and baptism.

Having known the will of God, I desired to come to the Lord and fulfill His commandments. I always thank God through Jesus Christ for sending his ministers to bear the light of God's truth to people walking in darkness, of whom I also used to be. For there is no greater joy for a person than abiding in the love of God and serving our glorious Lord for ever."

> Marina
> 28 year old, former Atheist, country of Belarus

- "Stephen's lessons are understandable and convincing. Having his lessons, I felt every seed was growing in my heart. I was eager to have several lessons at once. I felt myself thirsty and these lessons were a spring in a desert. I was gulping precious drops to quench my thirst, and every drop brought me great pleasure, joy and happiness.

  When he asked if I wanted to be baptized, my answer was, "YES." Baptism was for me desired and necessary. When I was being baptized, a though flashed across my mind, 'My Lord, forgive me, I want to become your daughter and serve you.'"

> Ludmilla
> English Teacher, country of Belarus

- "I have learned more about the Bible from these thirteen weeks of study than I did in sixty five years at the Catholic Church."

  Gerald McBride
  65 year old, former Catholic

- "Before I started studying these lessons, I had no knowledge of the Bible. The lessons were laid out in such a way that it took you step by step in learning the information necessary to become a Christian. They were simple and easy to follow.

  Without these lessons, I don't know if I could have made that choice.

  These lessons were very beneficial to me in preparing to go overseas to teach others because all you need to do is follow the outline of the lesson. By doing this, it helped you to keep on track of the message you were trying to get across to your student."

  Tony Tanner
  44 year old former Pentecostal, member at Washington Avenue Church of Christ in Evansville, taught on overseas trips, Evansville, IN

These are but a few examples of stories we could provide you of students who have become Christians using this strategy during the last ten years. Brethren are using this method in several places in the U.S. and overseas. I simply encourage you to consider it, and use it if you find it helpful. I am not promoting this as the only, or the best methodology. I want you to find a method with which you are comfortable and which is Biblical and "get busy about the Lord's work."

I commend you for spending so much time in study to prepare yourself to excel in teaching God's Word. My prayer is that our lives will radiate love for Christ, for our own salvation, and for the privilege to tell others of His saving power and hope! I urge you to GO, GROW, and GLOW as you SHOW others His Message and see Its power.

I send this book forth with prayers that it will be an effective tool in bringing more and more to Christ throughout the world. May none of us seek any glory for ourselves; rather, in the inspired words of the Apostle Paul, may we say, "To God only wise, be glory through Jesus Christ for ever. Amen." Rom. 16:27.

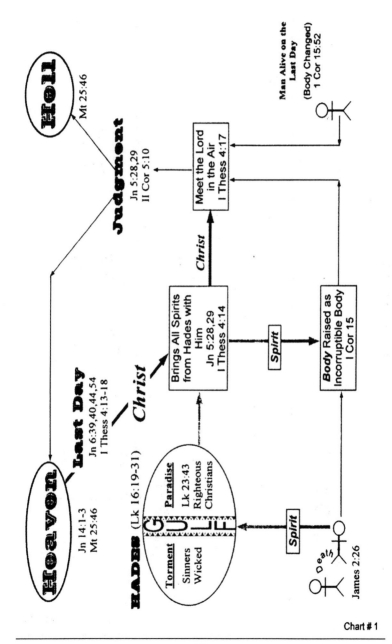

Hell
Mt 25:46

Judgment
Jn 5:28,29
II Cor 5:10

Man Alive on the Last Day
(Body Changed)
1 Cor 15:52

Meet the Lord in the Air
I Thess 4:17

Christ

Heaven
Jn 14:1-3
Mt 25:46

Last Day
Jn 6:39,40,44,54
I Thess 4:13-18

Christ

Brings All Spirits from Hades with Him
Jn 5:28,29
I Thess 4:14

Spirit

Body Raised as Incorruptible Body
I Cor 15

HADES (Lk 16:19-31)

Paradise
Lk 23:43
Righteous Christians

G U L F

Torment
Sinners
Wicked

Spirit

Death

James 2:26

Chart # 1

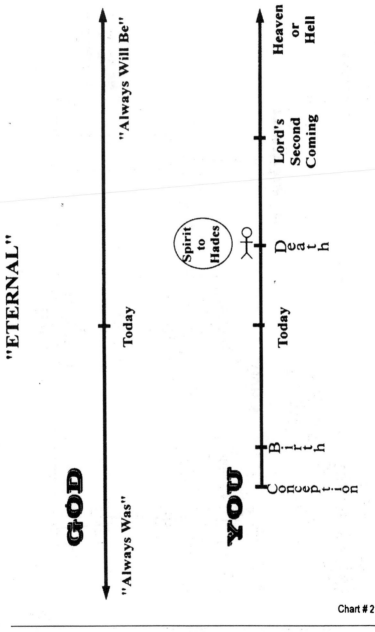

"ETERNAL"

GOD

"Always Was" — Today — "Always Will Be"

YOU

Conception — Birth — Today — Death — Spirit to Hades — Lord's Second Coming — Heaven or Hell

Chart # 2

UNDERSTANDING THE GODHEAD

DEITY
(Divine Being)

1. God – Father
2. God – Son
3. God – Holy Spirit

HUMANITY
(Human Being)

1. You
2. Me
3. The President

Chart # 3

435

"MEDIATOR"

Management ———|{ Mediator }|——— Union

Is He a Member of Management? NO!

Is He a Member of the Union? NO!

Is He an Impartial Person Equally Connected to Both Parties? ABSOLUTELY!

God ———|{ Mediator (Christ) }|——— Sinful Man

Could the Holy Spirit Be Our Mediator? NO!
(He is Divine Only!)

Could Any Man Be Our Mediator? NO!
(He is Human Only!)

Christ -- One Who is Equally Connected to Both (God and Man) Understands Both Sides!
(He is Deity and Humanity)

Chart # 4

436

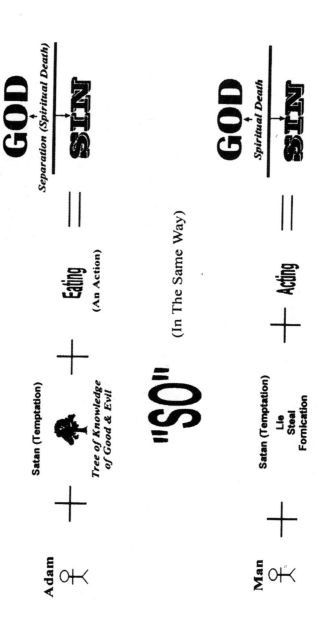

Romans 5:12

Adam + Satan (Temptation) *Tree of Knowledge of Good & Evil* + Eating (An Action) = GOD / SIN — *Separation (Spiritual Death)*

"SO" (In The Same Way)

Man + Satan (Temptation) Lie Steal Fornication + Acting = GOD / SIN — *Spiritual Death*

Chart # 5

437

GOD'S LAWS FOR MANKIND
THROUGH THE AGES

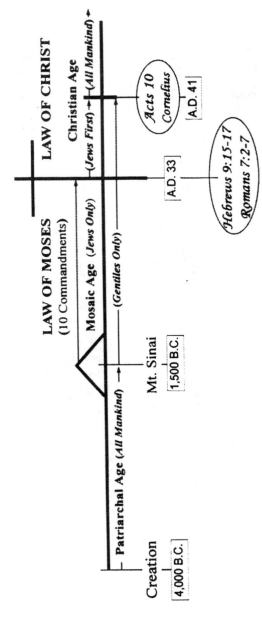

Chart # 6

ENDNOTES

[1] **Doctrine and Covenants**, 130:22

[2] Personal discussion with members of the United Pentecostal Church.

[3] **Let God Be True** (Brooklyn, NY: Watch Tower Bible & Tract Society, 1946), pp. 81-89.

[4] **Make Sure Of All Things** (Brooklyn, NY: Watch Tower Bible & Tract Society of Pennsylvania, 1965), pp. 132, 282, 283. **Let God Be True**, pp. 35, 82.

[5] **Let God Be True**, p. 89. The Truth That Leads to Eternal Life (Brooklyn, NY: Watch Tower Bible & Tract Society of Pennsylvania, 1968), p. 24.

[6] "In Search of Jesus," **U.S. News & World Report** (April 8, 1996), pp. 47-53. "Funk's Radical Reformation Roadshow," U.S. News & World Report (August 4, 1997), pp. 55,56.

[7] Ibid, p. 49.

[8] Steele, David N. and Thomas, Curtis C. **The Five Points of Calvinism Defined, Defended, Documented** (Philadelphia, PA: Presbyterian and Reformed Publishing Co., 1976), p. 16.

[9] Ibid, pp. 16,17.

[10] Ibid, p. 17.

11 Ibid, p. 18.

12 Ibid, p. 18.

13 Patterson, James and Kim, Peter. **The Day America Told the Truth** (New York: Prentice Hall Press, 1991), p. 202.

14 Williams, Robert. Just As I Am (New York: Crown Publishers, Inc., 1992), p. 150.

15 Ibid, p. 48.

16 Patterson and Kim, op. cit. p. 89.

17 Ibid, p. 95.

18 Ibid, p. 45.

19 Ibid, p. 65.

20 Williams, op. cit. p. 156.

21 McCollister, John. **Christian Book of Why?** (New York: Jonathan David Publishing Co., 1983). **World Almanac And Book of Facts** (NY: Newspaper Enterprise Association, Inc. World Almanac Division, 1967). "Catholics' Friday To Be Meatless Again?" **The Record On Line** (Bergin, NJ, November 12, 1997).

22 "Catholics Are Turning To Immersion Baptism," **Evansville Courier** (April 14, 1990).

23 "Musician Urges Elevation of Mary's Status," **Evansville Courier** (August 26, 1997). "Movement To

Give Mary Special Role Creates Concern, Anger," **Evansville Courier** (October 18, 1997).

24 "American Nuns Call For Female Priesthood," **Evansville Courier** (October 14, 1994). "Catholic Activists Push For Changes," **Evansville Courier** (February 17, 1997). "Poll: Let Women Into Priesthood," **Evansville Courier** (February 22, 1997).

25 "Easter Is Stadium Hit," **Evansville Courier** (April 13, 1998). This article discusses the use of instruments in the previous day's Easter service of the Crossroads Christian church at Robert's Stadium in Evansville. "Steve Wyatt had enough musicians, singers, electrical sound equipment and video cameras to make most rock bands envious."

26 "Proposal Ponders Non-Christians' Salvation," **Evansville Courier** (April 18, 1998), discussion about proposed catechism of Presbyterian Church (USA) which suggests Jews, Muslims, Buddhists and others might be destined for the life of eternal peace and happiness many Christians used to envision only for themselves.

27 Steele and Thomas, op. cit. pp. 13-19.

28 Ibid.

29 Thayer, Joseph H. **Greek-English Lexicon of the New Testament** (Grand Rapids, MI: Zondervan Publishing House,1974), pp. 79,80.